50
PROBLEM-SOLVING
LESSONS

The Best from 10 Years of Math Solutions Newsletters

50
PROBLEM-SOLVING
LESSONS

Grades 1–6

by Marilyn Burns

MATH SOLUTIONS PUBLICATIONS

Editorial Direction: Lorri Ungaretti
Art direction and design: Aileen Friedman
Illustrations: David Healy, First Image; Gordon Silveria
Cover by Aileen Friedman and Gordon Silveria

Printed in the United States of America.

ISBN 0-941355-16-0

This book is printed on recycled paper (at least
50 percent post-consumer waste).

Math Solutions Publications

A division of
Marilyn Burns Education Associates
150 Gate 5 Road, Suite 101
Sausalito, CA 94965
Telephone: (800) 868-9092 or (415) 332-4181
Fax: (415) 331-1931

www.mathsolutions.com

A Message from Marilyn Burns

We at Marilyn Burns Education Associates believe that teaching mathematics well calls for continually reflecting on and improving one's instructional practice. Our Math Solutions Publications include a wide range of choices, from books that describe problem-solving lessons, to *Math By All Means* units that show how to teach specific topics, to resources that help link math with writing and literature, to children's books that help students develop an appreciation for math while learning basic concepts.

Along with our large collection of teacher resource books, we have a more general collection of books, videotapes, and audiotapes that can help teachers and parents bridge the gap between home and school. All of our materials are available at education stores, from distributors, and through major teacher catalogs.

In addition, Math Solutions Inservice offers five-day courses and one-day workshops throughout the country. We also work in partnership with school districts to help implement and sustain long-term improvement in mathematics instruction in all classrooms.

To find a complete listing of our publications and workshops, please visit our Web site at *www.mathsolutions.com*. Or contact us by calling (800) 868-9092 or sending an e-mail to *info@mathsolutions.com*.

We're eager for your feedback and interested in learning about your particular needs. We look forward to hearing from you.

SOLUTIONS® Publications
A DIVISION OF MARILYN BURNS EDUCATION ASSOCIATES

Contents

Introduction

When I was a new teacher, I was constantly searching for teaching ideas to use with my students. I combed every resource book I could find. I subscribed to teacher magazines. I talked with other teachers. I signed up for workshops whenever I could. As with all new teachers, my classroom experience was limited and my store of ideas was slim. Sunday nights typically wound up in a frenzied struggle to plan the week's curriculum in ways that (I hoped) would be motivating for the students and manageable for me.

Now, 33 years later, my store of ideas is no longer slim, and I can rely on my years of experience. But I'm still searching for ideas to enhance and expand my teaching repertoire. While I'm no longer looking for ideas to fill an empty larder, I realize the benefit of refining and expanding my teaching by adding new ideas and approaches. And even with my years of experience, trying new lessons is still a challenge. Focusing on doing something new in the classroom calls for teaching and thinking at the same time, without

the experience of being able to predict how students will respond. It's this challenge that has always helped keep teaching alive and exciting for me.

In the summer of 1984, I began teaching Math Solutions five-day summer courses for teachers in kindergarten through grade 8 and established the Math Solutions faculty to offer the courses nationwide. Previously, I had been involved with several mathematics inservice projects and enjoyed helping teachers think in new ways about teaching mathematics. As the Math Solutions courses grew, I realized that teachers needed help beyond the five-day summer experience. We began presenting Math Solutions one-day workshops during the school year, both to offer follow-up support to teachers who had attended a summer course and to provide beginning experiences for teachers who were interested in thinking more about their math teaching.

In the spring of 1986, in order to provide another way to offer support to teachers searching for new ways to teach mathematics, I wrote the first Math Solutions newsletter and mailed it to all of the teachers who had attended Math Solutions courses and workshops. Since then, I've written one or two newsletters each year, and our mailing list has grown to more than 40,000 teachers. Over the years, I've tried to keep all of the articles grounded in the realities of the classroom by presenting new ideas for classroom teaching, sharing new approaches to existing ideas, offering tips for classroom organization, and addressing general issues about math education.

To write the newsletters, I depended on the teaching ideas and classroom experiences of other teachers. Many ideas came from colleagues I worked with on a regular basis; some came from correspondence I received from teachers who had attended courses. Some articles offered activities that were new to me; others recycled familiar ideas, giving them new twists and energy. I wrote the classroom activities as vignettes, including details about classroom management as well as information about the mathematics being presented. As often as possible, articles were illustrated with samples of actual student work.

Over the years, writing the newsletters sparked other projects. I used articles from newsletters for the bulk of the ideas in *Math and Literature (K-3)*. I expanded some articles and included them in the series of *A Collection of Math Lessons*, and some ideas found their way into *Math By All Means* units.

For this book, I combed all of the back issues of the Math Solutions newsletters and identified articles that hadn't appeared in other publications or, if they did appear, had been much revised. I chose articles that presented practical, classroom-tested instructional ideas and compiled them into this resource of 50 lessons for teaching mathematics in grades 1 through 6. In some cases, I used my more recent experiences with the lessons to boost articles with additional instructional ideas or samples of children's work.

On the first page of each lesson, I indicate the span of grades for which the lesson is appropriate and the mathematics strands it addresses. The charts on pages 4–7 provide an overview of the strands and recommended grade levels for all the lessons.

Revisiting the past newsletters reminded me that teaching never stays the same. Improving and refining ideas is an ongoing part of the craft of teaching, and I hope that this book helps teachers examine and expand their classroom repertoires.

GRADE LEVEL
AND STRAND
CHARTS

Grade Levels for Activities

ACTIVITY	1	2	3	4	5	6
Acrobats, Grandmas, and Ivan				■	■	■
Anno's Magic Hat Tricks			■	■	■	■
Assessing Understanding of Fractions				■	■	
Beginning Experience with Recording	■					
Budgie Problem					■	■
Calculators in Math Class			■	■		
Comparing Alphabet Letters	■	■				
Comparing Fractions				■	■	
Counting Cats	■	■				
Counting Feet	■	■	■			
Cutting the Cake			■	■	■	
Dividing Cakes		■	■	■		
Exploring Halves		■	■			
Firehouse Problem			■	■	■	■
From the Ceiling to Algebra					■	■
Game of Leftovers			■	■		
Guess Our Number					■	■
Hands and Beans	■	■				
How Many Animals?	■	■	■			
How Many Days of School?		■	■	■		
How Many Dots?	■	■				
How Many Pockets?	■	■				
How Much Ribbon?			■	■		
Largest Square Problem			■	■	■	■
Lessons with Geoboards	■	■				

4

GRADE	1	2	3	4	5	6
Long Division Activity				■	■	
Making Generalizations			■	■	■	■
Making Recording Books	■	■				
Match or No Match			■	■		
Math from the Ceiling			■	■		
Mathematics and Poetry			■	■	■	■
Measurement Problem				■	■	■
Multiplication and Division					■	■
Name Graph		■	■	■	■	■
Penticubes					■	■
Pioneers, Candles, and Math			■	■		
Place Value Game		■	■	■	■	■
Planting Bulbs	■	■				
Probability Tile Games					■	■
Raccoon Problem	■	■				
Roll for $1.00		■	■	■		
Rubber Band Ball		■	■	■		
Sharing 50 Cents		■	■			
Sharing an Apple	■	■	■			
Statistical Experiment			■	■	■	■
Tiles in the Bag				■	■	■
What Is a Polygon?					■	■
When Is the Cup Half Full?					■	■
Where's the Penny?	■	■				
Writing Questions from Graphs				■	■	■

Strands in Activities

ACTIVITY	NUMBER	GEOMETRY	MEASUREMENT	STATISTICS	PROBABILITY	PATTERNS AND FUNCTIONS	ALGEBRA	LOGIC
Acrobats, Grandmas, and Ivan	■						■	■
Anno's Magic Hat Tricks								■
Assessing Understanding of Fractions	■							
Beginning Experience with Recording	■							
Budgie Problem	■						■	■
Calculators in Math Class	■					■		
Comparing Alphabet Letters		■						
Comparing Fractions	■	■						
Counting Cats	■			■				
Counting Feet	■			■				
Cutting the Cake	■	■	■					
Dividing Cakes	■	■						
Exploring Halves	■	■	■					
Firehouse Problem		■						■
From the Ceiling to Algebra	■	■				■	■	
Game of Leftovers	■							
Guess Our Number	■							■
Hands and Beans	■		■	■				
How Many Animals?	■							
How Many Days of School?	■		■					
How Many Dots?	■							
How Many Pockets?	■							
How Much Ribbon?	■	■	■					
Largest Square Problem		■	■					
Lessons with Geoboards		■		■				

ACTIVITY	NUMBER	GEOMETRY	MEASUREMENT	STATISTICS	PROBABILITY	PATTERNS AND FUNCTIONS	ALGEBRA	LOGIC
Long Division Activity	■							
Making Generalizations	■					■		
Making Recording Books	■	■						
Match or No Match	■			■	■			
Math from the Ceiling	■	■				■		
Mathematics and Poetry	■	■	■	■	■	■	■	■
Measurement Problem	■		■					
Multiplication and Division	■	■	■					
Name Graph	■			■				
Penticubes		■						
Pioneers, Candles, and Math	■		■					
Place Value Game	■				■			■
Planting Bulbs	■		■	■				
Probability Tile Games					■			■
Raccoon Problem	■							
Roll for $1.00	■							
Rubber Band Ball	■	■	■					
Sharing 50 Cents	■							
Sharing an Apple	■		■					
Statistical Experiment				■				
Tiles in the Bag	■				■			
What Is a Polygon?		■						
When Is the Cup Half Full?	■		■					
Where's the Penny?	■							■
Writing Questions from Graphs	■			■				

THE LESSONS

GRADE
1
2
3
4
5
6

STRAND
NUMBER
GEOMETRY
MEASUREMENT
STATISTICS
PROBABILITY
PATTERNS AND FUNCTIONS
ALGEBRA
LOGIC

A Beginning Experience with Recording

Bonnie Tank taught this lesson to first graders in San Francisco, California, early in the school year as she was getting to know the children. Bonnie used this lesson to learn about how the students would represent a situation mathematically.

Materials

— Color Tiles

— Lunch bags with fewer than 10 Color Tiles in each (tiles in varying combinations of three colors), one per pair of students

Typically, young children's early experiences with mathematical recording come from completing problems on workbook pages. These pages often present isolated exercises that do not relate to children's concrete experiences. They do not give children the opportunity to learn how to formulate and record their own ideas, and they do little to reveal to teachers how children think and what they understand.

This lesson had a different focus. To prepare for the lesson, Bonnie prepared 15 lunch bags, each with fewer than 10 Color Tiles in varying combinations of three colors. (For example, she put 7 red, 1 green, and 1 blue in one bag; 3 yellow, 3 green, and 2 red in another; and so on.)

Bonnie organized the students into pairs and gave each pair a bag of tiles and a sheet of paper. She then explained their task to them.

"Your job is to work with your partner and record on your paper exactly what's in your bag," she said. "You can use pictures, words, numbers—whatever makes sense to both of you so that someone else can tell from your paper what you have in the bag."

The Children's Work

The children used various ways to approach the problem and to record the contents of their bags. Alan and Maura, for example, divided the tiles between them. Maura took one of each color, Alan took the rest, and they each recorded what they had. Alan drew red squares to represent the six red tiles he had; Maura wrote *1 red, 1 blue, 1 green* and drew one square of each color.

Alan drew six red tiles, and Maura drew one red, one blue, and one green tile.

Zheng and Jonah each took on a different job. Jonah wanted to build, and Zheng wanted to draw. So Jonah built a structure with their nine tiles, and Zheng drew a picture of it. The boys talked as they worked.

Lawrence and Margaret drew a line to divide their paper into two parts. They also divided the tiles between them, and each recorded what he

or she had on one side of the paper by tracing the tiles and coloring them in. Anthony and Jennifer worked the same way.

Kate and Ryan also divided their paper in half. However, each drew a picture of all the tiles, producing two records. When they compared, Kate found that she had made an error by including an extra tile. She crossed it out. They agreed to write the number 9 to show how many tiles they had.

Kate and Ryan both drew pictures showing all the tiles in their bag.

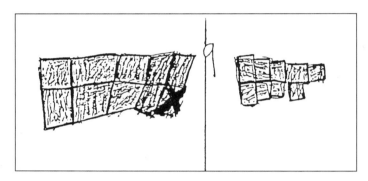

All of the students knew how many tiles they had and could report the colors when asked, though some were unable to record this information accurately, either pictorially or numerically. However, the activity engaged all of the children, and it helped Bonnie gain beginning insights into individuals' thinking and ability to use mathematical symbols to represent their thinking.

GRADE
1
2
3
4
5
6

STRAND
NUMBER
GEOMETRY
MEASUREMENT
STATISTICS
PROBABILITY
PATTERNS AND FUNCTIONS
ALGEBRA
LOGIC

Counting Cats

This lesson draws on information about pets to provide students with a graphing experience and an opportunity to count and compare numbers. Carolyn Felux taught the lesson to first graders in San Antonio, Texas.

Materials
- Interlocking (Multilink, Snap, or Unifix) cubes, one per student
- Two lunch bags, one labeled "Yes," one labeled "No"

"I'm interested in learning who has a cat for a pet," Carolyn said to the first graders. She quickly circulated through the class, giving each child one Snap Cube.

Then Carolyn showed the students the two lunch bags and asked them to read the label on each one. She then explained, "As I walk around the room, you'll each put your cube in one of the bags. Put your cube in the Yes bag if you have a cat and in the No bag if you don't. Then we'll use the cubes to find out how many of you do and do not have cats."

After Carolyn had collected the children's cubes, she said, "First we'll find out how many of you have cats. Count with me as I remove the cubes from the Yes bag." As the students counted,

13

Carolyn snapped the cubes together to make a train. The train had seven cubes.

Before doing the same with the other bag, Carolyn asked, "How many students do we have in class today?" A buzz of conversation broke out in the room. A few children stood up to take a head count, and then several children raised their hands. Carolyn had several of them explain how they knew there were 21 children present.

Carolyn then asked, "Do you think there are more or fewer cubes in the No bag than in the Yes bag?" Again, a buzz of conversation broke out.

Carolyn called the class to attention and asked the children to raise their hands if they thought the No bag had more. Then she had them raise their hands if they thought the Yes bag had more. A few thought there were probably the same in each. Some weren't sure and didn't raise their hands at all.

"The Yes bag has seven cubes," Carolyn reminded the class. "How many cubes do you think are in the No bag? Talk with your neighbor about this."

After a minute or so, Carolyn called on volunteers to report their ideas. Some children reported a number and were able to explain how they figured. For example, Ali said, "We counted," and demonstrated with her fingers.

Other children, however, were willing to give answers but couldn't explain. Sally just shrugged when Carolyn asked for her reasoning, and Elliot said, "I guessed."

Carolyn then removed the cubes from the No bag and snapped them into a train. The children counted along. This train was 14 cubes long. Standing the two trains together gave the children a concrete comparison.

Carolyn continued with more questions, all designed to probe the students' thinking and help her assess their understanding.

- What can you tell me about these two stacks of cubes?

- How can we use the cubes to figure out how many children are in class altogether?

- How many more children do not have cats than do have cats?

- We can tell how many children have cats, but I don't think we can tell how many pet cats we have from these cubes. Who can explain why I think that?

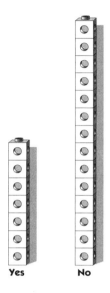

Yes No

GRADE

| 1 |
| 2 |
| 3 |
| 4 |
| 5 |
| 6 |

STRAND

NUMBER
GEOMETRY
MEASUREMENT
STATISTICS
PROBABILITY
PATTERNS AND FUNCTIONS
ALGEBRA
LOGIC

Where's the Penny?

Bonnie Tank got the idea for this lesson from *Games for Math,* by Peggy Kaye, a book for parents about helping their K–3 children learn math. (See the Bibliography on page 179.) Bonnie taught the lesson to a first grade class in San Francisco, California.

Materials

- 10 small paper cups
- One penny

To prepare for the lesson, Bonnie labeled the cups "1st," "2nd," "3rd," and so on, up to "10th." She placed them upside down in order on the table at the front of the room and hid a penny under the seventh cup.

"Your job is to guess under which cup I hid the penny," Bonnie told the children. "If you make a guess that isn't right, I'll give you a clue. I'll tell you whether I put the penny under a cup before or after the one you chose."

English was not the first language for more than half of the children. Not only was Bonnie interested in having the children become familiar with ordinal numbers and learn to interpret clues logically, she was also interested in providing them with experiences hearing and speaking English. For that reason, she asked them to give their clues in complete sentences.

"When you guess," she told them, "say 'I think the penny is under the third cup.' Or the sixth cup. Or whatever cup you'd like to guess."

Gregory guessed first. "I think you put it in the first cup," he said. Even though this wasn't exactly the wording Bonnie had given, she accepted it because it was a complete sentence.

"The penny is under a cup that comes after the first cup," Bonnie said.

Cynthia guessed next. "The tenth one," she said.

"Can you say your guess in a whole sentence?" Bonnie asked "Start with 'I think . . .'"

"I think the penny is under the tenth one," Cynthia said.

"I put the penny under a cup before the tenth one," Bonnie responded.

Marcie gave the next guess. "I think it's under the fifth cup," she guessed.

"I put the penny under a cup after the fifth one," Bonnie answered.

"I think the penny is under the second cup," Lawrence offered next. Neither Lawrence nor any of the other children seemed aware that this guess was redundant. Bonnie did not call this to the children's attention, but responded as she had for the other guesses.

"I put the penny under a cup after the second one," she said.

The guessing continued. Though the children guessed different cups each time, their guesses were random. Finally, on the eighth guess, Ryan gave the correct answer.

The children were eager to play again. To prepare, Bonnie blocked their view of the cups and moved the penny to another cup. For this round, the children again began by guessing the first and tenth cups. Still, none made use of the information from the clues. The game took six guesses.

Bonnie handled the third game differently. In response to the first three guesses, she told the class that the penny was in a cup after the first

cup, before the tenth cup, and before the sixth cup. Then she asked the children a question.

"What do you now know from the clues?" she asked.

The next three children Bonnie called on did not answer her question but made new guesses. To each Bonnie gave the same response: "I'm not interested in a new guess now," she said. "Instead, I'm interested in what the clues you already have tell you."

Finally, Jessamy responded. "I don't remember the first two clues," she said, "but I remember the last clue. It comes before the sixth."

"What does that tell you?" Bonnie probed.

"Oh yeah," Jessamy continued, "it's not under the first, so it's under the second, third, fourth, or fifth."

Some of the children agreed with Jessamy; others didn't understand. Bonnie continued with more children's guesses. With each clue, more children were able to explain what information they now had. It took the class four guesses in the third and fourth games.

Bonnie thought that it might have helped the children if after each guess she lifted the cup and turned it upright. However, the children's strategies seemed to improve as they played more games, so this extra hint didn't seem essential.

Over the next several days, the class played the game with children taking turns hiding the penny and giving clues.

GRADE
1
2
3
4
5
6

STRAND
NUMBER
GEOMETRY
MEASUREMENT
STATISTICS
PROBABILITY
PATTERNS AND FUNCTIONS
ALGEBRA
LOGIC

How Many Pockets?

Marge Genolio, a first grade teacher in San Francisco, California, gives her students regular experiences with estimating and comparing numbers. In this lesson, she had the children count the number of pockets on their clothing. The lesson gave students experience that helped build their understanding of large numbers and place value.

Materials

— Interlocking (Multilink, Snap, or Unifix) cubes

"How many pockets do you think we are wearing today altogether?" Marge asked her class one Monday morning. After giving the children a chance to share their estimates, Marge organized a way for them to find out.

She put a supply of Unifix cubes at each table and directed the children to put one cube in each of their pockets. Once they had done this, Marge removed the remaining cubes.

She directed the students to remove the cubes from their pockets, snap them into trains, and compare their trains with those of the other students at their table. Then Marge called the class to attention.

"Raise your hand if you have a train that's the same length as someone else's at your table," she said. Marge had a few children show their trains, report how many cubes they had, and tell who had a train the same length.

"Now raise your hand if your train is longer than someone else's train," Marge said. After a few children reported, she said, "Raise your hand if your train is shorter than someone else's train." Again, she had several students report.

Marge gave further directions. "Now let's find out how many cubes we have altogether. This will tell us how many pockets we have on our clothing today. I'd like you to combine the cubes at your table by snapping them into trains of 10."

Marge collected the trains of 10 from each table and then combined the extra cubes from each group to make additional 10s. The class counted the 10s and extras and found that there were 68 pockets. Marge recorded on the board:

6 tens and 8 ones = 68

Although it's obvious to adults that the digits in 68 represent how many 10s and 1s there are, this is not obvious to children. Experiences like these can help them make this connection.

Marge posted a sheet of paper, then wrote the date and recorded the number 68 on it. She told the children that they would try the activity again the next day.

"I wonder if we'll get the same results tomorrow," she mused. The children's reactions were mixed.

The count rose on Tuesday and Wednesday, and by Thursday there were 95 pockets. On Friday, however, there was a slump—only 89 pockets. Some children were disappointed; they were hoping for 100. Obviously, the children had exhausted the pocket potential of their wardrobes by that time!

A Literature Connection

When Stephanie Sheffield did this lesson with her first graders, she first read aloud *Peter's Pockets* by Eve Rice. The story is about a boy who puts on a new pair of pants and takes a walk with his uncle. As he finds treasures he wants to keep, Peter discovers that his pants have a serious flaw —no pockets! When Peter gets home, his mother solves the problem by sewing enough pockets on Peter's pants to hold all of his treasures. You can read Stephanie's version of the lesson in her book *Math and Literature (K–3), Book Two*. (See the Bibliography on page 179.)

GRADE

1
2
3
4
5
6

STRAND
NUMBER
GEOMETRY
MEASUREMENT
STATISTICS
PROBABILITY
PATTERNS AND FUNCTIONS
ALGEBRA
LOGIC

Planting Bulbs

Each December, Carole Clarin's K–1 students in New York City plant narcissus bulbs. For several weeks, children measure the growth of their bulbs, graph data, record findings in individual books, and contribute to a class time line. This month-long project integrates reading, writing, math, science, and art, and results in a room full of delicious smelling flowers in time for the holidays.

Materials

— Narcissus bulbs, one per student (plus a few extra in case some students' bulbs don't grow)
— Toothpicks, one box
— Clear plastic cups, one per bulb
— Centicubes
— Two sheets of chart paper
— Circle stickers (available at stationery stores)
— Potting soil

To begin this project each year, Carole has each child select a bulb, support it with three toothpicks, and put it into water in a plastic cup. The children label their cups with their names. (Carole always plants several extra bulbs in case some don't grow.)

Carole creates a class chart. She lists all of the students' names, rules four columns, and titles the columns "Roots," "Shoots," "Buds," and "Flowers." Each child posts a circle sticker in the appropriate column when he or she first sees roots, shoots, buds, or flowers.

19

On one of the class charts, each child posts a circle sticker when he or she notices roots, shoots, buds, or flowers.

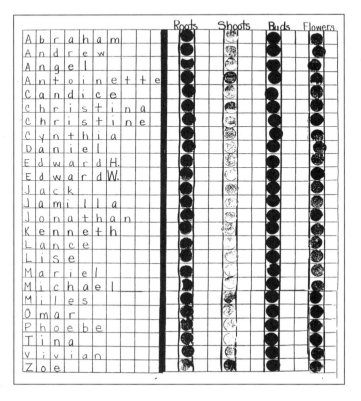

When all the bulbs have sprouted, which takes about a week, the children use Centicubes to measure the height of their shoots. Carole posts another chart on which the students record the lengths of their shoots by coloring in columns of centimeter squares.

A week later, each child takes a new measurement and adds the information to the graph, coloring his or her column so it represents the current height in Centicubes. Carole chooses a different color crayon for each week so that the children can see how much their bulbs grow each week.

As roots begin to grow, the students plant their bulbs in gravel or soil and continue to measure and record their data each week.

There is a great deal of discussion about the data on the graph. Carole asks questions such as:

- What does the graph tell?
- Whose shoot is the longest?
- Whose bulb grew the most in one week?
- How tall is Andrew's? Daniel's? Anne's?
- How much longer is Tina's than Mike's?
- How many are 18 centimeters long?
- Whose bulb grew the most evenly?

Carole also gives the students blank books in which to make drawings and record information about their study. A time line, usually kept on a hallway wall, illustrates the project as the study progresses. Sometimes Carole records the information on the time line, and other times the children do. The time line often includes Polaroid photos and the children's artwork.

The children record regularly in their bulb books.

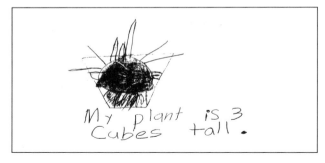

STRAND

NUMBER
GEOMETRY
MEASUREMENT
STATISTICS
PROBABILITY
PATTERNS AND FUNCTIONS
ALGEBRA
LOGIC

Making Recording Books

Relating math to classroom routines gives children the opportunity to see the usefulness of mathematics in real settings. The following is an example of a math experience that emerged from students needing to have books in which to record classroom activities. Bonnie Tank presented this lesson to first graders in San Francisco, California.

Materials

— 12-by-18-inch construction paper, one sheet per student

— 12-by-18-inch newsprint, several sheets per student

The students in this class were accustomed to making recording books by folding 12-by-18-inch newsprint pages and stapling them inside construction paper covers. They wrote only on the right-hand pages. (Newsprint is thin, so writing on both sides makes student work difficult to read. Also, when students erase, the paper becomes even more fragile.)

Before they made new recording books one day, Bonnie asked the students to figure out how many sheets of newsprint they would each need. "For this book," Bonnie told the children, "you'll need 12 pages to write on."

Bonnie had the children work in pairs to solve the problem. She asked them to explain the problem to each other, figure out an answer, record it on a sheet of paper, and prepare to explain their thinking to the rest of the class.

All but four pairs of children arrived at the correct answer of six sheets. Of the others, two pairs decided the answer was seven, and one pair decided it was eight. The fourth pair worked on a different problem, trying to figure out how many sheets were needed for all 30 children.

All of the students worked diligently and were pleased with their efforts. After the children had shared their solutions, they assembled their books.

This lesson helped students see that there is more than one way to solve a problem. It related mathematics to a real-life purpose. It also gave Bonnie insights into the children's individual abilities.

These students illustrated how they would fold each of the six sheets they needed.

This pair of children made an intricate drawing to show their solution.

Tiffany and Michael tried to figure out how many sheets of paper were needed for the entire class. They decided each child would need 12 sheets.

GRADE

| 1 |
| 2 |
| 3 |
| 4 |
| 5 |
| 6 |

STRAND

NUMBER
GEOMETRY
MEASUREMENT
STATISTICS
PROBABILITY
PATTERNS AND FUNCTIONS
ALGEBRA
LOGIC

Comparing Alphabet Letters

Sorting experiences encourage students to identify properties of objects, notice their similarities and differences, create classifications, and discriminate between objects. This sorting activity uses letters of the alphabet. Bonnie Tank presented it to first graders in San Francisco, California. Brenda Mercado reported doing a version of the lesson with her multiage primary students in Tucson, Arizona.

Materials

— 3-by-5-inch index cards, one per student

Bonnie began by writing on the board:

B   M

"Look at these letters," she directed the class. "What's the same about them?"

There was a variety of responses: "Both have a straight line." "They're both letters." "They're both capitals." "They're not numbers." "Both are in the alphabet." "Both are not creatures."

Bonnie then posed another question: "What do you notice that's different about these letters?"

Again, the answers varied: "One's M and one's B." "One has four lines; one has one line and two bumps." "The B has curves and the M has straight lines and slanted lines." "M has the shape of a V, and the B doesn't." "M has more lines."

Bonnie then asked each student to write his or her first initial on a 3-by-5-inch card. Bonnie organized the students into pairs and had them talk about what was the same and what was different about their letters. Then, in a class discussion, the children reported what they had noticed.

Brandon and Anthony focused on the shapes in their letters. "The B has half circles and the A has a triangle," they reported.

Zheng and Nektaria discovered a similarity when they rotated their cards. "The Z, can turn into an N, and the N can turn into a Z," Zheng explained.

This sparked a discovery from Hoi Shan and Sammy. "When we turn our initials upside down, they're still the same," they reported.

Kimmy reported for her and Jonah: "J comes before K in the alphabet," she said.

Bonnie then explained to the class that each pair of students was to record how their initials were alike and different. She modeled for them how to fold a sheet of paper in half, label one half "Same" and the other "Different," write both their names on the paper, and record in complete sentences what they noticed.

The Children's Work

Zheng and Nektaria repeated what they had reported in class. They wrote: *Our names are interesting be cause the Z can turn in to a N and the N can turn in to a Z. the N comes Befor Z. the Z's sound is like this zzzzzz and the N's sounds like this nnnnn.*

Sammy and Hoi Shan also reported what they had discovered during the class discussion. Under "Same," they wrote: *If you turn it around it is the same.*

Sylvia and Katherine looked at various types of similarities between their letters. They wrote: *1. we Both have Curves. 2. In the Aphabet we are 8 letrs apert. 3. they are both Capitals.*

English was not the first language of many of the children in this class, and this was evident in sentences such as: *We don't have same letters. His is a J and Mys is a M.* But all the children's papers revealed that they seemed to understand what *same* and *different* meant, and many were able to use geometric properties in their descriptions.

Zheng and Nektaria's paper included information about the different sounds their letters make.

Sammy and Hoi Shan focused on the lines and curves in their two letters.

Sylvia and Katherine looked at the letters in various ways.

Another Approach

Brenda Mercado does a similar lesson during the first week of school. Rather than have each child write the first letter of his or her name on an index card, she makes cutout letters available to her class. (Brenda has templates for block letters, and parent volunteers cut out a supply.)

"The children can compare their letters more easily when they're cut out," she reports. "Also, they can fold them in various ways to find lines of symmetry. And I introduce the idea of closed shapes by having them put a bean on their letters to see if it's a good fence to keep a dog in the yard."

GRADE		STRAND
1		NUMBER
2		GEOMETRY
3		MEASUREMENT
4		STATISTICS
5		PROBABILITY
6		PATTERNS AND FUNCTIONS
		ALGEBRA
		LOGIC

How Many Dots?

Children benefit from activities that ask them to apply what they understand about numbers in situations that are new to them. Students' responses help teachers assess their ability to use what they know. Bonnie Tank presented this problem to first graders in San Francisco, California.

Materials

— One 3-by-12-inch strip of tagboard

— An envelope or covering that the tagboard can slide into

To prepare for the lesson, Bonnie drew 12 dots on a 3-by-12-inch strip of tagboard. She made an envelope that allowed 8 dots to show when she slipped the strip into it.

Bonnie began the lesson by showing the students the entire strip. She didn't give them time to count the dots. Instead, she slipped the strip into the envelope so that the children could see only some of the dots.

"You can't see all the dots now," Bonnie said, "because some of them are hidden. Your problem is to figure out how many dots are on the whole strip. Because you can't see the dots that are hidden, I'm going to give you a clue."

Bonnie took a paper clip. "This dot," she said, putting the paper clip above the dot she was showing them, "is the sixth dot. Use that information to figure out how many dots there are altogether."

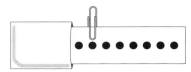

Bonnie often has students work in pairs or in groups. With this activity, however, she wanted to assess individual students' understanding. "You're to work on this problem by yourself," she said and gave each child an unlined sheet of newsprint. "Put your answer on this paper and also explain how you figured it out. Your explanation is very important because it tells me what you're thinking. You can also draw pictures to help you figure or explain your reasoning."

The Children's Work

Children's responses to the problem differed. Stephanie counted on from the sixth dot and wrote: *I think there are 12 dots. I counted the dots from the 6th dot And I counted 12 dots.*

Stephanie counted on from the sixth dot to reach the answer of 12 dots.

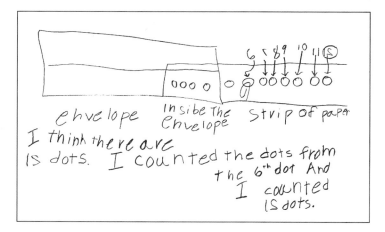

Carlos solved the problem by trial and error. He wrote: *I figered it ote droring and arasing there are 4 insid The envelop there are 12 all twogether.*

Carlos used trial and error, drawing, erasing, and counting, to arrive at a solution.

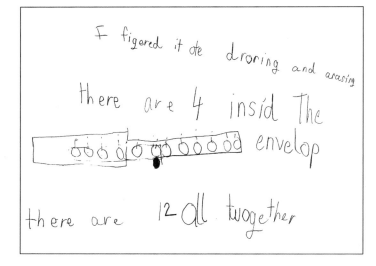

Some students guessed or were unable to explain their reasoning. Most included pictures, some of which were elaborate but had little to do with the problem. A few children solved different problems, figuring out how many dots were inside the envelope or focusing just on the dots they could see.

While the children's writing revealed the reasoning strategies of individuals, it's not possible to draw definitive conclusions about a child's mathematical prowess from just one problem. The information from each problem is valuable when analyzed in conjunction with that child's responses in other problem-solving situations.

Angie's drawing didn't explain how she got her answer.

I think it was 12 dots.

Eric guessed that there were 11 dots, but he did not explain his reasoning.

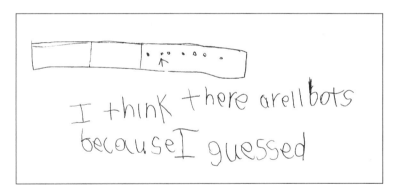

I think there are 11 bots because I guessed

GRADE

1

2

3

4

5

6

STRAND

NUMBER

GEOMETRY

MEASUREMENT

STATISTICS

PROBABILITY

PATTERNS AND FUNCTIONS

ALGEBRA

LOGIC

The Raccoon Problem

Children benefit from problem-solving experiences that help develop their number sense. Christie Brinkley developed this problem for her first graders in Urbana, Illinois. Bonnie Tank presented the problem to first graders in San Francisco, California. She organized the students into pairs and had them explain their solutions in writing.

"Today I have a problem for you to work on with your partner," Bonnie said. Before presenting the problem, Bonnie described the procedure for how the students would work.

"First, you need to tell the problem to each other to be sure you both understand it," she explained. "Then, before writing anything, talk about what you'll write and how you'll share the work."

Bonnie then stated the problem: Four raccoons went down to the lake for a drink. Two got their front feet wet. One got its back feet wet. How many dry feet were there?

Bonnie talked about what the students should be writing. "What you put on the paper should help explain your thinking. It can be a drawing, numbers, or anything you think will help. You may also use blocks or counters if you'd like. When you arrive at an answer on which you both agree, put that on your paper as well."

Before beginning a class discussion about the children's work, Bonnie gave the students a direction to help them prepare their presentations. She asked them to review what they had written on their papers.

"Then practice explaining to each other what you did," Bonnie told them, "so you'll be ready to share with the whole class. Also, decide how you'll share. Maybe one of you will hold the paper while the other does the talking, or maybe you'll decide to share both of those jobs." Bonnie finds that preparation like this helps students' presentations go more smoothly.

Following are similar problems that Christie and Bonnie have given to their students:

- A manufacturer needs wheels for 5 bicycles and 4 tricycles. How many wheels does he need?

- Some children went out to play in the snow. When they went back inside, they put their boots by the door to dry. There were 12 boots. How many children had gone out?

- There were 4 cows and 3 chickens in a field. How many tails and legs were there altogether? (See sample of student work below.)

Jessica and Lisa accidentally drew five raccoons, then crossed out one and wrote Xs on the feet that got wet.

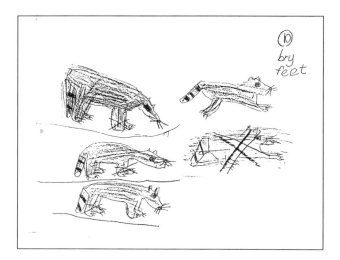

These two students drew four cows and three chickens, then counted 7 tails, 22 legs, and 29 in all.

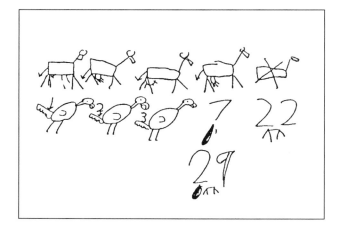

Mohammad and Mark carefully drew two raccoons with their front feet in the water, one with its back feet in the water, and a third outside the water.

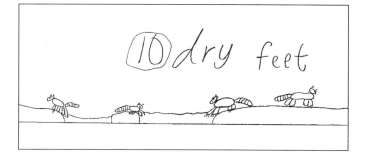

GRADE

1
2
3
4
5
6

STRAND

NUMBER
GEOMETRY
MEASUREMENT
STATISTICS
PROBABILITY
PATTERNS AND FUNCTIONS
ALGEBRA
LOGIC

Lessons with Geoboards

The geoboard is an excellent tool for helping students explore shapes and examine their properties. Bonnie Tank taught these two lessons to a class of second graders in San Francisco, California.

Materials

— Geoboards, one per student
— Rubber bands
— Geoboard dot paper, at least one sheet per student (See the blackline master on page 167.)
— One long sheet of butcher paper
— 2-by-6-inch strips of paper, one per student
— Scissors

For a first experience with geoboards, Bonnie gave each student one geoboard and a supply of rubber bands. After giving the children time to explore making shapes, Bonnie asked them to create something that could fly.

"When you find a shape that pleases you," Bonnie said, "use crayons to draw it on dot paper and then cut it out." (Transferring geoboard shapes to dot paper is useful for helping young children develop spatial skills and hand-eye coordination.) Bonnie modeled how to do this and then passed out sheets of geoboard dot paper. (See the blackline master on page 167.)

While the students drew their shapes, Bonnie stretched a long piece of butcher paper across the chalkboard to use for a class graph. She also cut a supply of 2-by-6-inch strips of paper.

When the children had finished their drawings, Bonnie began a class discussion. "Edward, what shape did you make that can fly?" she asked.

"A rocket," Edward replied, holding up his paper.

Bonnie wrote *rocket* on a 2-by-6-inch strip, taped it near the bottom edge of the butcher paper, and told Edward to post his dot paper above the label.

"Did anyone else make a rocket?" Bonnie asked. Several students raised their hands. Bonnie had them go to the front of the room and post their designs, making a column above Edward's rocket. Bonnie then had the students discuss how the rockets were alike and how they were different.

Bonnie continued this process for all the other shapes the children had made. She made labels for each category and had the children post their shapes, creating a large bar graph. There were 11 categories—rocket, kite, airplane, flying TV, bird, bubble, spaceship, Pegasus, helicopter, butterfly, and bumblebee.

When she finished making the graph, Bonnie said, "Describe what you see."

"I see that only four people made rockets and six people made butterflies," said Ana.

"Who can describe what's on the graph in a different way?" asked Bonnie.

Jesse observed that there were nine kites in the Kites column. Then another child spoke up. "There are seven more kites than spaceships. The spaceships have only two, and the kites have nine."

During the class discussion, the students talked about differences and similarities among the shapes; which shape they had the most of, least of, and the same number of; how many more rockets there were than birds; and so on. This classifying activity was preparation for a class exploration to focus children on the properties of geometric shapes.

The children drew pictures of their geoboard objects.

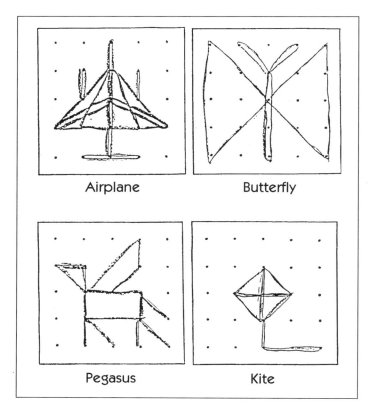

Airplane

Butterfly

Pegasus

Kite

Another Geoboard Lesson

Bonnie began a second geoboard lesson by saying, "I'm going to make a shape on my geoboard that follows three rules: 1. It's made from only one rubber band. 2. It has no loops, twists, or crossovers. 3. It's like a fence—it could keep a horse from running away."

Bonnie made a triangle and reviewed with the children why it followed the three rules.

"Each of you is to make a shape that also follows the three rules," she said. "Your shape doesn't have to be a triangle." She wrote on the board:

1. Only one rubber band
2. No loops, twists, or crossovers
3. Like a fence

When all of the students had made their shapes, Bonnie called for their attention and invited Rebecca to come to the front of the room and show the class the triangle she had made. Bonnie then led a class discussion, asking: "How many sides does Rebecca's shape have? Has anyone else made a shape that also has three sides? Come up and show it. How are these alike? How are they different?"

The children discussed the similarities and differences among the three-, four-, five-, and six-sided shapes they had made. Bonnie also talked about the names of the various shapes with the students, introducing the proper terminology to describe what they had created.

Bonnie then invited three children to come to the front of the room and show their shapes to the rest of the class.

Note: These lessons appear on the geoboard videotape in the "Mathematics with Manipulatives" series. (See the Bibliography on page 179.)

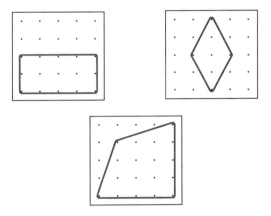

Bonnie said, "I'd like you to think about what's the same about all three shapes. First, talk to someone next to you about this."

After giving the students a minute or two to talk, Bonnie asked for volunteers.

"They all have four corners," offered Scott.

"They all have four sides," Jennifer said.

"They all have space in the middle of them," added Jodi.

"What's different about all three shapes?" Bonnie asked.

Aaron had an opinion. "Jamie's isn't a real shape like those two—the rectangle and the diamond," he said.

Bonnie continued the discussion, inviting other sets of students to show their shapes to the class.

GRADE		STRAND
1		**NUMBER**
2		GEOMETRY
3		**MEASUREMENT**
4		**STATISTICS**
5		PROBABILITY
6		PATTERNS AND FUNCTIONS
		ALGEBRA
		LOGIC

Hands and Beans

The story "Jack and the Beanstalk" can be a springboard to a class investigation that involves children in estimating, measuring area, and collecting and representing data. Sharon Dentler taught this lesson to her first graders in Orlando, Florida.

Materials
— The story "Jack and the Beanstalk" (any version)
— Dried beans
— Scissors
— One sheet of chart paper

After reading "Jack and the Beanstalk" aloud, Sharon introduced an estimation lesson. She reminded her students that Jack had received only a few beans for the cow. She asked the class, "How many beans do you think Jack would have had if he'd received a whole handful instead of just a few?"

After the children gave their estimates, Sharon asked, "How many large lima beans do you think you can hold in a handful?" Again, the children offered their ideas.

Sharon then gave directions for what the students were to do. "Think about how many beans you think you can hold in a handful," she said. "Trace one of your hands onto paper, cut it out, and write your estimate on the paper thumb."

37

Sharon modeled this procedure for the class and then continued with the directions.

"Then take a handful of beans and count," she said. "Work with a partner and check each other's answer. Then write your actual count on a small paper bean, and glue it to your cutout hand." Again, Sharon modeled for the children what they were to do.

A Class Graph

Sharon gathered the students on the rug in front of the board so they could help her arrange their cutout hands into a graph. She had ruled a sheet of chart paper into vertical columns wide enough for the children's cutout hands. She wanted to involve the children in making the decisions necessary to create a graph and in considering different ways to group the numerical data.

First, the children identified the smallest number of beans anyone had held—16—and placed that paper hand in the first column. They continued placing their paper hands on the chart, assigning a different number to each column. Counts ranged from 16 to 65, and there weren't enough columns for all the numbers. (There was some suspicion about the 65, but they didn't deal with that until later.)

The students then tried grouping the hands by 10s: 1–10, 11–20, 21–30, and so on up to 61–70. Sharon talked with them about eliminating the column for 1–10 since the smallest count was 16. This arrangement fit on the paper, but since more than half of the children's counts were in the 20s and 30s, their hands seemed too bunched up.

Then a child suggested giving pairs of numbers their own columns—16–17, 18–19, and so on. However, as with the first plan, there weren't enough columns on the paper. Finally, the class settled on five numbers to a column and labeled

the columns 16–20, 21–25, 26–30, 31–35, and so on to 61–65. This approach worked, and the children glued their cutout hands on the chart.

When they looked at the completed graph, the students noticed that some large hands held fewer beans than smaller hands. Sharon asked the students how this could happen, and they came up with a list of possible reasons:

1. Some students could have miscounted.

2. Partners didn't count because they were in a hurry.

3. The handful was taken with the palm turned down in the bag.

4. The handful was taken with the hand scooping under the beans.

5. Beans that had fallen off the handful on the way to the table had been added to the pile and counted.

Revisiting the Lesson

Sharon returned to the activity a week or so later. Children often benefit from trying an activity a second time. Their prior experience eliminates the confusion that new activities often generate and allows children to focus more easily on the mathematics.·

Sharon told the students that they would investigate more carefully how the sizes of their hands compared with the number of beans they could hold. They traced their hands again, this time keeping their fingers together. They cut out the paper hands and covered them with beans, using the beans as a nonstandard measure of area. Their areas ranged from 21 to 35 beans. Sharon thought the variation was due, in part, to some of the children's tracing and cutting skills.

The students again figured out the number of beans they could actually hold. First they set some rules for taking the beans, including making sure partners helped. (The partner of the boy who had recorded 65 the first time confessed that he had never checked.) They recorded the information on their paper hands the way they did the first time, but now their handfuls ranged from 18 to 42.

To help them look at the data in a different way, Sharon listed a pair of numbers on the board for each child—one telling the number of beans that covered the paper hand and the other telling the number of beans in the child's handful. This information showed that larger hands typically held more beans than smaller hands.

The children wrote about the activity in their math journals. Most wrote about learning that larger hands can hold more beans than smaller hands.

Sharon reported: "Like other estimation activities we had done, the children determined that an estimate was the best we could do to figure out the number of magic beans Jack could hold because we didn't know the size of his hand or the size of the magic beans."

The children wrote about the experience in their math journals. These two students wrote about their discovery that larger hands hold more than smaller hands.

We did Math Waith are red hands and We fagroot that big hands can hold More than Lotte hands

We Worked with Beans and Putthem on Our hands. and big hands hold more.

STRAND

NUMBER
GEOMETRY
MEASUREMENT
STATISTICS
PROBABILITY
PATTERNS AND FUNCTIONS
ALGEBRA
LOGIC

Counting Feet

In this lesson, students collect information in three different ways about how many feet there are for the adults living in their houses. The activity gives children the chance to think about numbers in a context related to their own lives. Carolyn Felux taught this lesson to second graders in Converse, Texas.

Materials

— Two sheets of chart paper

— Interlocking (Multilink, Snap, or Unifix) cubes, at least 100

"**H**ow many adult feet would there be in our room if all the adults living in your houses came to our class at the same time?" Carolyn asked the children.

The children were eager to respond to the question. Their initial estimates ranged from 20 to 10,000, with more than half of the children estimating between 20 and 45.

Carolyn posted two sheets of chart paper and brought out a supply of Unifix cubes. She told the children that each of them was to figure out how many adult feet there were in his or her house. Carolyn also gave the students directions about the three ways they were to report their information. She pointed to one of the sheets of graph paper she had posted. "On this chart," she said, "record the number of adult feet in your house. On the other chart, write an X to represent each adult foot in your house. Finally, make a train of Unifix cubes, with each cube representing one adult foot."

Carolyn had several children repeat the directions, and then had the class go to work. After all of the children had recorded the information, Carolyn called them together. She gathered all the trains of Unifix cubes and snapped them together to make one long train on the chalkboard tray. The students were surprised at its length. "Look how long!" "It's taller than me." "It almost covers half the board."

Some of the children wanted to change their original estimates of how many adult feet there would be altogether, some increasing them and others decreasing them.

Carolyn then asked the class, "Do you think we'll get the same number if we add the numbers on the chart, count the cubes, and count the Xs?" Most of the children were unsure.

"Let's find out," Carolyn suggested. She began with the cubes, breaking the train into 10s and then asking the students to count the cubes. There were 70 in all.

Carolyn then moved to the first class chart and used a calculator to add the numbers the children had written. She had a student check off each number as she added it. The total was 86.

Finally, Carolyn drew circles around groups of 10 Xs on the second class chart. There were eight 10s and eight extras—88 in all.

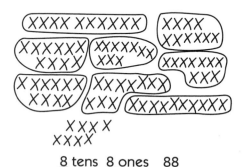

8 tens 8 ones   88

Most of the children were not concerned that the results differed. The few who were troubled couldn't explain why. Rather than try to resolve the discrepancy at this time, Carolyn ended the lesson by asking the children to continue thinking about the information they had gathered.

Revisiting the Lesson

A few days later, Carolyn returned to the data the children had collected. Although the cubes had been returned to their container, the children recalled that there had been 70 cubes in the train. She asked several children to describe what the information on the charts represented.

Carolyn again asked whether the children thought the totals should be the same or different. There were still differences of opinions. A few more students thought the totals should be the same, but many were still uncertain, and others were convinced the results could be different.

"I'm bothered by the differences in our numbers," Carolyn mused. "They all tell the same thing—the number of adult feet in your houses. I don't understand how they could be different. What ideas do you have about that?"

"Someone could have put in the wrong number of cubes," Monica said.

"The Xs looked like more than the numbers," Tommy said.

"Maybe we counted wrong," Stenna said.

"Maybe some people counted people instead of feet," Erin said.

Carolyn then reviewed the chart of numbers by having the children tell their numbers again. This revealed that in one case a 2 should have been a 4, changing the total from 86 to 88—matching the total on the chart of Xs.

Carolyn then asked the children to reconstruct their trains of cubes so they could investigate that information. Grouping the class train into 10s revealed 80 cubes this time.

April's observation resolved the discrepancy. "Matthew isn't here," she said. The class chart of numbers showed that no one present had recorded eight feet, so that must have been Matthew's number.

The experience gave Carolyn the chance to talk with the students about several things—how to make sense out of numbers, the importance of checking work, and the benefit of sharing ideas with others.

GRADE

1
2
3
4
5
6

STRAND

NUMBER
GEOMETRY
MEASUREMENT
STATISTICS
PROBABILITY
PATTERNS AND FUNCTIONS
ALGEBRA
LOGIC

Sharing an Apple

Sharing an apple equally among three people presents students with a problem that can be solved in different ways and provides a concrete experience with fractional parts. Joan Akers created the following problem for first graders when she was a math resource teacher in Santee, California. Bonnie Tank taught this lesson to first graders in San Francisco, California; Cheryl Rectanus taught it to second and third graders in Piedmont, California.

Materials

— Apples, enough for one-third of the students

"I've brought some apples for you," Bonnie began the lesson, showing the first graders a bag of apples. She removed one apple from the bag and posed a problem similar to the one the students would be solving.

"If I wanted two people to share this apple, what could I do?" she asked.

"You have to cut it," Matthew said.

"Does it matter how I cut it?" Bonnie asked.

"So we each get the same," Maria said.

"How much do you each get?" Bonnie asked.

"Half," several children called out. Though young children haven't learned the mathematical symbolism for one-half, they're familiar with the terminology and have had experiences with the concept in different situations.

Bonnie peered inside the bag. "Hmmm," she said, "I don't have enough apples for each of you to share with a partner. But I'm sure I have enough apples to give one to every three children."

Bonnie then introduced the problem the children were going to solve. "I'm going to put you into groups of three. Then you'll talk in your group about how you might share the apple equally, so you each get the same amount. After you share your ideas, agree on one plan that you think would work. Then write down that plan."

Bonnie showed the children the knife she had brought for cutting the apples. "When you show me your plan, I'll follow it and cut your apple, and then you can eat it. It may help to include drawings on your plan so it's clear to me what to do, but I also want you to explain your plan in words. Also, I'd like you to write how much each person gets."

"Do we have to eat the apple?" Jason asked.

"No," Bonnie said, "but I'd still like you to solve the problem of how three people can share one apple."

Bonnie then reviewed the instructions and wrote on the board:

How three people can share one apple.
Talk
Plan
Write

Bonnie wrote a prompt on the board to help the students as they began writing.

Each person gets _____.

Then she gave each group of three students an apple and a sheet of paper.

Several first graders found it easier to start by cutting the apple into fourths.

How Three people can share 1 apple. our plan is to take a knife and a apple and cut the apple into 4 pice is then we each get one pice then we cut the 4 Th pice in to 3 then were don Each person gets 2.

The children's writing showed a variety of methods. Bonnie was not surprised that none of the first graders used the language of fractions to describe how much each child would get. Although experience with the language of halves is common, young children haven't had similar experience with other fractions.

Albert, Meagan, and Jason each drew a different way to cut the apple into thirds.

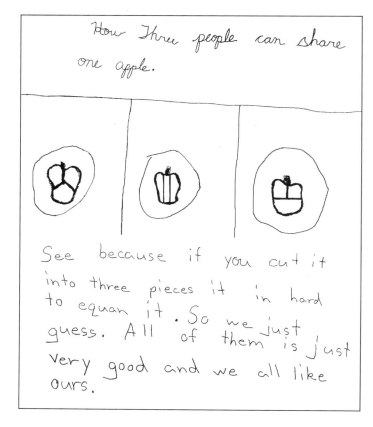

How Three people can share one apple.

See because if you cut it into three pieces it in hard to equan it. So we just guess. All of them is just very good and we all like ours.

The Lesson with Second and Third Graders

When Cheryl Rectanus's second and third graders worked on the problem, their solutions were more sophisticated. They divided the apples more precisely than the first graders had. Some students considered how to deal with the core of the apple when making equal pieces. Some included thirds or quarters in their solutions.

One group used scratch paper to draw the apple, then wrote extensively about the five methods they had tried for dividing it. They illustrated their fifth method and wrote: *Are last idea looks like a pie. but one piece is cut in 3 pieces.*

These third graders presented five different ideas for cutting the apple. Their scratch paper showed their work.

1 Are first idea was like a pie, but we found out that some pieces where to big. It looked like this. ⊕.
2 Are secent idea looked like stripes, but we found out that someone would get the core. It looked like this. ⊕.
3 Are third idea was like the letter Y, and that's are secent best one. It look like this. ⊗.

4 Are fourth idea looks like the letter V, but we found out that some one would get the core. It looks like this. ⓥ

5 Are last idea looks like a pie. but one piece is cut in 3 pieces. It looks like this.

This group's plan made sense, but the students' explanation revealed their confusion with naming fractional parts.

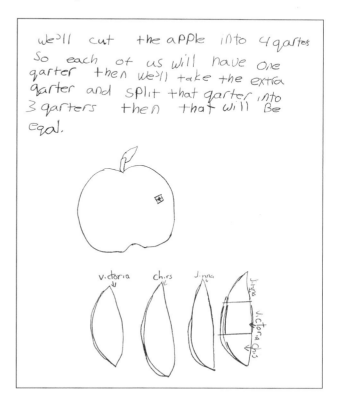

we'll cut the apple into 4 qartes so each of us will have one qarter then we'll take the extra qarter and split that qarter into 3 qarters then that will be equal.

victoria   chirs   Jinna

At all three grade levels, the activity provided a way for students to talk and think about fractions and the names of fractional parts in a problem-solving context.

GRADE

1	
2	
3	
4	
5	
6	

STRAND

NUMBER
GEOMETRY
MEASUREMENT
STATISTICS
PROBABILITY
PATTERNS AND FUNCTIONS
ALGEBRA
LOGIC

How Many Animals?

It's important that children experience problems with more than one possible answer, so they can learn that some math problems can have several solutions. David Ott taught this lesson to second graders in Albany, California.

After a storytelling session about safari adventures, David posed a problem to the second graders. "How many animals can there be if there are eight legs altogether?" he asked.

The question gave students a problem to solve that had more than one correct answer. The children worked on the problem in groups of four, describing alternatives and illustrating them.

Heather, Eunice, Aaron, and Rhonda wrote: *There are two four legged animals. or four two legged animals. or There cod be oun* [one] *four legged animal. and two two legged animals.*

Matthew, Stephen, Sara Rose, and Kirsten wrote: *There could be 8 and 4, 2, 3, 5, 6, 7. We thought this because there could be all kinds of animal.* They illustrated seven possibilities.

Stella, Min-Ki, Sherry, and Darren offered two possibilities: *Two animals that have 4 legs and 4 animals that have 2 legs.*

Dina, Minh, Michael, and Bonnie avoided the mathematical aspect of the problem. They simply wrote: *Monkeys, Lions, Girffs.*

This group illustrated their examples.

There are two four legged animals.
or four two legged animals.
or There cod be oun four legged animal.
and two two legged animals

This group lost sight of what the animals might be and drew solutions for combinations of one, two, and four legs.

These students figured out seven possible answers to the problem.

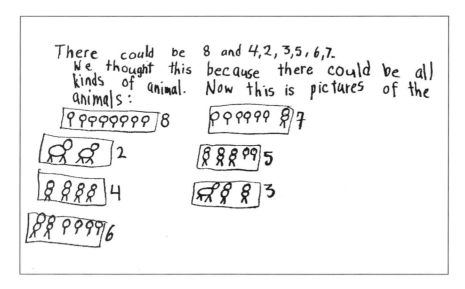

There could be 8 and 4,2,3,5,6,7. We thought this because there could be all kinds of animal. Now this is pictures of the animals:

STRAND

NUMBER
GEOMETRY
MEASUREMENT
STATISTICS
PROBABILITY
PATTERNS AND FUNCTIONS
ALGEBRA
LOGIC

Sharing 50 Cents

Chapter 5 of *A Collection of Math Lessons From Grades 1 Through 3* (see the Bibliography on page 179) presents four lessons designed to help third graders build their number sense and their understanding of division. David Ott adapted a problem from one of these lessons for second graders in Albany, California.

To present the problem to the second graders, David told them a story, incorporating himself and two boys in the class into the story.

"Craig, Roger, and I were walking to school, and we found 50 cents," he began.

Several students called out: "Where did you find it?" "Do you come to school together every day?" "Wow, 50 cents!"

"It's just a story," David responded.

"You mean it's make-believe?" Lauren asked.

David nodded, and the class settled down. He began again. "Craig, Roger, and I were walking to school, and we found 50 cents. We turned the money in to the office. But a week later, no one had claimed it, so we got to keep it."

"Too bad it's make-believe," Roger commented.

David then presented the problem to the class. He asked the students to figure out how much each of the three people would get if they shared the 50 cents equally. "Then write about how you solved the problem," David said.

The Children's Work

The children used different strategies to arrive at their solutions and presented different versions of correct answers. Their work is testimony to the uniqueness of children's thinking and the varied and partial understandings that exist in a class.

Lina and Monica H. wrote: *We gave 16 cents to every body and then we saw the 2 more cents were left so we gave then to the teacher. We figuord 15 before we thought 16 but then we saw that it was not inof.*

Lina and Monica H. verified their answer with an addition calculation.

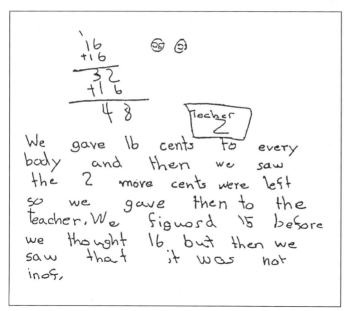

Monica S. came up with the same numerical conclusion but didn't offer advice about what to do with the extra money. She began counting by 3s, writing the multiples 3, 6, 9, 12, and so on. She abandoned this approach when she reached 18. Then she made three columns and wrote the numbers from 1 to 48, putting one in each column. She counted how many in each column by numbering (incorrectly) each entry, but eventually reported the correct answer.

Monica S. drew three columns and wrote the numbers from 1 to 48, one by one.

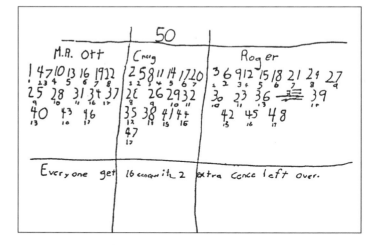

Erica and Elizabeth presented a different solution. They decided that each would get 15 cents, and they would give away 5 cents. They provided several alternatives: donating the nickel to the office or the PTA, turning it over to the teacher, or throwing it in the river.

Mia drew marks in three columns and wrote: *I put a dot in each colum (each colums dot's stand for one cent) until I had put down fifty dot's but then one person would only have sixteen cent's and the other people would have seventeen cent's.* Mia's writing reflected her enthusiasm for the apostrophe and her partial understanding of its purpose.

Odysseus and William's method was similar to Mia's. They drew three stick figures and put tally marks under each. The arrived at an incorrect conclusion, however, but were satisfied with their results. They wrote: *We drew three seventeens and it added up to fifty.*

Lauren drew 17 squares for each person and checked her answer by adding 17 three times. After figuring that 7 + 7 + 7 was 21, she made the common error of writing the larger digit in the 1s place and carrying the smaller. This resulted in the incorrect sum of 42. Confused, she tried adding 15 three times, and arrived at 45. That's as far as she went. Lauren's erroneous arithmetic is a reminder that we can't count on the symbolism of mathematics to clarify children's thinking.

Lauren drew pictures and tried to represent the problem symbolically but became confused.

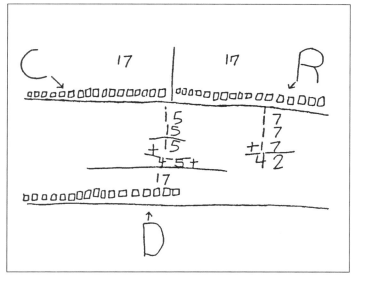

STRAND

NUMBER
GEOMETRY
MEASUREMENT
STATISTICS
PROBABILITY
PATTERNS AND FUNCTIONS
ALGEBRA
LOGIC

Exploring Halves

This lesson gives students the challenge of exploring different ways to divide squares into halves and involves them with geometry and measurement. David Ott taught the lesson to second graders in Albany, California. David followed this lesson with *Dividing Cakes* (see page 55), which asks students to divide rectangles into different numbers of equal shares. A similar lesson, *Cutting the Cake* (see page 97), has students divide rectangles into fourths and compare the resulting shapes.

Materials

— Paper ruled into six 2¾-by-2¾-inch squares, one sheet per student (See the blackline master on page 168.)

David drew a circle on the board and asked the children how he might divide it in half. After listening to several responses, David drew a diameter of the circle to divide the circle into two equal parts. He shaded one part to model for the children how to show one-half.

David then introduced the activity. "You're going to experiment with ways to divide squares in half," he said. He held up a sheet with six squares on it.

"You'll work in pairs," David said. "Find different ways to divide each square in half, and then shade half of each square. Be sure that both of you can explain how you divided the squares and why you're sure each part equals one-half."

After about 15 minutes, David called the class to attention. "Each pair will show the class one square that you divided," he said. "Pick a square that you think is unique, that nobody else would have."

As each pair came to the front of the room, David drew a square on the board on which the two students showed their method. The children had to explain why the part they shaded was one-half of the square. David invited others in the class to ask questions and challenge the results if they disagreed.

It was hard for some of the children to duplicate their squares on the board. Sarah and Amika had a particularly difficult time. Once they drew it, however, they were able to explain why what they shaded represented half.

"See, this corner part is the same as this part," Sarah explained as Amika pointed. "Then these two long pieces are the same, and we cut the middle one in half."

Jeremy's example raised the question of how to prove whether what was shaded really was half. He wasn't sure how to explain it, but he was convinced that he was correct. Children made suggestions, and soon Jeremy was cutting up the square to compare areas.

Monica and Allison explained their drawing by measuring and showing that the line was the same distance from the upper left and lower right corners. Their method opened up many other possible ways to divide a square in half.

David followed this lesson with an exploration of the ways to divide rectangles into 2 through 10 equal shares. (See *Dividing Cakes* on the facing page.)

The students used various ways to divide squares in half.

GRADE

1
2
3
4
5
6

STRAND

NUMBER
GEOMETRY
MEASUREMENT
STATISTICS
PROBABILITY
PATTERNS AND FUNCTIONS
ALGEBRA
LOGIC

Dividing Cakes

In this lesson, students explore how to divide rectangles into different numbers of equal shares. David Ott reported the following experience with second graders in Albany, California. He introduced this activity after his students had completed *Exploring Halves* (see page 53). In another lesson, *Cutting the Cake* (see page 97), students divide rectangles into four equal shares, then compare the resulting shapes.

Materials

— 8½-by-11-inch paper, about four sheets per student, cut as described below

— Rulers, one per student

David told the students that they would work in pairs to divide rectangular cakes so that groups of 2 to 10 people would have equal portions. He cut 8½-by-11-inch paper into fourths to make rectangular "cakes" and gave each pair of children about 15 of them.

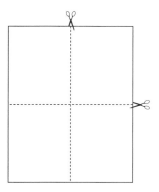

"Draw lines on each cake to divide it into equal shares for different numbers of people," he explained. "You may want to fold the paper first. Also, be prepared to explain for each of your cakes why you think the shares are equal."

As David circulated and observed the children, he overheard some of their comments. "I wish he had given us squares." "Sharing with five people is real hard." "Odd numbers of people all seem hard."

Some of the children folded and then drew lines. Others began by drawing. Some pairs worked together on each cake. Other pairs divided the rectangles and worked individually. David reminded these pairs to discuss their solutions with each other.

One pair of students used a ruler successfully but in an unconventional way. They discovered that the length of a rectangle was exactly the same as five widths of a ruler and used that information to draw fifths!

One pair divided their "cake" as shown below and felt satisfied that there were 16 equal pieces.

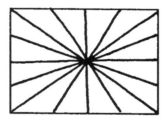

"Some are short and fat and some are long and skinny and it all evens out," the two children explained to David.

"That's just how it looked to me," David reported later, "but I had to think a bit to decide how to prove or disprove it."

The students divided their "cakes" in various ways.

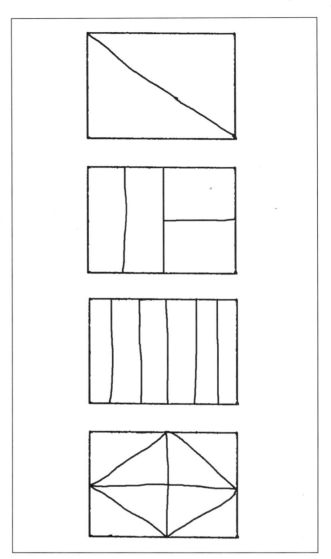

STRAND

NUMBER
GEOMETRY
MEASUREMENT
STATISTICS
PROBABILITY
PATTERNS AND FUNCTIONS
ALGEBRA
LOGIC

Roll for $1.00

Having children write in math class helps them reflect on their experiences and also serves to give the teacher insights into the children's thinking. In this lesson, Carolyn Felux taught second graders in Converse, Texas, how to play *Roll for $1.00* and then had them write about the game and explain the strategies they used.

Materials

- Dimes
- Pennies
- *Roll for $1.00* Directions (See the blackline master on page 169.)
- Dice, one die per group of students

Carolyn organized the class so the students could play *Roll for $1.00* in small groups. "You each need to make a playing board that looks like this," Carolyn began. She drew an example on the board.

Dimes	Pennies

"Use a full page," Carolyn advised, "and leave enough space so you can fit a small pile of pennies or dimes in each box. Be sure you have seven boxes in each column."

Carolyn gave the children time to make their playing boards. She chose not to prepare and duplicate playing boards in advance. It's important that children learn how to organize their work on paper, and this game provided another opportunity for them to practice doing so.

"You'll play *Roll for $1.00* in your groups," Carolyn said. "The object of the game is to get as close as possible to $1.00 without going over." Carolyn wrote the rules of the game on the board and read them aloud.

1. Each person takes a turn rolling one die.

2. On each turn, all players use the number rolled.

3. Each player takes as many pennies OR dimes as the number rolled. A player may not take both pennies and dimes on the same turn.

4. Each player puts pennies in the Pennies column and dimes in the Dimes column.

5. Whenever a player has 10 or more pennies, he or she MUST exchange 10 pennies for a dime. Put the dime in any box in the Dimes column.

6. Players who go over $1.00 are out of the game and must wait for the next round.

7. The game is over after seven rolls. The winner is the player who has the closest to but not more than $1.00.

Carolyn distributed a die and a supply of pennies and dimes to each group. She also gave each group a copy of the directions. (See the blackline master on page 169.) As with all new activities, there was confusion during the first round of the game. Carolyn gave assistance as needed—answering questions, explaining again, and resolving differences. The children soon were able to play easily.

Writing About the Game

After the students were familiar with the game, Carolyn asked them to write about their experiences. She was interested in having them evaluate the game and also explain the strategies they used when playing.

"There are two parts to this writing assignment," Carolyn told the children. She wrote prompts on the board to help the children get organized:

1. I think the game is _____.
2. The best way to play the game is

_____.

Most of the children reported that they liked the game. Liz's response was typical. She wrote: *I think the game is fun because you get to play with money and you get to count it.*

From April: *I think the game is a good game becase if you know how to count money it will help you practice.*

Stenna wrote: *I think the game is fun because it is a learning game.*

Sarah had a complaint. She wrote: *I think the game is noisy because the children play with the money on the desk!*

Clint panned the game. He wrote: *I think the game is boring because all you do is roll and put on money.* In response to the second question, however, he had a clear and concise strategy: *The best way to play this game is you count every time. When I rolled a big number I put pennies and when I rolled a low number I put dimes.*

Greg gave the game a mixed review. He wrote: *I think the game is good and bad because I like to count but then you get stuck you have nine pennies and 90 but I can't go over ten pennies and also I can't go over a dollar.* Greg's idea about how to play the game was operational rather than strategic. He wrote: *The best way to play the game is to count the money every few minnites so that you don't get over ten pennies or ten dimes so if you do you can trade in the pennies for dimes.*

Greg had mixed feelings about *Roll for $1.00.*

> ## Roll for $1
>
> I think the game is good and bad because I like to count but then you get stuck you have nine pennies and I go but I can't go over ten pennies and also I can't go over a dollar.
> The best way to play the game is to count the money every few minnites. so that you don't get over ten pennies or ten dimes so if you do you can trade in the pennies for dimes

Liz combined both approaches in a lengthy response: *The best way to play the game is to count the money because if you don't and you keep on playing you might already be over a dollar and you won't know it and you won't win. The way I knew to choose a dime or pennies is if I roll over a four I used pennies and if it was lower than a four or a four I used dimes.*

April's idea was similar. She wrote: *The best way to play the game is to yous strategy. Becase if you roll a five if you put five dimes you mite go over a $1. But if you roll a five and you put pennys you will mabe not go over a $1. When you yous dimes is when you roll a little numer like 4, 3, 2, and 1. And when you roll a big numer like 5 and 6 you yous pennys if you want to.*

Erin took a broader focus in her response. She wrote: *The best way to play the game is to first learn the rules and don't go over a dollar. You use dimes and pennies. I like the game because it is a thinking and a money game too because I like playing with money a lot. How I win on big rolls I put pennies and on little rolls I put dimes. I like to buy stuff with money like gum toys and presents the best. Money is inmortent to me because you need it to buy clothing, shellter and food.*

Stenna's strategy was to use dimes for 1s, 2s, 3s, and 4s, and pennies for 5s and 6s.

> ## Roll for a $100
>
> 1 I think the game is fun because it is a learning game.
> 2 The best way to play the game is with good strategy because you can not go over a dollar. I played the game by using one, twos, three, fours for dimes and fives and sixes for pennies

GRADE		STRAND
1		NUMBER
2		GEOMETRY
3		MEASUREMENT
4		STATISTICS
5		PROBABILITY
6		PATTERNS AND FUNCTIONS
		ALGEBRA
		LOGIC

The Rubber Band Ball

Sometimes the inspiration for a math activity comes naturally from conversations with students about things in which they're interested or involved. In this case, a third grader in Mill Valley, California, brought to school a rubber band ball she had made and was showing it to other students. I used the opportunity to focus the children on estimation, ratio, proportion, and patterns.

Materials

— Rubber bands, at least 600

Brandie had brought a rubber band ball to school, and I overheard her tell the other students at her table that her father had given her the rubber bands. She had worked on the ball for two days and used 320 rubber bands.

"I have an idea," I said to Brandie and the others at her table. "How about showing the ball to the rest of the class without saying how many rubber bands you used? Then they can guess."

I called the other students to attention, and Brandie showed them the ball. "When you make a guess," I said, "Brandie will tell you whether your guess is too large or too small. Listen to all the guesses and to Brandie's clues. They can give helpful information for figuring out how many rubber bands there are in all."

Most of the children were eager to guess. Few of them, however, made use of the clues. For example, Michael guessed 400, and Brandie told him that was "too high." Then Vanessa guessed 500, and everyone looked expectantly at Brandie for the clue. It was only after about 10 guesses that some children started to notice that some guesses weren't useful or necessary.

As the guesses got closer to the correct number, I began recording them on the board. (I think I should have recorded the guesses and clues from the start, as seeing the numbers seemed to be useful for some of the children.) Finally, Timmy guessed correctly.

I then measured the diameter of the ball for the children by propping a chalkboard eraser on each side of the ball and measuring the distance between. It was $3\frac{1}{2}$ inches. The word *diameter* was new for the children, so I added it to our class list of geometry words.

"I wonder what the diameter would measure," I said to the children, "if we added more rubber bands to the ball."

Brandie's hand shot up. "My dad said he has 300 more rubber bands that I could have," she said excitedly. Brandie is a quiet child who generally doesn't ask for or receive a great deal of attention. She was enjoying center stage right now and was eager for it to continue.

"Suppose Brandie added 300 more rubber bands, 100 at a time," I said to the class. "After adding 100 more, how many rubber bands would there be on the ball?" Patrick answered that there would be 420.

"And then 100 more?" I asked. Grace answered with 520.

"And the last 100?" I asked. I received a chorus of 620. I recorded on the chalkboard:

Rubber Bands	Diameter
320	$3\frac{1}{2}$ inches
420	
520	
620	

"With 100 more rubber bands," I asked the class, "what would the diameter measure?"

Timmy guessed 5 inches, but couldn't explain why. Erika guessed 6 inches, and then Michael guessed 7 inches; neither had an explanation.

Grace thought it would be $4\frac{1}{2}$ inches. "I figured that it took about 100 rubber bands to make

an inch," she explained, "so another inch would make it $4\frac{1}{2}$." Grace's idea made sense to others who nodded in agreement.

Patrick had a different thought. "I don't think it would get so big," he said, "because when you put rubber bands on, they have to stretch more because the ball is bigger, and when they stretch more they'll be thinner. So I think it'll be 4 inches." This idea appealed to some of the other children.

I asked Brandie to bring in 100 rubber bands, so others could help her add them to the rubber band ball.

The Next Day

Brandie came to school the next day with a plastic bag of 1,000 rubber bands. "My dad said I could have these because it was for math," she announced.

I gave the children at Brandie's table the task of counting out three piles of 100 rubber bands and adding the first 100 to the ball. When they were finished, I called the class to attention and measured the diameter. It measured $3\frac{3}{4}$ inches.

"Does anyone have an idea about why the diameter is less than you predicted?" I asked.

"I think it's like what Patrick said," Jill answered. "They stretch more because the ball is bigger, so it didn't grow much."

Bayard, who had helped put the extra rubber bands on, had another idea. "I think these rubber bands are thinner than the others," he said.

"With this new measurement," I then asked, "think about what the diameter will measure with 100 more rubber bands. Tomorrow we'll discuss your ideas, add more rubber bands, and measure again."

We took the time the next few days to continue the investigation. I purposely spread the activity over time to allow the children to reconsider their ideas. Too often, we race for answers and push for conclusions. Missing is time for musing, reflecting, and letting ideas sit. Over several days, more of the children used reasoning techniques and made predictions they could explain. The time was well spent.

GRADE
1
2
3
4
5
6

ST
N
GE
MEASUREMENT
STATISTICS
PROBABILITY
PATTERNS AND FUNCTIONS
ALGEBRA
LOGIC

How Many Days of School?

These two problems require students to apply number and measurement skills as well as their understanding about the calendar. I got the idea for the lesson from Marge Tsukamoto, a teacher in San Francisco, California. I presented it to third graders in Mill Valley, California, at the beginning of the school year.

Materials

— One 1-inch strip of paper, ruled into 1-inch squares

"How many days have you come to school so far this year?" I asked the third graders.

The students weren't sure. We looked at the calendar together and verified that this was the eleventh day of school.

I took a 1-by-12-inch strip of paper ruled into 1-inch squares and taped it horizontally at the top of the chalkboard. With a marker, I numbered the first 11 squares.

1	2	3	4	5	6	7	8	9	10	11	

"Why do you think I numbered up to 11?" I asked.

Laura volunteered that it was because they'd been in school 11 days so far.

"I have two problems for you to solve in your groups of four," I then told the class. "First, I want

63

you to figure out how many days you'll come to school this year. Next, I want you to decide where the strip will end if we continue numbering it for all the days of school until summer vacation."

The Children's Work

The discussions in the groups were extremely animated. Children brought different bits of information and approaches to their groups. There was disagreement in some groups about how many days were in a year. Some knew exactly, some had a close idea, and some had no idea at all.

Most of the groups figured that they came to school for nine months and focused on how many days were in each month that they came to school. One girl started to write down the "30 days has September" poem to help her group figure the differences among months. One group figured that there were either 20 or 21 school days in each month. But Teddy knew something about February and said they should count only 18 days for it.

There was much adding and figuring on scratch paper. Then, when I reminded the students about writing down their ideas, they scurried to record their thoughts.

Only three groups tackled the problem of how far the strip would stretch. They used rulers and yardsticks and relied on visual estimating.

One group had three students in it: Patrick, Mairead, and Bryce. Patrick was working separately from the other two. He concluded that there were 213 days of school, while the other two thought there were 192 days. However, Patrick marked a spot for the strip to end that wasn't as far around the room as the spot that the other two had marked.

"That can't be," Mairead said, "because your guess for the number of days is higher."

These three students wrote the following about their different answers: *Patrick thinks there are 213 days in school. Bryce and Mairead think there are 192 days in a school year. Patrick thinks it is 213 bucause it is not a hole year. Bryce and Mairead think it is 192 bucause it sounds like the rite number.*

Bryce and Mairead estimated 192 days. Patrick disagreed, believing there were 213 days in a school year.

> Patrick thinks there are 213 days in school. Bryce and Mairead think there are 192 days in a school year. Patrick thinks it is 213 bucause it is not a hole year. Bryce and Mairead think it is 192 bucause it sounds like the rite number.

The numbers in the problem posed difficulties for the children. Still, they were interested and engaged in thinking and reasoning. This was a good reminder that even when a complicated problem poses difficulties for children, if their curiosity is engaged, the problem can provide a valuable experience.

Both of these groups mentioned removing vacations and weekends, but each came up with a different answer.

> We think that thare are 177 days of school because there are 305 days in a year so we took off Holladas and vacations.

GRADE

1
2
3
4
5
6

STRAND

NUMBER
GEOMETRY
MEASUREMENT
STATISTICS
PROBABILITY
PATTERNS AND FUNCTIONS
ALGEBRA
LOGIC

The Place Value Game

The *Place Value Game* has long been one of the standard activities I give to students of all ages. It blends probability with place value in a game that has an element of chance and gives children practice reading large numbers and writing decision-making strategies. I taught this lesson to third graders and sixth graders in Mill Valley, California.

Materials

— Dice or spinners with numbers 1 to 6, one per group of students

The Lesson with Third Graders

The object of the *Place Value Game* is to try to make the largest number possible with the digits determined by a die or spinner. I introduced a four-digit game to third graders, but it's possible for younger children to play with two- or three-digit numbers and for older students to play a five-digit game.

Although I planned to have the children play the game in groups of four, I introduced the game to the entire class. I drew on the board a game board and asked that each student copy it on a sheet of paper.

"Make the boxes large enough so that you can write a numeral in each one," I said. "And draw the game board near the top of your page so that you can fit many games on one sheet of paper."

I purposely did not prepare a worksheet for the students to use. I think that children benefit from having the responsibility to organize their own recording, and this game gave them practice doing so.

"To play the game," I said, "I'll roll the die, and you'll write each number that comes up in one of the boxes in your game board. Once you write a numeral, you can't move it to another box. The object is to end up with the largest number possible."

"Why do we have a reject box?" Andreas wanted to know.

"I may roll a number that you don't think will help you get the largest number possible," I answered. "So you have one chance to reject a number. But the rule is the same: Once you write a numeral in the reject box, you can't change it."

I know to expect confusion the first time I try any new activity with students. "Let's just try a game," I said, "and we'll see if that helps you understand how to play."

I rolled the die five times, stopping each time to give all of the students a chance to record the number. There were groans and cheers when I rolled a 6. I already had rolled a 5, and some students had written it in the 1,000s place, while others had held out, hoping for a 6.

At the end of the game, I asked students to read their numbers aloud to the others at their tables. This would give them practice reading numbers in the thousands. "Each of you should read your number aloud," I said. "Then the person with the largest number should raise his or her hand."

"We had a tie," Jill said.

"Then both of you can raise your hands," I responded. I called on several children to report their results. I recorded their numbers on the board and reviewed the names of the 1s, 10s, 100s, and 1,000s places with them.

After playing one more game with the class, I had the students play in small groups. The chil-

dren liked the game, and after they had played it on and off for several days, I initiated a class discussion to hear their ideas about how to win the game.

The children offered a variety of approaches: "It's a good idea to put a 6 in the first box." "I always put a 1 in the reject box." "I put a 5 or 6 in the 1,000s place." "You have to decide if you'll take a chance with a 3."

I didn't comment or probe their ideas but merely gave all who volunteered the chance to report.

"When people play games," I said, "they often have a strategy, a plan for deciding what to do." I wrote the word *strategy* on the board. I then explained that I wanted the students to write about the strategies they used to decide where to write numbers as they came up.

"Think about how you'd give someone else advice about how to win," I said.

Grace developed a strategy for playing the game but was also philosophical about winning and losing.

Our table got 9 all ties and 8 all in a row. One of them was all 1s. My stratagy was that if there was one I put it in the regect box. I put 6s in the thousands box. I put 3s in the ones box. I put 4s in the tens box. I put 5s in the hundreds box. I never won alone but I was in a few winning ties and a few losing ties. I was dissapointed when I lost but I know games are for fun not winning.

Teddy thought it was a good idea to take chances in the game.

> I thought taking chances on low numbers like 2 is better than putting it in the reject box. Thats how I won a game. We all almost had the same stratege. Thats how we got 9 all ties. I lost three games from not taking chances. So I changed my stratege.

The Lesson with Sixth Graders

After I explained the rules to the sixth graders, I rolled the die, listing the numbers on the board after each roll. After all of the students had filled in their boxes, it was clear to them from the numbers on my list what the largest number could be. Some students were pleased that they'd made choices that turned out to be advantageous; others were disappointed in their choices.

I played the game several more times with the class, and then I described their assignment. "Work in your groups, and write a decision-making strategy that you think would give the best chance of producing the largest number possible," I said. "Imagine that you're programming a computer to play the game. Describe how you would tell the computer to decide where to place each number as it comes up."

After the students wrote and shared their strategies, they were interested in doing some comparison testing with them. We played several games as a class. I rolled the die, and each group used its strategy to decide where to record the number. Doing this pointed out to some students that their strategies weren't complete or clear enough, and some groups had to revise their directions. Also, the students decided that it

would be necessary to play many games before they had convincing evidence that some strategies were more effective than others.

As an extension, some students wrote strategies for two-, three-, and five-digit games. There was a good deal of discussion among students about which game was easiest to win.

These students wrote a step-by-step procedure for playing the game.

> 1. Rolls of 1 and 2, put in reject box; if reject box filled, put farthest right as possible.
> 2. In rolling a six, put it farthest left as possible.
> 3. 5 and 4 on first roll go in 100's place.
> 4. 4 on first roll or three on first roll go in 10's place
> 5. 4 on second roll goes in 10's place.
> 6. on 4th roll, 5 goes to thousandth
> 7. 4 rolled after a four in the 10's place put in the 100's place.
> 8. rolling a 3 on other than 1st roll, put farthest right as possible.

After explaining how to play the game, this group described its strategy.

> Roll the die—
> You must put the number you roll in a box and you may not change it to a different box after you roll again. Put the 6 in the top left box. If you get a 5 or a 4 put them in the hundrenths or tenths box. If you get a 3, 2, or 1 put them in the ones box or the reject box. If the space of a 1, 2, or 3 is taken move it to the nearest right hand box. If the space for a 4, 5, or 6 is taken move it to the nearest left hand box.

STRAND
NUMBER
GEOMETRY
MEASUREMENT
STATISTICS
PROBABILITY
PATTERNS AND FUNCTIONS
ALGEBRA
LOGIC

The Name Graph

Making classroom graphs gives students experience with collecting and interpreting statistical data. This lesson uses children's interest in their names and their classmates' names to help them learn to create a graph, make generalizations from the data, and think about number relationships. A similar activity gives older students the opportunity to think about fractional relationships. I taught the lesson to second graders in Mill Valley, California and to fifth graders in San Francisco, California.

I began the lesson with second graders by ruling four columns on the board and numbering them 1, 2, 3, and 4. I wrote *Marilyn* in column 3.

1	2	3	4
		Marilyn	

"Why do you think I wrote my name in column number 3?" I asked.

Several students had theories. "You wrote it there because you have three names—a first

69

name, a middle name, and a last name," Marisa said.

"It's true that I have three names," I replied, "but that isn't why I put my name in column 3."

Sara had a different idea. "Maybe it's because you are 30 years old," she said.

I informed her that I was not 30 years old, and my age had nothing to do with my reason.

Edward spoke next. "Because it's your favorite number," he suggested.

I told him that wasn't my reason either.

Marie came up with the correct answer. "Is it because your name has three syllables?"

I was surprised by Marie's response. I didn't expect the children to figure it out—or know the word *syllable*.

"Yes, that's why," I responded, without revealing my surprise.

I then said my name, clapping each syllable as I did so. "My name has three claps. That's three syllables."

I wrote above the columns:

How many syllables are in your name?

I erased my name and had each student in turn come up, say his or her name, clap for each syllable, and then write the name in the correct column.

Encouraging Mental Calculation

I stopped after about half of the class had recorded. To engage the students in calculating mentally, I asked them to look at what had been written so far.

"How many people on the chart have one-syllable names?" I asked. There were four. We then counted and found that there were nine two-syllable names and three three-syllable names. I wrote *4, 9,* and *3* on the chalkboard.

"Let's figure out how many names are posted so far," I said. "How much is 4 plus 9?"

About half the children immediately raised their hands. "Say the sum together," I said, and received a chorus of "13."

"And 13 plus 3?" I continued. The class answered "16" in unison.

"Since there are 27 of you altogether, how many more names need to be written on the chart?" I then asked. There was some hesitation. After a few moments, three children raised their hands, though tentatively. After a few more moments, one more child raised her hand. I had the four volunteers report, and I received different answers: 9, 12, 11, and 13.

Next, I asked the students who had not yet written their names on the chart to raise their hands. We counted and found that 11 children still had to record.

We completed the chart. There were 7 names in the one-syllable column, 13 in the two-syllable column, 7 in the three-syllable column, and zero names in the four-syllable column.

How many syllables are in your name?			
1	2	3	4
Nick	Sara	Marisa	
Doug	Edward	Allison	
Jon	Marie	Tiara	
Beth	Timmy	Angela	
Jill	Michael	Jonathan	
Matt	Phillip	Angela	
Anne	Suzanne	Christopher	
	Eli		
	Laura		
	Marco		
	Andy		
	Julie		
	Martin		

Analyzing the Data

I wanted the children to draw conclusions from the information posted, so I gave several examples.

"Let me tell you some things I notice from examining this chart," I said. "There are more names in the two-syllable column than in any of the other columns. Also, zero children have four-syllable first names." The students nodded.

"I'm interested in what you notice," I then said. "Who can tell us something else from looking at the information on the chart?"

Edward spoke first. "All the children have different handwriting," he said.

Grades 2–6: The Name Graph

Though the children had indicated their agreement with my generalizations, they were much more enthusiastic about Edward's idea. "Look Allison's name is big." "Marisa used cursive." "Phillip's name is the smallest."

Sara had a different thought. "Timmy could've written his name in the 1, 2, or 3 column, but I could only write mine in the 2 column."

Again, the children were interested and talked about how Timmy could have written his name as Tim or Timothy. They found others with that same option—Nick, Doug, Michael, Edward, Phillip. Doug wanted to move his name and write it as Douglas instead.

Suzanne added, "All the names that can be written in more than one column are boys' names."

Nick focused on another aspect of the names. "Marisa was the only one who wrote her name in cursive," he said.

This was not going in the direction I had hoped for. I was looking for generalizations from the numerical relationships on the graph. My plan was to use these generalizations to create word problems for the students to solve. However, their generalizations were obviously more interesting to them than mine, so I let them continue.

After all of the children had had a chance to share their thoughts, I wrote two problems on the board:

1. Do more or less than half the children have two-syllable names? Explain why.

2. How many more children have two-syllable than one-syllable names? Explain why.

I asked the students to write group responses. They were accustomed to doing this in math class. One child from each group got a sheet of paper, and the children negotiated who would do the writing. I was interested in their responses, as we had done no formal work with fractions.

All but one group answered both questions. That group spent a lot of time copying the chart. They answered the first question but ran out of time and steam.

These groups had no problem answering the two questions about the name graph.

① The 2-syllable colom has thirteen, and the 1 collom and three colom have 7 each. 7+7=14 and 13 is not half the class. 14 is grater than 13. It is less.

② Colom 2 has 6 more than colom 1. 7+6=13, If you add one more it will be 14.

The ↓1st one answer is less. We think it is less because 7+7=14 and there is 13 in the two syallable group.

2nd one ↓
6 people. We think this because 13-7=6.

There is 7 in the 1s colem and 7 in the 3's colem
① less than half because 7+7=14 and there is 13 2-syllable names.

②.) 6 because there is 7 in the 1-syllable colem and 13 in the 2-syllable colem and 6+7=13.

71

The Lesson with Fifth Graders

At the beginning of class one day, I wrote on the board:

How many syllables are there in your first name?

Under the question, I drew four columns, numbering them 1, 2, 3, and 4. I modeled what I meant by syllables by saying my name, *Marilyn,* and clapping for each syllable. Then I wrote my name in column 3.

"I'd like each of you to come up and write your name in the correct column," I said. The children in this class sat in groups of five or six, and I called the students to the board in groups.

There was much discussion and questioning about what they were to write. "Should I write Matt or Matthew?" "Most people call me Jerry, but my real name is Gerald, and some people call me Jer." "I can't decide whether to write Jennifer or Jenny."

I repeated several times that the choice was theirs, but that they each could sign only once.

After all of the students had recorded, I focused them on interpreting the information on the graph. We counted how many people had signed in each category, and I recorded these counts at the bottom of each column. There were 9 names with one syllable, 14 with two syllables, 6 with three, and 1 with four.

"I'm going to ask you some questions that you're to answer using the information on this chart," I told the students. "When I ask a question, please don't call out the answer or raise your hand to reply. Rather, I'd like you to put your heads together in your groups and quietly discuss what you think the answer is. When you've done this, raise your hands to show you're ready with a response."

I then asked my first question. "How many people signed their names on the chart altogether?"

After a moment, all hands were raised. "When I count to 3," I said, "I'd like you all to say the answer together, softly."

I counted, and got a chorus of 30.

"Here's my next question," I continued. "Do more or less than half the names have two sylla-

bles?" Some of the children immediately raised their hands, so I reminded them, "Talk about this in your groups, raise your hands when you agree on an answer, and then I'll call on someone to respond."

After a few moments, I called on Irene. "Less than half," she said.

"Can you explain why you think that's true?" I asked.

"Because 14 and 14 add to 28, and that's less than 30," Irene explained.

Sean raised his hand. "I figured it another way. Half of 30 is 15, and that's more than 14," he said.

"Any other thoughts?" I asked.

There were none, so I asked another question, writing it on the board as well:

Do more or less than ½ of the names have more than one syllable?

This seemed easy for the students, and their explanations were similar to the ones they had given for the first question.

I then asked, "Do more or less than ¼ of the names have three syllables?" I wrote the question under the first question on the board.

This also seemed easy, and students again offered two explanations.

David said, "It's less because 6 times 4 is 24 and that's less than 30."

Geneva said, "It's less because if you divide 30 by 4, you get . . . " After hesitating, she added, "more than 6."

"How much is 30 divided by 4?" I asked.

Matt answered, "Seven and some left over."

I continued with several more questions of this type, each time having students mentally figure answers and explain their thinking. The discussion gave students practice with calculating mentally, contributed to their learning about fractions, and helped their development of number sense.

STRAND

NUMBER
GEOMETRY
MEASUREMENT
STATISTICS
PROBABILITY
PATTERNS AND FUNCTIONS
ALGEBRA
LOGIC

Calculators in Math Class

The National Council of Teachers of Mathematics' position statement, "Calculators and the Education of Youth," recommends that calculators be used "at all grade levels in class work, home-work, and evaluation." Because my third graders in Mill Valley, California, had limited experience with calculators, I planned some introductory explorations.

Materials:

—Calculators, at least one per group of students

—Calculator Explorations (See the blackline master on page 170.)

—NCTM Position Statement (See the blackline master on page 171.)

"**H**ow many of you have calculators at home?" I asked the class. Most of the students raised their hands.

I then held up one of the calculators we had in the classroom.

"What number do you think you'll see on the display if I press 2 plus 2?" I asked. The children answered "4" in unison.

I pressed 2 + 2 and asked the children sitting directly in front of me to report what number they saw on the display.

"It says 2," Chris said, surprised.

"It must be broken," Andreas said from the back of the room.

"No," I answered, "I just haven't asked it for the answer yet."

Mairead's hand shot up. "You have to press the equals," she said.

I did so. Now Chris reported that he saw a 4. Everyone seemed relieved.

"What I'm going to do now," I said, "is press equals again and again. Each time I press the equals key, Chris, Jason, and Brandie will report what they see." I did this and the three students called out the numbers as they appeared—6, 8, 10, 12. As they continued, all the children began chiming in—14, 16, 18. I stopped and called the class to attention.

"How can those of you who are sitting in the back of the room know what numbers are coming up when you can't see the display on the calculator?" I asked.

"Easy," Erika said. "They go by 2s."

"Ahh," I said, "you've noticed a pattern. That's just what you're to do when you explore the calculators—look for patterns."

I showed them how the "C" button cleared the display. I then asked another question, "If I press 3 plus 2, what will be on the display?" Some said 5; some answered 2; some said to press equals.

I pressed the buttons 3 + 2 =, and 5 was displayed.

"Now watch what happens," I said, "when I press the equals button again."

"You'll get 10," Ann called out.

I pressed it.

"No, it's a 7," Chris said.

I pressed the equals sign several more times, and the children seated in the front of the room reported—9, 11, 13, 15.

"What's the calculator doing?" I asked.

"It's adding 2 again," Teddy said.

I cleared the calculator.

"This time," I told the class, "I'll start with '2 plus 3 equals' instead of '3 plus 2 equals.' What pattern do you think will be displayed as I keep pressing equals, equals, equals?"

The children had various ideas. Rather than answer them, I suggested that they work in groups to find out.

I then showed them the sheet of explorations I had prepared. (See the blackline master on page 170.) I explained to the students that when they saw three periods (. . .), it meant "and on and on."

The Children's Discoveries

The children made a variety of discoveries. One group wrote: *We learned that if you press 2 + 2 it equals 4 but if you keep pressing the equals sign it will keep adding by twos. The next thing we learned is that when you add something like two plus three the last number that you add is the number that will keep adding together when you press the equals sign. I think the reason it always adds the last number when you press the equal sign more than once is because it is the number you add on to the first number.*

Another group, however, was confused by what happened. They wrote: *We found out if we press 2 + 3 10 times it will add up to 32. And 3 + 2 will = 23. We thought it would come out the same because it was the same numbers. We pressed 2 + 2 10 times. It came out 22. We pressed it again it came out 22. We think it is weird because we pressed 3 + 2 and it came out 23 and we pressed 2 + 3 and it is the same numbers. Others, we pressed 8 + 9 10 times. It came out 98. We pressed 9 + 8 it came out 89. We thought it would come out the same numbers.*

This group noticed that the calculator repeats the second number in a two-addend addition problem.

Plus Patterns
2+2=4=6=8=10 It goes by twos
3+2=5=7=9=11 It goes by two's
2+3=5=8=11=14 It goes by three's
The second numder in the probolom is the one you add on.
6+3=9=12=15=18 It goes by three's
3+9=12=21=30=39 It goes by nine's
8+6=14=20=26=32 it goes by sixs

A third group related addition to multiplication. They wrote: *We found out about patterns when we pushed 2 + 2 patterns then we pushed = and it went 2, 4, 6, 8, 10, and so on and then it's just like multiplication because when we pushed the 3's it went like 3, 6, 9, 12 and so on and the 4's, 5's, 6's, 7's, 8's, 9's, 10's, 11's and 12's and they all went in a pattern.*

Included in another report was an explanation of the associative principle: *When you add three numbers it adds the first two numbers together. Then it adds the answer and the last number. Then when you keep pushing = it will add the last number.*

One group found: *Odd + odd is always even. Even + even is always even.*

These students found an addition pattern that they "tried with hundreds and it worked."

Plus Patterns

Odd + odd is always even. Even + even is always even. We did 8+8 and 8+12. It always adds up by the last number. The second number is always the one you count by, like six plus 4 counts by four. The same thing with 1, 2, 3, 5, 6, 7, 8, and 9. It works with any number. Jill and Laura tried with hundreds and it worked.

Minus Patterns

When investigating patterns with the minus button, one group generalized about odds and evens: *Odd – odd turns out to be even. Even – even*

turns out to be even. Three odds turns out to be odd. Three evens turns out to be even.

One group explained their discovery about negative numbers: *The negative numbers are wen after you get down to one and then keep pressing the eqwells sighn it will look like it went back up to 26 but it is really going down to negative numbers because if you look at the side of the number there is a tacaway and that means that those numbers are numbers below zero.*

These students discovered that if they continued to press the minus button, the calculator would go beyond 1 and show negative numbers.

Minus Patterns

We found out that if you press on odd number and an even number and press the eqwells sighn it will go down to one and then if you press the eqwells sighn some more it will start going down to negative numbers.

The negative numbers are wen after you get down to one and then keep pressing the eqwells sighn it will look like it went back up to 26 but it is really going down to negative numbers because if you look at the side of the number there is a tacaway and that means that those numbers are numbers below zero.

For another group, however, numbers just got smaller and then larger: *When you do 20 – 2 after 0 it starts counting up to as high as you want to. And when you do 20 – 2 you go down by two and go up by two.*

These introductory activities provided just what I had hoped for. The children were involved.

While learning about a useful tool, they also were exploring mathematical patterns. In addition, from watching the children, listening to their discussions, and reading what they wrote, I learned more about each student's thinking process and understanding.

Some children brought in calculators from home. Some of these calculators, however, didn't have the capability of adding a constant when the equals button was pressed repeatedly. This difference fascinated the children.

A Note About Communicating with Parents

It's important that we communicate with parents about what their children are experiencing and learning in classroom mathematics instruction. I duplicated the NCTM position statement (see page 171) and sent it home. Also, I asked the children to share with their families the patterns they discovered.

GRADE
1
2
3
4
5
6

STRAND
NUMBER
GEOMETRY
MEASUREMENT
STATISTICS
PROBABILITY
PATTERNS AND FUNCTIONS
ALGEBRA
LOGIC

Pioneers, Candles, and Math

One recommendation in the NCTM *Curriculum and Evaluation Standards for School Mathematics* calls for having students "apply mathematical thinking and modeling to solve problems that arise in other disciplines" (p. 84). Joanne Curran made this happen with her third graders in Olivette, Missouri. The following describes five days of activities in her class during which she integrated the children's math work with their study of pioneers.

Materials

— Post-it Notes, 1-by-2 inches, at least two per student
— Paraffin wax, one 10-pound block
— Two 5-pound coffee cans
— Candlewick string
— One large pot
— One hot plate (or stove burner)
— Pot holders
— One box, approximately 1 cubic foot

"How many dips do you think it would take to make a candle with a base that measures 1 inch in diameter?" Joanne asked the class. The children had been studying pioneers and had learned about life in log cabins.

Joanne gave the children Post-its on which they wrote their estimates. The children went one at a time to the board and posted their estimates, which ranged from 100 to 300 dips, with estimates close to 250 being the most common.

Joanne had assembled the materials needed for each child to make a candle. She filled the large pan about half full of water and put it on the hot plate to heat. Using a hammer, she broke the wax into chunks and put them into one of the coffee cans. Then she put the can in the pot of water to melt the wax. She filled the other coffee can with cold water.

Joanne showed the children how to make their candles.

"First you cut a 6-inch length of candlewick string and tie one end of it around a pencil," she explained.

"Then you dip the string in the wax and slowly count to 10." She demonstrated.

"Lift it out," she continued, "and immerse it in the cold water to speed up the cooling process. Dip again and again, until the candle is the right size." To help the children get a sense of the process, Joanne repeated the procedure several more times, dipping her string into the hot wax and then plunging it into the cold water.

She organized the children into pairs. She explained that partners would take turns, one dipping while the other kept track of the dips by tallying.

"When the diameter of the base measures 1 inch," Joanne said, "record the number of dips on a Post-it. Then switch jobs and make another candle. When you're finished, the next pair goes." She gave each pair a number, so all the students would know the order of their turns.

"Save your Post-its," Joanne concluded, "so when the entire class is finished, we can post the data and compare them with our estimates."

Joanne went on with her day's plan of activities, and pairs of students made their candles throughout the morning.

Later, when all the candles were made and the students had posted their data, Joanne led a discussion about the range of the data of their actual dips, what occurred most often, and how the two sets of data compared. She also talked informally about the average number of dips, referring to what was "most typical." (The number of actual dips ranged from 30 to 60, with close to 50 being most common.)

Day 2

Joanne read to the students an article in the *St. Louis Post Dispatch* reporting that a candle could light approximately 1 cubic foot. She had brought in a box about that size to show the children, then posed a problem for the class to investigate.

"How many candles do you think a pioneer family would need to light a log cabin?" Joanne asked the class.

The children worked on this problem in groups of four. Most groups drew pictures of a one-room log cabin, decided on the lengths of the walls, and figured the area of the floor. A few groups tried to figure the volume of the cabin as well. One group drew a rectangle and divided it into small squares, each representing what a cubic foot box would occupy on the floor of the cabin.

"I wasn't looking for any single right answer," Joanne reported. "I was interested in the students' thinking processes and methods for solving this problem." Joanne had the children share their ideas in a class discussion.

Lindsey pointed out that pioneer families didn't really need to light the entire log cabin. "There's always a fire in the fireplace or the stove," she said, "and that gives light."

Scott had a different idea. "They would only light part of the cabin at a time," he said, "and carry the candles with them when they had to go to a darker part of the cabin."

Doug pointed out that they needed more candles in the winter when it was darker longer. "They wouldn't need so many in spring and summer," he added. This gave Joanne the opportunity to talk with the children about why days are different lengths in summer than in winter.

"How many candles would they need to use each night?" Derek wanted to know.

Adam suggested that they burn one of their hand-dipped candles to see how long it lasted. Joanne agreed. The class went on to other work while the candle burned. It lasted for 2 hours and 45 minutes.

Grades 3–4: Pioneers, Candles, and Math

Day 3

After reviewing the previous day's experience, Joanne posed another problem. "How many candles would a pioneer family need for a full year's supply?" she asked.

Joanne listed three assumptions on the board.

1. The family's one-room log cabin was no bigger than 20-by-20 feet.
2. The family had candles about the same size as the ones the students had made.
3. The family would light only the part of the cabin they were using.

The class measured 20 feet by 20 feet in the classroom to get a sense of the size of a log cabin. Also, the children thought they should say that the candles lasted about three hours, since candles might be different.

Groups approached the problem different ways. One group said it got dark in winter at about 5 p.m., and the family would need to burn two to three candles each night until 8 p.m., when they'd all go to bed. They figured that Ma needed two candles near her to light 2 cubic feet of space so she could sew, while Pa needed only one candle to read because he sat near the fire.

Then the students were stuck. Finally, they decided to multiply 365 by 2½. Not knowing how to multiply by fractions, they multiplied 365 by 2 and then added ½ of 365 to get 914 candles. (Later they lowered their estimate, reasoning that in the summer the family needed less than one candle per day since it stayed light until 8 p.m.)

Another group used a similar line of thinking, but decided that in the winter the family also needed half a candle each morning. They wrote: *They got up when it was still dark and needed light to dress and eat breakfast.*

A particularly energetic group divided the year into four parts with 91 days in each. (They ignored the extra day.) They decided the family needed one candle per day in summer, two per day in spring and fall, and three per day in winter. They arrived at a total of 728 candles for the year.

Two groups divided the year into winter and summer, figured the number of hours per day

they needed candlelight in each half year, and used that information to estimate a year's supply of candles.

Three groups came up with answers between 900 and 1,000; two groups estimated 528 and 789. Joanne instructed the groups to record their thinking processes. She found their methods remarkably complex. One group recorded 27 steps they had used; another recorded 12.

"The children were pleased and congratulated each other profusely," Joanne reported.

Day 4

Joanne began the lesson by telling the students that it had taken the class more than three hours to make 20 candles. "If the pioneer family needed between 500 and 1,000 candles each year, how many hours would they need to make them?" she asked.

The children worked in the same groups as before. Some groups found the problem easy; others were confused. One group figured the time for 500, 750, and 1,000 candles, not sure how many the family would need. Two groups divided 1,000 by 20 to get 50 but then forgot to multiply this by the three hours it took them to make the 20 candles.

Two other groups figured the total hours and divided by 24 to find the number of days. Another group contested this approach "because they had to sleep and nobody works for 24 hours straight." Then the students chose to divide by 10. "It's easier and rounder," they said, "and pioneers had to work at least 10 hours a day." In situations such as this, calculators allow children to work with numbers that otherwise might be out of their reach.

Day 5

Joanne gave the class the problem of finding a quicker and easier way to dip the candles. "Pioneer women had dozens of jobs to do each day," she told the children, "and couldn't spend all their time dipping candles! How could they approach this problem?"

Surprisingly to Joanne, this problem was the most difficult for the students to solve. Only one group came up with an option that they felt good about. They wrote: *Get a long stick and a huge pot of wax. Tie about 20 strings on at one time and get two people to dip for a day.*

A Final Note

Joanne felt that the time for these activities over the five days was well spent. The children were involved, interested, and engaged in thinking mathematically. They were pleased with their work—and so was Joanne.

Joanne presented one additional problem to the children: If they had made 12-inch candles instead of 6-inch candles, how would their answers change? This problem encouraged the children to reexamine their work and reflect on their thinking.

STRAND

NUMBER
GEOMETRY
MEASUREMENT
STATISTICS
PROBABILITY
PATTERNS AND FUNCTIONS
ALGEBRA
LOGIC

The Game of Leftovers

*M*ath By All Means: Division, Grades 3–4, which I co-authored with Susan Ohanian (see the Bibliography on page 179), is a five-week replacement unit. Lynne Zolli taught the unit to third graders in San Francisco, California. Here is an abbreviated description of a whole class lesson that uses Color Tiles to give students experience with division and remainders.

Materials

—Color Tiles, 15 per pair of students

—Paper cups or other containers to hold 15 tiles, one per pair of students

—Dice, one die per pair of students

—Small paper plates or paper squares, six per pair of students

—Directions for Playing *Leftovers* (See the blackline master on page 172.)

—One sheet of chart paper

"I'm going to teach you how to play a game called *Leftovers*," Lynne announced to her third graders. "It's a game of chance for partners and uses remainders. The winner is the person who gets more leftovers. I'm going to play the game with Irene, so you can see the way it works." Lynne invited Irene to join her at the board.

Lynne cautioned the class, "The game isn't hard to play, but you have to count carefully and keep careful records." She picked up a plastic cup containing tiles. "Your first job is to make sure you have 15 tiles. Irene, will you make sure we have 15?" Irene counted the tiles and nodded her head.

"Also, you need a die and six squares of paper," Lynne said, showing these items to the children. "We'll call these squares 'plates.'"

Lynne turned to Irene and said, "You go first. Roll the die."

Irene rolled a 4. Lynne directed Irene to lay out four plates and divide the tiles among them. "Be sure you put the same number of tiles on each plate," Lynne said.

Irene first put 2 tiles on each plate. After counting what was left in the cup, she put 1 more tile on each plate. "There aren't enough to go around again," Irene said. "There are 3 left over." Lynne illustrated on the board what Irene had done.

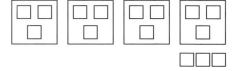

"Next, both people record the division sentence," Lynne said and wrote the equation $15 \div 4 = 3\ R3$. Then she wrote the letter I in front of it.

"This I will help me remember that Irene rolled the die," Lynne explained. Lynne designated a place on the board for Irene to record, and Irene copied what Lynne had written.

"Irene rolled the die, so she gets to keep the 3 leftovers, but she puts the rest back in the cup," Lynne said. "How many tiles do we have now?"

"Fifteen!" exclaimed Reggie.

"We have 15 altogether," Lynne said, "but how many are in the cup now that Irene got to keep the 3 left over?" Irene counted and reported 12 tiles.

"Now it's my turn to roll the die," Lynne said. She rolled a 6, put out six paper squares and divided the 12 tiles among them. She then illustrated on the board 2 tiles in each of six squares.

"There's nothing left over," Brittany said.

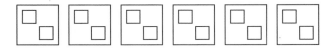

"That's right," Lynne said. "Who can tell us what to write?" She called on Amari. She and Irene recorded as Amari dictated: $12 \div 6 = 2\ R0$. Then she added a Z in front to indicate that it had been her roll.

Next, Irene rolled a 5. She put out five plates and divided the tiles as Lynne drew on the board. Aaron dictated the equation, and Lynne and Irene both recorded it: $I\ 12 \div 5 = 2\ R2$.

Lynne and Irene continued to play the game, recording the plays on the board. When all the tiles had been distributed, the game was over.

$$
\begin{array}{l}
I\ \ 15 \div 4 = 3\ R3 \\
Z\ 12 \div 6 = 2\ R0 \\
I\ \ 12 \div 5 = 2\ R2 \\
Z\ 10 \div 3 = 3\ R1 \\
I\ \ \ \ 9 \div 3 = 3\ R0 \\
Z\ \ \ 9 \div 6 = 1\ R3 \\
I\ \ \ \ 6 \div 3 = 2\ R0 \\
Z\ \ \ 6 \div 3 = 2\ R0 \\
I\ \ \ \ 6 \div 6 = 1\ R0 \\
Z\ \ \ 6 \div 4 = 1\ R2 \\
I\ \ \ \ 4 \div 5 = 0\ R4
\end{array}
$$

"Who won?" Truc wanted to know.

"Let's each count the tiles we kept," Lynne said. Irene reported that she had 9, and Lynne reported 6.

"Do we have all 15?" asked Lynne. Irene counted the tiles; others figured in their heads or used their fingers.

"You and your partner have to do one more thing before you start another game," Lynne said. She posted a large sheet of chart paper and titled it "Division with R0."

"On this chart, write all the sentences from your papers that have a remainder of zero," Lynne instructed. "But don't record any that are already on the chart." Lynne recorded the four different sentences that had remainders of zero.

Division with R0
12 ÷ 6 = 2 R0
9 ÷ 3 = 3 R0
6 ÷ 3 = 2 R0
6 ÷ 6 = 1 R0

The students were accustomed to working with partners, and they went right to work.

Observing the Children

Lynne circulated among the pairs. When children rushed through the game, she tried to slow them down, encouraging them to be methodical in laying out the paper squares and counting the tiles they had at the start of each round.

Matthew and Irene were typical of the children who valued speed over care. Both confident of their mathematical ability, they didn't share their tiles on the paper squares and didn't count the tiles at the beginning of each round. They relied on thinking they knew the right answers to the division problems. Lynne scanned their paper.

"You've made two errors," she told them.

"Where?" Matthew demanded to know.

"You can find them if you replay the game," Lynne said. She sat with them as they got started, checking each of their sentences with the tiles.

When Matthew found the error he had made dividing 14 into four groups, he said, "Oh, no. Then it all changes from here." Lynne agreed. After reminding them to slow down and be careful with their calculations, Lynne left them to redo the rest of their game.

Lynne noticed two errors and asked Matthew and Irene to replay the game.

A Class Discussion

The next day, Lynne called the class to the meeting area at the front of the room. "When you play *Leftovers*, you have to have a remainder to get out of a number," she said. "What was a very hard number to get out of?"

Demetrius and Wesley exclaimed together, "Twelve! It's impossible."

Lynne copied onto the board division sentences from the class chart that began with 12:

$$12 \div 1 = 12 \text{ R0}$$
$$12 \div 3 = 4 \text{ R0}$$
$$12 \div 6 = 2 \text{ R0}$$
$$12 \div 2 = 6 \text{ R0}$$
$$12 \div 4 = 3 \text{ R0}$$

"The only thing left to throw is a 5," Lynne said and added $12 \div 5 =$ to the list on the board.

"What happens with this number?" she asked.

"It's 2 remainder 2," Matthew said. Lynne completed the last sentence:

$$12 \div 5 = 2 \text{ R2}$$

"Wow!" Demetrius said. "Every number on the die except 5 comes out even, with no remainders. That's what makes it so hard."

Lynne later introduced an extension of the game—*Leftovers with Any Number.* In this game, students play *Leftovers* with one difference: They choose how many Color Tiles to start with. Giving students the choice is a way to allow them to gauge their own comfort level with numbers.

When playing *Leftovers with Any Number,* Samantha and Juliette were surprised by how many times they rolled before getting a remainder for 20.

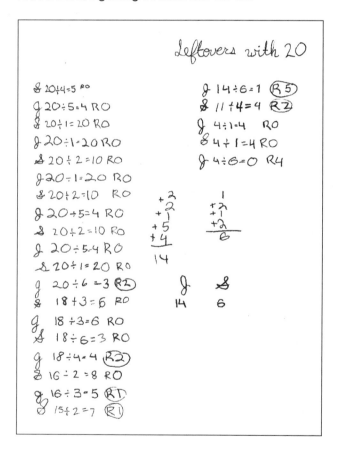

GRADE

1
2
3
4
5
6

STRAND

NUMBER
GEOMETRY
MEASUREMENT
STATISTICS
PROBABILITY
PATTERNS AND FUNCTIONS
ALGEBRA
LOGIC

How Much Ribbon?

One day, I purchased a gift for a friend and brought it to the gift wrapping desk. While I waited, I watched the two women working there wrap several presents. Their spatial skills were impressive. Each would pick up a box, tear off paper from a huge roll, and have just the right amount. Then they would cut a length of ribbon that, again, was just what they needed.

"How do you know how much to cut?" I asked the woman who took my box.

"I just judge, I guess," she answered with a shrug.

"Are you usually close?" I asked.

"Pretty much," she said. "I get a lot of practice."

As she wrapped my gift, I wondered about the ribbon. I couldn't even imagine how much ribbon I would need for the bow, much less the whole package.

Months later, Bonnie Tank and I were talking about lesson ideas for third graders. Bonnie wanted problems that would involve children with two-digit numbers.

"How much ribbon does the bow on a gift take?" I asked her.

"How big a bow?" Bonnie asked.

"A nice bow," I answered.

We both made estimates. We each got ribbon and tied a bow. Our thinking about how much ribbon we needed inspired the following problem-solving lesson, which involves third graders with geometry, measurement, and number. There's no end to the real-world sources for problem-solving ideas!

Bonnie taught this lesson to third graders in Mill Valley, California.

Materials

— Boxes of various sizes, one per group of four students

— Yarn, one yard-long piece per group

— Ribbon or yarn (Use yarn that doesn't stretch much.)

"**W**e're going to investigate how much ribbon you would need to wrap a present," Bonnie told a class of third graders. She showed the class one of the boxes she had collected.

"Let's start by thinking about the bow," Bonnie went on. "In your groups, estimate how much ribbon you think you would need just for the bow. Discuss your estimates in your group."

Bonnie gave a yard-long piece of yarn to each group. "We're going to use yarn instead of real ribbon," she explained. "Use this yarn to tie a bow around a pencil. It's up to your group to decide what size bow you'd like and how long the ends should be. After you make the bow and trim the ends, measure the yarn you used."

The children were interested in the problem. There was a great deal of discussion. Some children got rulers. Some made estimates with their hands. After a little more than 10 minutes, all groups were ready to report. Bonnie had one child in each group hold up the bow as another in the group reported. Bonnie recorded the lengths on the board:

12 inches
19 inches
26 inches
19 inches
24 inches
13 inches

"What do you notice about these lengths?" Bonnie asked the class.

There was a variety of responses: "They're all in the teens or in the 20s." "None are more than 30 inches." "None are more than 26." "All are more than 10." "Most of them are more than 12." "They go even-odd-even-odd-even-odd." "Two are 19 inches."

Because of an assembly, the math period was cut short. Bonnie continued the lesson the next day.

"Today," Bonnie began, "each group will get a box to wrap." Bonnie had a box for each group of four children. The collection included two shoe boxes, one box large enough for a shirt, one box that had held a ream of paper, the box that held the class Color Tiles, and two small cartons.

"Your group's job is to figure out how many inches of ribbon you need to wrap your box, including the bow." Bonnie demonstrated how to wrap the yarn around in two directions with a bow on top.

Then Bonnie explained to the children how they were to work. She wrote the directions on the board and elaborated on them:

1. Talk about a plan to solve the problem.
2. Decide on the length of yarn you need.
3. Write about how you got your answer.
4. Measure and cut yarn to test your answer.

The Children's Work

There was much talking, measuring, drawing, writing—and thinking. All but one group reported that their estimates were short. For example, one group drew an illustration of their box and explained clearly how they made their estimate. They wrote: *This is how we figured it out we measured acros the bottom and dubbled that then we measured the side and dubbled that then we dubbled it again and then we added 19 inches for the bow. We tested it and it barly fit we think we measured it well. but we needed one or two inches more.*

These students made a careful estimate but found that they needed 1 or 2 inches more ribbon.

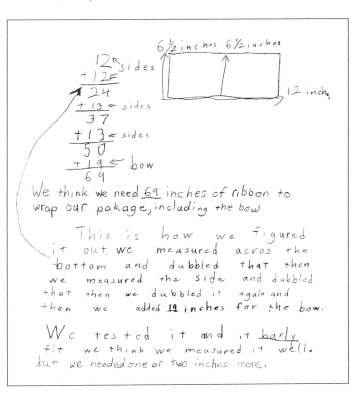

We think we need **69** inches of ribbon to wrap our pakage, including the bow

This is how we figured it out. we measured acros the bottom and dubbled that then we measured the side and dubbled that then we dubbled it again and then we added **19** inches for the bow.

We tested it and it <u>barly</u> fit we think we measured it well. but we needed one or two inches more.

These students were surprised when the ribbon didn't fit around their box.

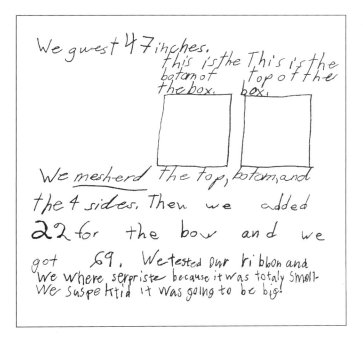

We gwest **47** inches.
This is the bottom of the box. This is the top of the box.

We mesherd the top, botom, and the 4 sides. Then we added **22** for the bow and we got **69**. We tested our ribbon and we where serpriste because it was totaly smoll. We suspektid it was going to be big!

Another group whose estimate was too short explained: *We mesherd the top, botom, and the 4 sides. Then we added 22 for the bow and we got 69. We tested our ribbon and we where serpriste because it was totaly small. We suspktid it was going to be big!*

One group dealt with the dilemma of too little ribbon by wrapping the package around the corners instead of the way Bonnie had demonstrated. They wrote: *We tested our ribbon and it was just right for us or We think we should of had 10 more inches for the regular way.*

The activity engaged the children and gave them valuable hands-on experience with estimating and measuring.

GRADE

1
2
3
4
5
6

STRAND

NUMBER
GEOMETRY
MEASUREMENT
STATISTICS
PROBABILITY
PATTERNS AND FUNCTIONS
ALGEBRA
LOGIC

Match or No Match

Materials

- Color Tiles
- Lunch bags, about 10

In 1994, I taught a unit I had developed on probability to a class of third graders in Mill Valley, California. This was the third time I had taught a version of this unit, and I felt ready to write the replacement unit *Math By All Means: Probability, Grades 3–4.* (See the Bibliography on page 179.) Following is an abbreviated description of *Match or No Match,* one of the menu activities.

I think it's valuable, as often as possible, to relate a new activity to children's real-life experiences. Therefore, before introducing this activity to the class, I talked with the children about how they decide among themselves who gets to pick first or go first in a game.

The students reported several different ways they used. The most common was playing ro-sham-bo (their name for Scissors-Paper-Rock). Other methods included tossing a coin and calling heads or tails; one person putting an object in one hand and the other person guessing which hand it's in; and both people showing one or two fingers, with one person winning if there's a match and the other if not.

"Although you have different ways of choosing," I said, "it seems to me that they're all the same in one way. They each give both people the same chance of winning. They're fair games because both people have an equal chance. In this activity, I'm going to explain three ways to choose, and you'll investigate whether or not each version is fair."

As the students watched, I put two blue tiles and one red tile into a paper lunch bag. "Suppose you and your partner decide to choose who goes first in an activity by reaching into the bag and drawing out two tiles," I said. "One of you is the match player and the other is the no-match player. When you look at the two tiles you remove, the match player wins if they're the same color, and the no-match player wins if they're different colors."

To demonstrate for the class, I asked Lori to join me at the front of the room. "Would you rather be the match player or the no-match player?" I asked her. She chose match.

I asked Lori to reach into the bag and remove two tiles. She did so and held them up for the class to see—a red and a blue.

"I'm going to record what happens so we can begin to collect some data," I said. I wrote *Match* and *No Match* on the board and made a tally mark next to *No Match*.

I asked Lori to replace the tiles. I shook the bag, explaining to the class that I did this to make sure I had mixed up the tiles. Then Lori drew again. Again, she got one of each color. I made another tally mark. We repeated this a third time with the same result. The students began discussing whether they believed match or no match was better.

"The game that Lori and I were playing is one of three versions that you'll investigate," I said. "Each version is played the same way, by drawing two tiles out of the bag and seeing if they match or not. The difference in the three versions is what you put into the bag." I listed on the board:

Version 1	2 Blue 1 Red
Version 2	2 Blue 2 Red
Version 3	3 Blue 1 Red

I explained to the children that they were to put the tiles in the bag and take 20 samples. Then they were to write about whether they thought the game was fair, or take more samples and then write.

After the students had explored all three versions of the game, I initiated a class discussion. The discussion was animated, and students argued about the fairness of the different versions. We examined the data they had collected, determined how many matches and no matches were in each version, and then talked about the fairness of each game.

Writing About the Game

After several days of discussion, I asked the children to write about the game. I circulated as the children worked. I noticed that some children drew conclusions from the data they collected, without thinking about the mathematical theory. Mercedes, for example, wrote the following: *I think for version 1 it's fair because we got 10 matches and 10 No matches. We thought it was really werd but thats just what happens. I think for version 2 it's fair also because there were 2 blues and 2 reds and match and no match got 10 and I new that it would be fair because 2 blues and 2 reds sound like they would be fair. I think for version 3 match is going to win because there are one red and 3 blues and on our sheet it's 9 to 11 and no match wins. My data doesn't mak any scents.* When I asked Mercedes why her data didn't make sense, she replied, "That's not what I thought was going to win."

I sorted the students' papers into three piles: those who were able to analyze the versions of the game completely and correctly (11 children), those whose reasoning was partially correct (10 children), and those who didn't seem to have much understanding at all (4 children). I noticed which children were able to list the possibilities and use the information to decide about the fairness of the game; who relied primarily on the data, either on the class chart or from his or her own individual experiments; and who wasn't able to think at all about the mathematics of the situation.

Mercedes drew conclusions from the data she collected, without thinking about the mathematical theory.

> Is IT Fair? No Match/Match
> I think for version 1 it's fair because we got 10 matches and 10 No matches. We thought it was really werd but thats just what happens.
> I think for version 2 it's fair also because there were 2 blues and 2 reds and match and no match got 10 and I new that it would be fair because 2 blues and 2 reds sound like they would be fair.
> I think for version 3 match is going to win because there are one red and 2 blues and on our sheet it's 9 to 11 and no match wins. My data doesn't mak any scents.

Abby's explanation was clear and succinct.

> Is It Fair
> (Match/No Match)
>
> V1 Version one is unfair because there are three possibilitys and in version one ~~and~~ match only has one possibility to win but no match has two possibilitys to win.
>
> V2 Version two is also unfair because in version two there are six possibilitys to win and no match has four of those possibititys. That only leaves two possibilitys for match to win.
>
> V3 Version ~~three~~ is fair because there are six ways to win, and match got three possibilitys and so did no match so it is fair. Our data was very close to what it should be and when I played it match won ten times and no match came up ten times so acourding to my data it should be fair.

Elliot wrote only about version 1 and did not deal at all with the probability aspect of the game.

> IS It Fair? Match/No Match
> I think version 1 is not fair because there is a bigger to get red or blue. I think they are the same because when I shake the bag, the red goes on top of the two blues. So I think when I stick my hand in the bag I pick up the red and the blue. But hear is a trick. You can have a red tiel with tow bumps on it. And then I touch the red and I don't pick it up and so I pick up the two blues. And when I want to get No macht I pick up the the red and the blue.

A Mathematical Note

Of the three versions of the game, only version 3 is mathematically fair. This seems counter-intuitive to many children (and adults), and the data from your class may or may not support the conclusion. It's important to remember that collecting a larger sample of data provides more reliable information. Also, although data are useful for thinking about and discussing the game, data are not sufficient to prove a theory.

One way to analyze version 1 is to list the three possible combinations of drawing two tiles:

B1, B2—match

B1, R—no match

B2, R—no match

This shows a 2/3 probability of getting no match and a 1/3 probability of getting a match. (Try analyzing version 2 this way to prove that it's more likely to get no match than match.)

Version 3, with three blue tiles and one red tile, disturbs some people when they analyze the possible combinations. Listing the possible pairs of tiles you can draw reveals that half of them produce a match and half produce no match.

B1, B2—match

B1, B3—match

B2, B3—match

B1, R—no match

B2, R—no match

B3, R—no match

Some people aren't sure that the six pairs are really equally likely and think that the blues make a match much more possible. I believe that the six possibilities above represent all the ways and that the game is fair, but you'll have to think about it to convince yourself.

STRAND

NUMBER
GEOMETRY
MEASUREMENT
STATISTICS
PROBABILITY
PATTERNS AND FUNCTIONS
ALGEBRA
LOGIC

Math from the Ceiling

Inspiration for problem-solving lessons comes from many sources. I got the original idea for this lesson from Jason, a third grader in Mill Valley, California. (A variation of the second activity in this lesson appears on page 141.)

One day, in response to one of my math-is-everywhere discussions with the class, Jason said, "We could do a math problem about the ceiling. We could figure out how many holes there are in the ceiling." The ceiling was covered with 12-inch-square acoustical tiles, each with a pattern of holes in a square array.

"How could we figure it out?" I asked.

"We need to know how many tiles there are," Michelle answered.

All eyes were drawn to the ceiling. The children began to count. It was a funny sight—27 little children looking at the ceiling intently, their heads bobbing as they counted. They counted, disagreed, counted again, argued, and finally came to an agreement. There were 32 tiles counting one way and 24 the other way.

"Now you multiply," Laura said. And though others nodded in agreement, no one was able to explain why multiplying made sense. However, the children used their calculators to find that there were 768 tiles. Some checked by adding 24 32 times or vice versa.

"Now we need to know how many holes in one tile," Patrick said.

None of us, however, could face counting the holes in one tile from our vantage points. We'd had enough for one day.

I was able to get an extra tile from the custodian and brought it into class the next day. This made the problem more accessible. The tile had 23 holes on each side. The children used their calculators again, first to find that each tile had 529 holes and then to calculate that there were 406,272 holes in the ceiling. They seemed proud of their work, even though they weren't able to read the number. I had them write about what they had done.

Michelle, Mike, and Tim wrote about how to figure out the number of holes in the ceiling.

> ## Holes in the Ceiling
> First count the numbers on one side. Then count the numbers on the other side. Multiply the two numbers, 23 and 23. Then then do the same for the ceiling. Multiply the number you got on the ceiling, 768, with the number you got from the tiles, 529, and the answer will be 406,272. That's what we got.

The Around-the-Edge Problem

"I have another problem for you to solve," I said. "I'll call it the 'around-the-edge-problem.' How many holes do you think there are around the edge of each tile? You could count them, but I'd like you to think about other ways to figure it out. Talk about this in your group and see if you can agree on an answer. Then each of you write about your thinking."

The groups' discussions were animated. I was surprised and delighted by the variety of

approaches that emerged. For example, Grace wrote: *I think there are 88 holes around the edge. I think this because if you add 23 + 23 + 23 + 23 you get 92 but that is not correct because you are counting the corners twice. I thought if you could pretend the corners weren't there and you added what was left which is 21, 4 times, you get 84. Then you add the corners on and you have 88.*

Grace suggested pretending that the corners weren't there, then adding them back in later.

> ## Around the Edge
> I think there are 88 holes around the edge. I think this because if you add 23+23+23+23 you get 92 but that is not correct because you are counting the corners twice. I thought if you could pretend the corners weren't there and you added what was left which is 21, 4 times you get 84. Then you add the corners on and you have 88.

Marina found a different way to approach the problem: *I think there are 88 holes around the edge. I think this because if you take away the corners there will be 21 holes on each side and then you add one corner to each side and will have 22 holes on each side. 22 + 22 + 22 + 22 = 88.*

Teddy wrote: *I think there are 88 holes around the edge because there are 23 holes on one side and you can't count the hole on the corner twice so it would be 22 on two sides and on the last one, it would be 21 because you can't count the same one twice on both corners. If you add 23 + 22 + 22 + 21, it equals 88.*

Ann explained: *I think there are 88 holes around the edge because there are 23 holes on two sides and on the other two sides there could not be 23 because the two end holes would be already counted so I subtrackted 23 tackaway 2 and I got 21 so there is twenty one holes on the other two sides so I added 23 + 23 + 21 + 21 and I got the number 88.*

Nick had a variation on Ann's method. He wrote: *There are twenty-three holes across the top and bottom and twenty-one along the sides. I added twenty-three plus twenty-one and I got forty-four. I timesed that by two and got eighty-eight.*

Nick counted the corners only for the top and bottom edges.

> *Around the Edge*
> I think there are 88 holes around the edge. I think this becuase there are twenty-three holes across the top and bottom and twenty-one along the sides. I added twenty-three plus twenty-one and I got forty-four. I timesed that by two and got eighty-eight.
>
> $$23 + 21 = \underline{44} \times 2 = \underline{88}$$
>
> $$\begin{array}{r} 23 \\ +21 \\ \hline 44 \\ \times\ 2 \\ \hline 88 \end{array}$$

GRADE
1
2
3
4
5
6

STRAND
NUMBER
GEOMETRY
MEASUREMENT
STATISTICS
PROBABILITY
PATTERNS AND FUNCTIONS
ALGEBRA
LOGIC

Cutting the Cake

This geometric problem gives students experience with exploring the fractional concept of fourths and with measuring to compare areas. Carolyn Felux developed and taught this lesson to fourth graders in Converse, Texas. Two similar lessons are designed for younger students: *Exploring Halves* (see page 53) has students divide squares into halves, and *Dividing Cakes* (see page 55) has students divide rectangles into different numbers of equal shares.

Materials

— 8½-by-11-inch sheets of paper

Carolyn asked the fourth graders to explore ways to cut a cake into four equal pieces. She gave the children 8½-by-11-inch sheets of paper to use as "cakes," and she asked them to sketch the different ways they found to divide them.

All of the children quickly found three ways to cut the cake into fourths.

Some children explored further and found additional solutions.

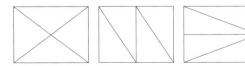

This activity is not unlike textbook problems that ask students to divide shapes into fourths. However, Carolyn extended the task by asking the children to respond in writing to the following direction: "Take one piece from each cake you cut. Compare the pieces to see if each one gives the same amount of cake as the others. Explain your reasoning."

The children's papers revealed that almost half of them thought that fourths in different shapes were different sizes. These children did not understand that all pieces that are one-fourth of the same whole are the same amount.

Megan wrote: *I do not think the pieces are the same size because they aren't the same shape.*

Susan wrote: *No, because some of them are short. And some of them are long. Because they are not all the same size.*

Others, however, understood that the pieces were the same size. Brandon explained how he verified his thinking with the pieces. He wrote: *Yes I do think they are all the same amount of cake. Why I think that is because I measured them or in other words I investigated. I cut one to measure the other one so that it fit it right.*

Sara wrote: *yes, I do think they are the same because all of the objects or shapes are ¼. No matter if you stretch & pull they are still the same size. But if you cut the cakes into smaller pieces of course they will not be ¼ any more.*

Carolyn might not have been aware of the students' misconceptions if she hadn't asked them to write about their thinking. With this information, she knew to provide additional investigations with geometric shapes to give the students opportunities to see that different shapes can have the same area. Having students make rectangular "cakes" with 24 Color Tiles, for example, can help them see that it's possible to build different shapes of rectangles with the same area. Cutting out tangram puzzles and learning that the square, parallelogram, and middle-sized triangle are all the same size also connects to the cake-cutting activity. Experiences with fractions in contexts other than geometric shapes are also important. With all activities, assessing what children truly understand is a key element.

Sara understood that the shape of the ¼ piece was not important.

yes, I do think they are the same because all of the objects or shapes are ¼. No matter if you stretch + pull they are still the same size. But if you cut the cakes into smaller pieces of course they will not be ¼ any more.

GRADE	
1	
2	
3	
4	
5	
6	

	STRAND
	NUMBER
	GEOMETRY
	MEASUREMENT
	STATISTICS
	PROBABILITY
	PATTERNS AND FUNCTIONS
	ALGEBRA
	LOGIC

Making Generalizations

Making generalizations—one of the important higher-order thinking skills—is difficult for some children. I derived this lesson from one of my long-time favorite activities— "The Consecutive Sums Problem"—which appears in *A Collection of Math Lessons From Grades 3 Through 6*. (See the Bibliography on page 179.) I taught this lesson to a fourth grade class in Bellevue, Washington.

The fourth graders were seated in groups of four and were accustomed to working cooperatively. To begin the lesson, I wrote five sets of numbers on the board:

1	2	3	4
8	9	10	11
42	43	44	45
19	20	21	22
77	78	79	80

"Each of these rows is a set of four consecutive numbers," I told the class. "What do you think I mean by *consecutive numbers?*"

The students described consecutive numbers in several ways: "They go in order." "They go up by 1s." "They don't skip any."

"When I examine these sets," I went on, "I notice that when I subtract the first number in each sequence from the last, I always get an answer of 3. For example, in the first one, 4 minus 1 equals 3. In your group, check to see if you agree this is true for all of these sequences."

While the students were talking this over, I wrote the generalization on the board:

The difference between the first and last numbers in a sequence of four consecutive numbers is always 3.

The students agreed that what I said was correct and that what I had written also expressed this characteristic.

"What I would like you to do in your groups," I then explained, "is to see what else you can say about sets of four consecutive numbers. What you are looking for are characteristics that hold for all sets. Write sentences to describe your group's generalizations."

Table 2 wrote three generalizations that used addition and one that used multiplication.

table 2

1. If you add the first and the last no. you always get an odd number
2. If you add the two middle numbers you always get an odd number.
3. If you add all four numbers you get an even number.
4 If you multiply the first and the last number you get an even number.

The students went right to work. After about 15 minutes, I asked for their attention and told each group to choose one person to read one of the group's generalizations.

"I'll go around the room," I said. "Each group will report just one conclusion on a turn. Listen carefully to the other generalizations because I want you to read one that hasn't been reported."

After each group read a statement, the others were instructed to check to see if it matched one they had written and to talk about whether they

agreed it was true. All six groups had different statements to report, and their statements stimulated new thinking.

Table 4 looked for patterns within the display of the four numbers.

Table 4
If you always start with an even number the last number will be odd, And if you always start with an odd # you come out with an even # last.
Every # next to each other, if you subtract you'll get the #1.

Throughout the lesson, I used the words *conclusion, characteristic,* and *generalization* as often as possible. Student understanding develops from hearing words in context. Also, students benefit from experiencing many such investigations, which support both their number sense and their ability to make generalizations.

Additional Explorations

Following are other explorations that engage students with making generalizations.

1. What can you say about any 2-by-2 array of numbers on a 0–99 chart? What about a 3-by-3 array?

2. What can you say about any three diagonally adjacent numbers on a 0–99 chart?

3. Try problems 1 and 2 but use numbers on a calendar instead. Do your generalizations still hold? Why or why not?

STRAND

NUMBER
GEOMETRY
MEASUREMENT
STATISTICS
PROBABILITY
PATTERNS AND FUNCTIONS
ALGEBRA
LOGIC

The Firehouse Problem

I found *The Firehouse Problem* in a lesson in "The Whole Language Connection," an article by Nancy Casey in the 1991 edition of *Washington Mathematics,* a publication of the Washington State Mathematics Council. Nancy Casey describes the whole language approach as one in which teaching is "organized around meaningful creative work by students." In the article, she describes four days she spent in a second grade classroom, "squinting over the wall that divides mathematics from language arts" to explore how the whole language approach to teaching reading and writing might transfer to the teaching of mathematics. I taught the lesson to third graders in Mill Valley, California.

Materials

— The Firehouse Problem recording sheet, at least one per student (See the blackline master on page 173.)
— Cubes, tiles, or other objects, at least seven per student (optional)

I held up a copy of the recording sheet and pointed to the pattern on it. "This is an unusual map of a town," I explained. "On this map, the lines represent streets, and the dots represent street corners. All the houses in this town are located at corners, and there's at least one house at each corner."

I then presented the problem. "The town needs firehouses," I said, "and the mayor has said that if a house catches on fire, fire trucks shouldn't have to drive more than one street to get to it. It's important that every house be on the same corner as a firehouse or only one street away."

To check that the children understood, I chose one dot as a possible firehouse location and asked which houses would be guarded by that station. After a few more demonstrations with different dots, all the children seemed to understand the parameters of the situation.

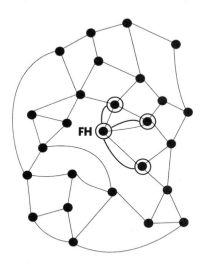

"Firehouses are expensive, and the people in the town would like to have some money left over for some swimming pools," I continued. "The problem is to figure out the fewest number of firehouses they can build and where to build them."

The students were fascinated by the problem and eager to get to work. I gave them a few more directions before distributing the recording sheet.

"Use cubes, tiles, or other objects to mark where you think firehouses might go," I said. "When you're satisfied with a solution, record it by circling the dots where the town should put firehouses." I also told the students that they could work individually, with a partner, or in a small group. They dove into their explorations.

This problem is from the area of graph theory. The map is a graph, but a different sort of graph from the types commonly used to represent a collection of data. This map comprises a set V of vertices (the dots) and a set E of edges (the lines). The solution—the fewest possible firehouses that meet the criteria—is called the minimum dominating set, and the only reliable way to find it is trial and error. However, there are many possible strategies for making guesses.

Observing the Children

As the children worked, I circulated, talking with them about their discoveries. Their theories were plentiful. Some looked for locations that serviced the most houses. Some noticed that a number of houses were particularly difficult to service. Some explored the different effect of locating firehouses near the outskirts of town or in the middle of town.

When students presented a solution to me, I gave them the choice of looking for a different solution or writing about the strategies they used to think about the problem. As students began finding solutions with the same number of firehouses, I had them compare their work to see if they had located the stations at the same corners.

At the end of the period, I asked the children to report what they had discovered so far. When we finished our discussion, no one was sure that the class had found the fewest number of firehouses possible, and all of the students were interested in continuing with the problem.

The next day, I started the class by having a few volunteers explain the problem for the two children who had been absent the day before. I also told the entire class that at some point they would have to write about their thinking. During this second class, some children continued to look for different solutions, even if they didn't find fewer firehouses, while others began writing about their strategies.

The Children's Work

Most of the students wrote about trying one strategy that wasn't successful, then finding another that they thought was better. For example, Gabe found a way to place seven firehouses in the town and believed his strategy would help him reduce that number to six. He wrote: *The way I figerd out how to do seven fire stations first by using Patricks idea that coverd five squars then I put a firehouse on the top of the triangle on the bottom right, and so on. I [In] the beginning I dident have a stratogy, but twords the end I started to pick up a stratogy I think you should put more on the side than in the middle. Now I'm pretty shere I can do six I'v almost got it.*

Gabe found a strategy he liked and believed he could use it to place even fewer firehouses.

Fire House Problems.
The way I Figerd out how to do seven fire stations First by using Patricks idea that coverd five squars then I put afire house on the top of the triangle on the bottom right, and so on. I the beginning I dident have a stratogy, but twords the end I started to pick up a stratogy I think you should put more on the side than in tha midle. Now I'm pretty shere I can do six I'v almost got it.

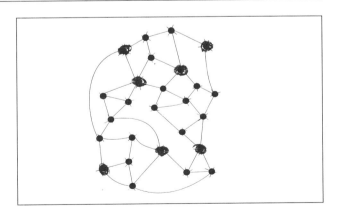

Bridget and Norah worked together. Bridget wrote: *At first Norah and I first would only put down a Fire Station if it would take care of four or five house, but we didn't get very far that way. Then we rellized that there were some places where fire house could only take care of one or two house but we need to put them down our [or] some house wouldnt get a Fire Station. The lest Fire Stations we could get is seven.*

Bridget described the strategies that she and Norah used.

At first Norah and I first would only put down a Fire Station if it would take care of four or five house, but we didn't get very far that way. Then we rellized that there were some places where fire house could only take care of one or two house but we need to put them down our some house wouldnt get a fire Station. The lest Fire Stations we could get is seven. I liked this problem a lot and I hope we do a nother problem like it again.

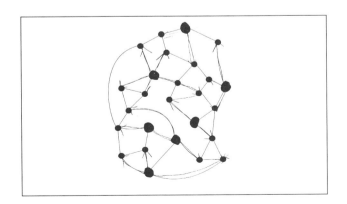

Most of the children continued working on the problem for a third day, and some stayed engaged with it even longer. Some made up their own "maps" to make firehouse problems for others to solve. After three days, I asked the children which grade levels they thought this problem was suitable for. After some discussion, the conclusion was unanimous that it was good for grades 3 through 8.

"It might be hard for second graders," Erin added, "but I think they could handle it."

Erin was pleased with the strategy that she and Jill used.

Firehouse Promblem
Jill and I got seven firehousese on the paper. Our strategy was to look for a place where there were most housese around one spot. There was one housese thet did not get coverd so we had to put a firehouse there. But our strategy worked.

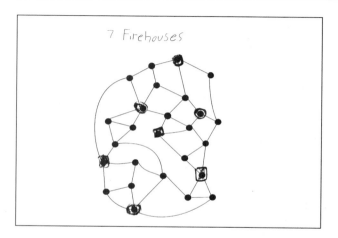

7 Firehouses

GRADE		STRAND
1		NUMBER
2		GEOMETRY
3		MEASUREMENT
4		STATISTICS
5		PROBABILITY
6		PATTERNS AND FUNCTIONS
		ALGEBRA
		LOGIC

The Largest Square Problem

Students in the intermediate grades are comfortable with the idea of what a square is. This activity gives them the challenge of examining their understanding more deeply and applying it to a problem-solving situation. It also helps students become familiar with the properties of other shapes and how shapes relate to one another. I taught this lesson to fourth graders in Mill Valley, California.

Materials

— Three paper shapes, each made from a sheet of 8½-by-11-inch paper as described below, one of each per student, plus extras

One right isosceles triangle made from folding and cutting a sheet of 8½-by-11-inch paper as shown.

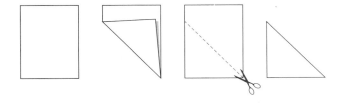

One pentagon

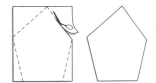

105

One irregular bloblike shape

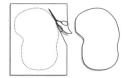

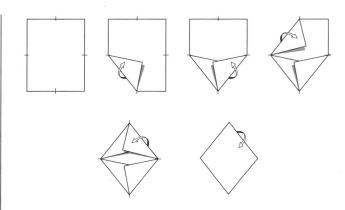

I began the lesson by giving each student a sheet of 8½-by-11-inch paper.

"Fold the paper to make a square," I said. "Do this so you make the largest square possible."

All the children got involved with the problem. As I expected, some were able to do this more easily and quickly than others. When I noticed that almost all of the students had finished, I asked for a volunteer to demonstrate a solution to the class. Marina did so, showing the class how she first folded a corner of the paper down to make a triangle and then folded up the flap.

"How can you be sure your shape really is a square?" I asked.

Marina didn't have an immediate answer, but several other students raised their hands.

"You could use a ruler," Jamie said.

"What would you do with the ruler?" I asked her.

"I'd measure it," Jamie responded.

"What would you measure?" I probed. Several other students raised their hands, but I let Jamie continue.

"I'd measure the sides to make sure they're the same," she said.

"I know another way," Gary said.

"How would you do it?" I asked.

"I'd fold it like this," he said, folding the square he had made on the diagonal into a triangle.

"How does that prove it's a square?" I asked.

"See, because the sides match," he said.

I then took a sheet of paper and folded it into a rhombus. I explained to the class what I did.

"First, I'm finding the midpoint of each side," I said. I folded each side in half and crimped it to mark its center. Then I folded each corner toward the middle of the paper, explaining that I made the midpoints the end points of each fold.

"Is this shape a square?" I asked.

"No!" A chorus of children answered.

"But look," I said. "If I measure the sides as Jamie did, they're all the same." I measured the sides for the class.

"And if I fold it to make a triangle as Gary did," I said, "the sides match." I did this for the children.

"So why isn't this a square?" I asked.

"The corners are wrong," Ann said.

"They have to be square," Jason added.

"Yes," I said, "measuring the sides is important but it's not enough to prove a shape is a square. The corners, which we call *angles*, are also important."

I demonstrated for the children how to compare a corner of a sheet of paper with the corners of the folded shape to determine whether it's a square. Then I held up one of each of the three paper shapes I had cut out and introduced the rest of the problem to the class.

"You're to work in pairs and investigate how to fold the largest square from these three shapes," I said. "I'd like you to describe in writing how you made each square—including the one you just made from the rectangle, which we've already discussed."

The children's methods and explanations differed. Some included drawings with their descriptions.

The activity also creates a reason for students to use mathematical terminology and therefore become more familiar with the language of geometry. Writing gives students the chance to describe their experiences with the shapes.

Marina wrote step-by-step directions for folding the triangle into a square.

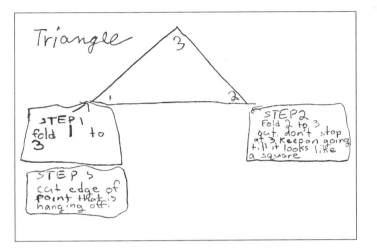

Jason found it too "hard to describe" how he had folded the triangle into a square and instead drew pictures.

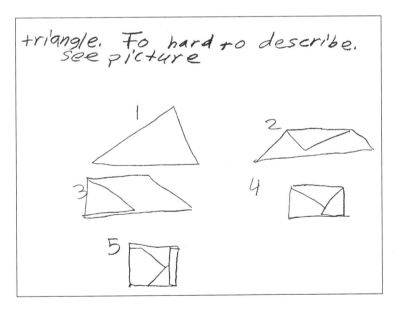

This lesson is valuable for both younger and older students. From tinkering with the shapes, students have the opportunity to learn concretely what a square corner is, that diagonals divide a square into triangles, and how to prove that a shape is a square.

GRADE		STRAND
1		NUMBER
2		GEOMETRY
3		MEASUREMENT
4		STATISTICS
5		PROBABILITY
6		PATTERNS AND FUNCTIONS
		ALGEBRA
		LOGIC

A Statistical Experiment

The lesson gives students experience with collecting, organizing, and interpreting data and making numerical inferences from a sample. Carolyn Felux taught this lesson to third graders in San Antonio, Texas.

To begin the lesson, Carolyn explained to the students that they were going to conduct an experiment.

"First, we'll collect data about how many children in our class are right-handed and how many are left-handed," she said. "Then you'll use that information to estimate how many right-handed and left-handed students there are altogether in all the third grade classes in our school."

Carolyn told the children that each, in turn, would report whether he or she was right-handed or left-handed. She organized the children into pairs. "You and your partner are to record the information as it's reported," Carolyn told them. "Talk together about how you'll collect the information." She gave the students time to organize their papers.

There were 3 left-handed and 25 right-handed students in the class.

"What information do you now need to estimate how many left-handed and right-handed third graders there are in all the classes together?" Carolyn asked.

The children wanted to know how many third grade rooms there were. Students volunteered the other teachers' names, and Carolyn listed them on the board. There were six other third grade classes.

The students seemed to feel that this was all the information they needed to make their estimates, so Carolyn gave them further directions. She said, "You and your partner should discuss and agree on an estimate." She wrote the word *hypothesis* on the board and continued with the directions. "Record your estimate and explain how you decided on it. Your explanation is your hypothesis. It should tell how you used the data to make your estimate."

The Children's Work

The children's estimates differed, ranging from 14 to 20 left-handers. Mark and Araceli based their estimate on the data that had been collected in our class and hypothesized that every class in the school (except one) had 3 left-handed students. They wrote: *We think there are 17 left handed and 136 right handed. We think this because we think there are 3 left handed people in every class but Mrs. Duncan we think she has only 2 left handers.*

Mark and Araceli based their hypothesis on the data collected in their own classroom.

None of the children seemed concerned about the lack of precise information about how many children were in each class. The children later collected the information from the other classes to compare with their estimates.

Louis and Mandy guessed, added, and subtracted, but their method wasn't clear.

Lettie and Sarah didn't explain how they reached their hypothesis.

GRADE

1
2
3
4
5
6

STRAND

NUMBER
GEOMETRY
MEASUREMENT
STATISTICS
PROBABILITY
PATTERNS AND FUNCTIONS
ALGEBRA
LOGIC

Anno's Magic Hat Tricks

Mitsumasa Anno's imaginative and thought-provoking books delight children and adults. He collaborated with Akihiro Nozaki to create *Anno's Magic Hat Tricks.* The tricks are logic problems that require students to make conjectures, test their validity, and draw conclusions. Although the initial warm-up problems in the book are simple, they should be read aloud slowly and carefully, as they prepare the reader for harder tricks. The last problem in the book will challenge older students—and even adults. The following describes my work with fourth graders in Mill Valley, California.

Materials

— *Anno's Magic Hat Tricks* by Akihiro Nozaki and Mitsumasa Anno (See the Bibliography on page 179.)

Anno's Magic Hat Tricks has four characters: a hatter, Tom, Hannah, and the reader. The book also has five props: three red hats and two white hats. The author gives the reader the name Shadowchild. Each trick asks the reader to figure out what color hat is on Shadowchild's head. Shadowchild appears throughout the book as a shadow, making it impossible to see what color hat he or she is wearing.

As I read each problem to the fourth graders, I asked them to offer solutions and explain their thinking. I kept the emphasis on the students clarifying their ideas and convincing one another. They found the early problems too easy.

In the first trick, the hatter has two hats—one red and one white. The illustration shows Tom wearing a red hat. The reader is asked to guess the color of Shadowchild's hat.

"Maybe this book is better for third graders," Noah said.

"I've read the book to third graders," I responded, "but it became too difficult for them later on. I wonder if the tricks will get too difficult for you as well." The children were curious to find out.

In each riddle, Tom can't see what color hat he's wearing, but he can see what color Hannah and Shadowchild are wearing. In the same way, Hannah and Shadowchild can't see their own hats but can see what color hats the other two characters are wearing.

In one riddle, the hatter uses three hats—two red and one white. The illustration shows Tom with a red hat and Hannah with a white hat. When Hannah is asked what color hat she's wearing, she knows and answers, "It's white." The fourth graders easily deduced that Hannah had to see red hats on Tom and Shadowchild in order to know that hers was white. Therefore, they knew that Shadowchild had to be wearing a red hat.

The problems in the book become more difficult when the hatter draws from three red hats and two white hats. The final trick shows Tom and Hannah each wearing a red hat. When Tom is asked the color of the hat he's wearing, he looks at Hannah's and Shadowchild's hats and responds, "I don't know." When Hannah is asked, she uses Tom's response and answers, "Mine is red." From that information, it's possible for the children conclusively to deduce the color of Shadowchild's hat.

After reading this last problem, I asked the children to put their solutions in writing. Sometimes it's difficult for me to respond to children's reasoning processes during class discussions when they present many different ideas. When children commit their thinking to writing, I'm better able to learn what each child understands. I can return to their papers later and reflect on their ideas. I can use what I learn from their individual points of view to prepare follow-up lessons.

The Children's Writing

While some students were unable to figure out a solution or explain their thinking, others were able to reason to a conclusive solution. Jacob, for example, wrote: *I think that Shadow childs Hat is White because Tom doesn't now because Shadow childs hat is white. Hanna's hat is red. Hanna knows the Shadowchild hat is white and tom's is red. She knows that tom doesn't know. So hers must be red.*

Jacob explained his reasons for believing that, in the last problem of the book, Shadowchild was wearing a white hat.

> I think that Shadow childs Hat is White because Tom doesn't now because Shodow childs hat is white Hanna's hat is red. Hanna knows the Shadowchild hat is white and tom's is red. She knows that tom doesn't know. SO hers must be red.
>
> ☐ too easy
> ■ Just right
> ☐ too hard

Peter wrote a run-on sentence that said it all: *I think that sadow child's hat is white because if Tom said "I don't know" there must be at least one red hat on either Hannah or sadow child and if she saw shadow child with a white hat he would know hers was red and she did so shadow child must have a white hat on.*

Some children reasoned differently. Lauren, for example, wrote: *I think that shadow child's hat is white. Because, we started out with 3 red and 2 white. Then Tom and Hana are wering red so now we have 1 red and 2 white. So there for, there is more chances for me to have a white hat.*

Peter's run-on sentence explained his reasoning.

> I think that sadow childs hat is white becausse if Tom said "I dont know!" there must be at least one red hat on either Hannah or sadow child and if she saw shadow child welh a whitehts he would now hers was red and she did so shadow child must a white hat on.
>
> ☑ too easy
> ☐ just right
> ☐ too hard

Lauren based her solution on chance, not on conclusive reasoning.

> I think that shadow child's hat is white. Because, we started out with 3 red and 2 white 🎩🎩. Then Tom and Hana are wering red so now we have 🎩🎩. So there for, there is more chances for me to have a white hat.

A Class Discussion

The next day, I returned to the problems, first returning to the simpler tricks. We acted them out, with students volunteering to be Tom, Hannah, and Shadowchild. This helped more of the children see how to use the information in the clues.

I asked the children for a thumbs-up or thumbs-down review of the activity. Seven of the children were intrigued and wanted more. Most of the class thought the beginning problems were okay but felt that the others were better for older children. A few children said they weren't interested.

"There are many different areas of mathematics," I reminded them, "and some people find some more interesting than others." I told them that logic was just one of the different strands they would be studying.

Sean's reasoning was incomplete.

> I think that Shadowchilds hat is white because Hannah said mine is reed So the only way she could tell is because there are two white so if you were wering a white and Hannah was wereing a white then she would a red.

Responses from Other Students

I've used this book with students in grades 3 through 7. When I read it to third graders, all of the children were engaged with the simpler tricks, but none could deal with the last several problems. With seventh graders, about three-fourths of the students engaged with the most challenging tricks, and their discussions continued for several days.

GRADE

1
2
3
4
5
6

STRAND
NUMBER
GEOMETRY
MEASUREMENT
STATISTICS
PROBABILITY
PATTERNS AND FUNCTIONS
ALGEBRA
LOGIC

Mathematics and Poetry

Every year, Dee Uyeda, a third grade teacher in Mill Valley, California, incorporates into her curriculum the study of haiku, an ancient Japanese form of verse that is composed of three non-rhyming lines. Traditionally, as written in Japanese, the first line has five syllables, the second has seven, and the third has five. Dee does not impose this structure on the children's haiku. She has them concentrate on their thoughts rather than on the number of syllables.

The following paragraph is an excerpt from a paper that Dee wrote:

"Young children, like almost everyone else, benefit from studying haiku. By reading and hearing haiku, thinking about it, and learning to write it, children learn to observe their world more closely and with greater care. They learn to trust their own perceptions since haiku records a personal, individual, and immediate experience—and no one else can see or hear or taste or think about or respond to something quite the way someone else can. Haiku is a way of communicating that personal experience to another person."

Dee became curious about how children might combine their thinking about math with writing haiku, about what they would choose to capture about mathematics. The following are some of the poems the children wrote.

Dee's third graders write haiku about mathematics.

Math
Complicated
Then easy.

5 jelly beans 4 people
So if I eat 1
It will be fair,

Calculator
Can't add or subtract
Without me.

Math
Just patterns
Waiting to be found

Triangle
You're half a square
But just as good.

Division
A copy cat
Of multiplication

Some of the third graders illustrate their haiku.

Tick Tock
Goes The clock
As I wait.

Zero
Is as important
As nine.

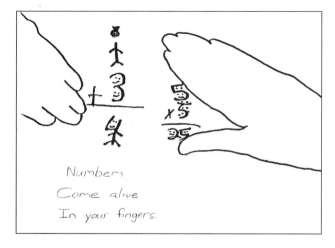

Numbers
Come alive
In your fingers.

STRAND

NUMBER
GEOMETRY
MEASUREMENT
STATISTICS
PROBABILITY
PATTERNS AND FUNCTIONS
ALGEBRA
LOGIC

A Long Division Activity

Bonnie Tank developed this lesson to present students with a problem-solving situation that called for division. Rather than focusing on teaching an algorithm, Bonnie had the students invent their own ways to divide. In this way, they had the opportunity to create procedures that made sense to them. Bonnie taught this lesson to fourth and fifth graders in Piedmont, California.

Materials

— One jar filled with dry beans (Note: Be sure that you know how many beans you put in the jar.)

— One coffee scoop

Bonnie showed the students the coffee scoop and the jar filled with beans.

"How many scoops of beans do you estimate are in the jar?" she asked.

After the students made estimates, Bonnie emptied the beans from the jar and put five scoops back in.

"Using this information," she asked, "what estimate would you now make about how many scoops would fill the jar?"

Bonnie asked the students to discuss their estimates with their partners. Then she had some students report their estimates and explain their reasoning as well.

Bonnie added more scoops of beans to the jar. As she did this, some students revised their estimates. There were both cheers and groans from the class when they learned it took 12 scoops to fill the jar.

"I knew it would take 12 scoops," Bonnie said, "because I filled the jar last night. I also know there are 334 beans in the jar because I counted them."

Bonnie then posed a problem. "Work with your partner," she said, " and find out how many beans you think would fill the scoop. Report the answer you get and also how you figured it out."

The Students' Work

The students approached the problem in different ways. Several pairs used multiplication with trial and error. Their papers showed a lot of figuring. Robbie and Christine, for example, wrote: *We multiplied numbers with 12 and if the answer was more than 334 the number should be lower. 336 was the closest we could get to 334. We got 28 beans in each cup.*

John and Rachel wrote: *We found out how many beans were in each scoop by multiplying 12 (the number of scoops) by what we thought was how many in each scoop. When we tried 27 × 12 we got 324 . . . not quite enough. Then we tried 28 . . . 336. The answer is between 27 and 28.*

Anne and April did the same, but reported their answer differently. They wrote: *10 of the cups have 28 in them and 2 of the cups have 27 in them.*

Some students drew circles to represent the scoops and either drew beans in each circle or wrote numbers. Adam and Erin, for example, drew 12 circles, wrote the number 10 in each, and found the total. They wrote another 10 in each and found the new total. Then they tried a few other numbers and finally decided on 8. They checked by multiplying.

Adam and Erin grouped and added, then multiplied to check their answer.

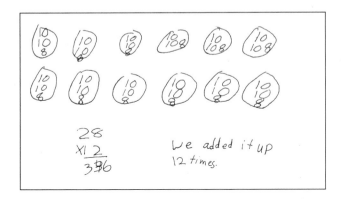

Gretchen and David used a different approach. They wrote: *We solved this problem by finding out what half of 334 is. Half was equal to 167. Then we divided it by 6 because we didn't know how to divide by 12. Then we checked it by multiplying 27 × 12 and that was too low. That answer is 324. So we tried 28 × 12 & we got 336. So the answer is inbetween 27 & 28.*

Gretchen and David used a combination of multiplication and division to find the number of beans in a scoop.

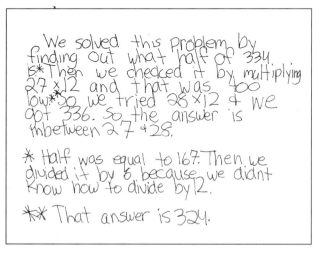

Two pairs of students solved the problem with the standard division algorithm. Nicole and Kelley divided 334 by 12 and got 27 with a remainder of 10. Their explanation outlined in detail how they divided to get an answer. They wrote: *Your answer is 27 remainder 10 beans can fit in each spoonful to put in the jar.* When Bonnie questioned the girls about filling a scoop with "27 remainder 10 beans," they amended their answer to: *Around 27.*

Bonnie gave students scoops of beans to verify their solutions. Of course, the number of beans varied, and this resulted in a lively discussion about the differences in sizes of beans and in how full each scoop was.

The emphasis in this lesson was on having students figure out what to do to solve a problem, decide on a method, and arrive at an answer that made sense to them. Problems such as this one can help students understand division and its relationship to multiplication.

STRAND

NUMBER
GEOMETRY
MEASUREMENT
STATISTICS
PROBABILITY
PATTERNS AND FUNCTIONS
ALGEBRA
LOGIC

Assessing Understanding of Fractions

I developed this lesson to assess students' understanding of fractions and learn about their ability to apply fractions in different problem-solving situations. I taught the lesson to fourth and fifth graders in West Babylon, New York, and to fifth graders in Mill Valley, California.

When teaching fractions, I find it's important to assess regularly what students understand. I gather information about what students are learning in three ways: from leading class discussions about students' reasoning, from observing and listening to students talk with one another as they work on problems, and from examining the written work that students produce. These types of assessments aren't perceived by students as "testing" situations. Rather, they're similar to other lessons in which students grapple with problems, share their solutions, and reflect on their thinking.

A Class Discussion

To initiate a class discussion about fractions, I wrote three statements on the board:

1. When pitching, Joe struck out 7 of 18 batters.
2. Sally blocked 5 field goals out of 9 attempts.

121

3. Dick did not collect at 14 of the 35 homes where he delivers papers.

I read the first statement aloud and asked the students whether Joe had struck out exactly half, about half, less than half, or more than half of the batters. Below the statements, I wrote:

Exactly half
About half
Less than (<) half
More than (>) half

I invited all of the students who were interested to express their ideas. Most thought that "less than half" made sense.

Philip said, "It's less than half because 7 and 7 is 14, and that's less than 18."

Sophia said, "I think the same, but I used multiplication and did 7 times 2. That's 14, and it's smaller than 18."

Mira said, "Nine is half of 18, and 7 isn't enough."

Emmy thought that "about half" was a better estimate. She was the only student who thought this. "It's pretty close," she said," because it's just 2 off from being exactly half."

Nick thought that "less than half" made better sense. "I did it with subtraction," he explained. "I did 7 take away 18, and that's 11 and that's more." I didn't correct Nick's explanation of the subtraction.

Several other students also expressed ideas that were similar to those already offered, so I moved on to the next statement: *Sally blocked 5 field goals out of 9 attempts.*

"It's more than half," Angelica said, "because it would have to be 10 to be exactly half."

"I think it's just about half," Josh said, "because 5 is about half of 9."

Chris was thinking about the situation numerically. He said, "You can't take half of 9 because it's an odd number.

"Yes, you can," Raquel responded. "You can take half of any number. The answer is just in the middle."

"What is half of 9?" I asked.

"It's 4½," Eli said. "I agree with Raquel that you can always take half."

"But you can't count half of 9 goals," Daniel argued. "That doesn't make any sense."

"Well, you *should* be able to take half of anything," Raquel said.

I offered my perspective. "Can you divide 9 apples in half?" I asked. Most of the students nodded.

"Half of 9 apples is 4½ apples," Ali said.

"What about 9 balloons?" I asked. The students laughed.

"You'd wreck a balloon," Eli said.

"It would be stupid," Sarah added.

"There are things we can divide in half and other things that we can't," I said. "When we study fractions, some things that make sense with numbers don't always make sense when you think about them in a real-life situation. It's important that we pay attention to how we use fractions as we learn about them."

Raquel's next comment shifted the direction of the discussion. "I have something to say about the first sentence, about Joe the pitcher," she said. "I think it's closer to ⅓ than ½."

"Why do you think that?" I asked.

Raquel explained, "Because you can divide 18 into thirds—6 plus 6 plus 6. And 7 is just one away from 18. But it's 2 away from 9, which is half. So it's closer to ⅓ than ½."

"Maybe I need to add another choice to the list," I said. I wrote *About one-third* on the board.

I then went on to the third statement: *Dick did not collect at 14 of the 35 homes where he delivers papers.* It seemed clear to most of the students that "less than half" was the best descriptor for that statement. The students' explanations were similar to the ones they had given for the other two statements.

Raquel surprised me with her observation. "I think that 14 is ⅖ of 35," she said. "Look, two 7s make 14, and three 7s make 21, and 14 plus 21 is 35, so 14 is ⅖."

I thought for a moment to understand Raquel's reasoning. None of the other students, however, seemed interested.

"I agree, Raquel," I said, to acknowledge her contribution, but I didn't pursue it further.

I have discussions such as this one frequently. I learn what some of the students are thinking, and the children have the opportunity to hear other points of view about reasoning with fractions.

At this time, I ended the discussion and introduced a fraction activity.

A Written Assessment

After a similar discussion with another class, I gave the students two written problems I had prepared for them to solve in groups. I asked the groups to find a solution to each problem and explain their reasoning. Also, I asked them to indicate if the problem was "Too hard," "OK," or "Too easy."

Problem 1. At her birthday party, Janie blew out ¾ of the candles. Draw a picture of the birthday cake and candles, showing which candles were blown out and which are still lit. P.S. How old is Janie?

After the students finished their papers, we discussed Janie's age. There were some giggles when the students realized that groups had arrived at three different answers to the question of Janie's age—12, 15, and 16.

Seeing the drawings with 12 candles and 16 candles convinced some that both answers made sense. The explanations offered by some of the students seemed to convince the others. The group that had said Janie was 15 had correctly drawn a cake with 16 candles and 4 left lit. They justified their answer by explaining that on birthday cakes there's an extra candle for good luck, and that's why they thought she was 15.

I asked the students if Janie could be 4 years old. They agreed that this was possible.

"Could she be 40?" I then asked. This sparked some students to suggest other ages she could be. "Could she be 212 years old?" I asked. Some started to figure in their heads until Kurt responded that she'd be dead and wouldn't have a birthday cake. The others groaned.

One group reported that they'd had a dispute about the problem. Jason thought Janie could be 12 with 3 candles left burning; Erica insisted she

had to be 16 with 4 candles burning. Using either 3 or 4 seemed to be important to the children because those numbers appeared in the problem's fraction. Erica explained how they resolved the problem. "I just took the paper and recorded my answer," she said, "and Jason said it was okay."

This group guessed that Janie was 16 years old and drew 4 candles still burning.

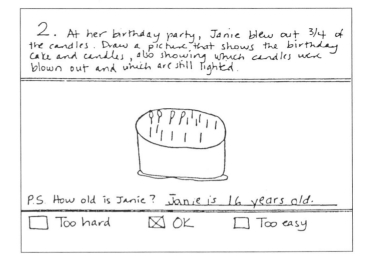

Problem 2. Three people are to share two small pepperoni pizzas equally. Shade in one person's share. Describe how much pizza each person gets.

Groups had different solutions to this problem. All four solutions shown on the next page are correct. Notice that the two groups reporting ⅔ shaded in the pizzas differently. The answer of ⅔ relies on the interpretation that the two pizzas together make one whole, so each person gets ⅔ of the two pizzas. The answer of 5⅓ pieces is also correct if the pizzas are divided into 8 slices each.

Children benefit from doing many problems in a variety of problem-solving contexts. Even when children have a basic understanding of fractions, they benefit from many opportunities to cement the concepts.

Here are four different ways that students correctly solved problem 3.

3. Three people are to share these two small pepperoni pizzas equally. Shade in one person's share.

Describe how much pizza one person gets.

2/3

☐ Too hard　　☒ OK　　☐ Too easy

3. Three people are to share these two small pepperoni pizzas equally. Shade in one person's share.

Describe how much pizza one person gets.

2/3 of one pizza.

☐ Too hard　　☐ OK　　☒ Too easy

3. Three people are to share these two small pepperoni pizzas equally. Shade in one person's share.

Describe how much pizza one person gets.

Each person gets 5 pieces and 1/3.

☒ Too hard　　☐ OK　　☐ Too easy

3. Three people are to share these two small pepperoni pizzas equally. Shade in one person's share.

Describe how much pizza one person gets. One person gets 2/6.

☐ Too hard　　☐ OK　　☒ Too easy

Another Class Discussion

After we discussed these two problems, I posed another problem for the students to consider. I was interested in seeing how the students would think about adding fractions.

"If I gave Jason ¾ of a chocolate bar and gave Tara ¾ of a chocolate bar, how much would I have given away?" I asked. The students offered several answers—6/4, 6/8, 2, 1½. Not many were sure of their answers.

"When I add the ¾ of a bar I gave Jason and the ¾ of a bar that I gave Tara, will my answer be greater or less than 1?"

It seemed clear to most of the children that it would be greater than 1. One student explained, "Because you are giving away more than one bar."

"Would the answer be greater or less than 2?" I asked. One student said that it had to be less because each got less than one chocolate bar.

But when I pushed the students to figure exactly how much chocolate I had given, they found it difficult. Eric said that he didn't think it could be 6/4 because fractions weren't supposed to have the big number on top. Erica's answer was 1½, but she couldn't explain how she got it.

Finally, I drew two chocolate bars on the board, divided each into fourths, and shaded in the two shares. That seemed to help. These kinds of examples help students form their own mental models for working with fractions in real-life situations.

GRADE

1
2
3
4
5
6

STRAND

NUMBER
GEOMETRY
MEASUREMENT
STATISTICS
PROBABILITY
PATTERNS AND FUNCTIONS
ALGEBRA
ALGEBRA
LOGIC

Comparing Fractions

Learning fractions is difficult for children. When teaching fractions, I engage students with games, problem-solving activities, and explorations with manipulative materials, all designed to provide a variety of ways for students to think about fractions. Recently, in my work with fifth graders in Mill Valley, California, I taught a game to help students learn to compare fractions and use fractional notation. After students had a chance to play the game during a few class periods, I used the context of the game to assess their understanding.

Materials

— Dice, one die per pair of students
— 1–9 spinner, one per pair of students

To give the fifth graders experience with comparing fractions, I introduced a game that involved both luck and strategy. I drew on the chalkboard:

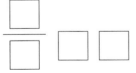

"This is a game for two people," I said. Hands flew up from students who were interested in volunteering to play. I drew another game board and invited Sarah to join me at the chalkboard.

I explained the rules. "To play this game, we'll use a regular die. We each roll the die four times, taking turns," I said. "Each time I roll, I write the number that comes up in one of my boxes. And you do the same for the numbers you roll."

I stopped to write on the chalkboard:

1. **Each player rolls four times and writes the numbers.**

I continued with the directions. "Once you write a number in a box, you can't move it. When we're done, we'll each have a fraction and two extra numbers."

"What are the two extras for?" Jeff asked.

"They're reject boxes," I answered. "They're places where you can write numbers that you don't want to use for your fraction."

"How do you win?" Paul asked.

I answered, "When you've each written your numbers, you compare your fractions. The larger fraction wins."

There were no more questions, so I said to Sarah, "Would you like to go first or second?"

"I'll go first," she said. She rolled the die and a 2 came up. Sarah hesitated, thinking about where to write it.

Other students called out suggestions. "Put it on top." "No, stick it in one of the extra boxes." "I'd put it on the bottom." "Yeah, the bottom is much better."

Sarah wasn't sure what to do but finally decided to write the 2 in the numerator.

Next, I rolled a 3. I put it in a reject box.

Sarah and I continued taking turns. After we each had rolled four numbers, the results were as follows:

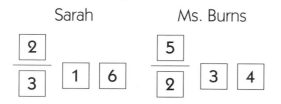

"You lost, Sarah," Maria said.

"By a lot," Seth added. Sarah shrugged, grinning.

Some students weren't as sure about the outcome. There was a large spread among the students in the range of their understanding about fractions. I continued by giving additional directions for the game.

"Let me explain the next part of the game," I said. "You each make a drawing to represent your fraction. Because you want to compare your two fractions, you first have to agree about the shapes you'll use for the whole—circles, rectangles, or something else. That way, you'll be able to compare fractional parts of the same wholes."

I turned to Sarah. "What should we draw?" I asked her.

"Circles," she said.

"You go first," I said. Sarah drew a circle, divided it into thirds, and shaded in two of the sections.

As I drew my fraction, I talked aloud to explain what I was doing. "My fraction says *five halves*. If I draw one circle and divide it into halves, that shows two halves. Another circle gives two more halves." I shaded in all four halves. "I still need one more half." I drew a third circle and shaded in just half of it.

"You win!" Ali said.

"There's one more part to playing the game," I said. "You have to write a math sentence that compares your two fractions. Here are two ways to do this." I wrote on the board:

$$\frac{2}{3} < \frac{5}{2}$$

$$\frac{5}{2} > \frac{2}{3}$$

I told Sarah that she could return to her seat, and then I completed writing the rules on the chalkboard:

1. Roll four times and write the numbers.
2. Each make a drawing.
3. Write at least one math sentence.

I then said to the students, "I know two other ways to write math sentences that compare these two fractions. Instead of writing ⁵⁄₂, I could count the whole circles I shaded in and then the extra part. That gives me two whole circles and half of another." I showed the children how to write the mixed number.

$$\frac{2}{3} < 2\frac{1}{2}$$
$$2\frac{1}{2} < \frac{2}{3}$$

"Who can explain why 2½ is worth the same as ⁵⁄₂?" I asked. I waited to see who would raise their hands, and then I called on Gwen.

"See, it takes two halves to make a whole circle," she said, pointing to one of the circles I had drawn. "So another circle is two more, and that's four, and there's one more half." Gwen delivered her explanation confidently.

"I have another way to show it," Kevin said. He came up to the board, drew five circles, and divided each one in half. Then he shaded in half of each circle and explained how you could put halves together to make wholes.

"These two make one whole," Kevin said, pointing to the shaded halves on the first two circles, "and these two make another, and you still have one left over."

I reminded the students of the three parts to playing the game and then had them play in pairs. As they played, I circulated, reminding some students to choose the same shape for their drawings, reminding others to write the sentences, helping some remember which way to draw the greater-than or less-than sign, and keeping others on task. By the end of the class, everyone seemed to understand the rules.

The Next Day

At the beginning of class the next day, Eli made a comment about the game. "I have a strategy for winning," he said. "Put big numbers on top and little numbers on the bottom."

"It didn't always work," his partner, his partner Joey said, "but it did most of the time."

"I'm going to give you time to play the game again," I said, "but this time you'll use spinners that have the numbers from 1 to 9 on them. That will give you new fractions to compare."

I had the students play for about 15 minutes before interrupting them for a class discussion. To begin the discussion, I wrote on the board the fractions from one of Tara and Doug's games.

Tara	Doug
$\frac{9}{5}$	$\frac{9}{8}$

"Talk with the person next to you about which fraction is greater," I said. "Then I'll have a volunteer come to the board and explain."

After a few moments, I called the students back to attention and asked for a volunteer. I called on Nick. He came to the board, drew rectangles, and divided them to draw each fraction. "It's hard to make five parts," he said, struggling with Tara's 9/5. He erased lines several times until he finally was pleased with what he had drawn. Dividing the other rectangles into eighths was easier for him.

Sophie then came up and showed how she would do it with circles.

127

Ali said that she didn't really need to draw the fractions. "I know that 10 fifths would be two wholes, so that's just a little less than 2. But 9 eighths is just a little more than 1."

Some students had difficulties with the fractions. Angie said that she was confused. "I don't get how to do this," she complained. Liz admitted that she was confused, too. Jason said, "It's hard to draw sometimes."

However, Seth said that he thought these fractions were easy and asked if he could come up and write the sentence. I agreed, and he wrote two versions:

$$\frac{9}{5} < \frac{9}{8}$$

$$1\frac{4}{5} < 1\frac{1}{8}$$

Over the next several days, I initiated other discussions like this and gave the students practice with drawing and comparing fractions and recording the results with correct fractional symbolism.

GRADE

1
2
3
4
5
6

STRAND

NUMBER
GEOMETRY
MEASUREMENT
STATISTICS
PROBABILITY
PATTERNS AND FUNCTIONS
ALGEBRA
ALGEBRA
LOGIC

A Measurement Problem

The NCTM Standards call for helping students learn to estimate, measure, and "select appropriate units and tools to measure to the degree of accuracy required in a particular situation." The Standards also suggest that students have experience with measuring inaccessible objects. To engage students with these ideas, Suzy Ronfeldt posed this problem to her fifth graders in Albany, California.

Suzy sent in the work for the Math Solutions newsletter quite a while ago, but I never included it because we couldn't figure out how to reproduce the large student work. We've learned more about computer scanning, so I can now show what the students did.

During the first week of school, Suzy often has her students explore manipulative materials. One year, as students were building trains with Unifix cubes, Suzy heard one child ask another, "Which do you think is longer, the fifth grade hall or the height of the building?" Suzy decided to turn the question into a lesson for the entire class.

The students had various opinions, so Suzy asked for ideas about how they might find the answer. Some children identified the different measuring tools they might use—rulers, yardsticks, meter sticks, and tape measures. Daniel suggested using a trundle wheel.

"It would make it easy to measure the hallway," he said.

"Yeah, but you couldn't walk it up the side of the building," Leonardo retorted.

"I think we'll need a ladder," Mariko said.

"What would you do with it?" Suzy asked. Mariko shrugged.

"Oooh, I know," Amy said. "You could go up to the roof and drop down some string."

"How do you get up to the roof?" Talia wanted to know. This time, Amy shrugged.

"Maybe we could get the blueprints of the building," Adam suggested.

Suzy then explained to the students how they would work on the problem. She told them to discuss the problem in small groups and then decide on one way to solve it.

"When you have an idea about what you'd like to do, talk with me about it," Suzy added. She realized that students would have to leave the classroom in order to do the measuring, and it was important that she know what they were planning to do.

Suzy gave further directions. "I'll give each group a sheet of 12-by-18-inch paper to report your plan and your results. Include sketches if they'll help explain what you did. Later, you'll post your papers so we can compare the results you got and the methods you used."

The students' interest was high, and they went to work eagerly.

The Students' Work

All of the groups decided that the hallway was longer, but their methods of measuring varied. One group estimated the height of the school building by using the height of the steps in the school staircases. They wrote: *First we used a meter stick and found out that each step in the staircase is 16 cm high. There are 28 steps in the staircase.* They figured that the building was 7 meters and 57 centimeters. Then they used the trundle wheel to measure the length of the hallway and reported it was 28 meters long. They concluded: *So the length of the hall is about 3 times longer than the height of the building.*

One group figured out a way to use rope to measure the height of the building by doing it in segments. They wrote: *What we did was got a wood chunk and tied it on to some rope and threw the wood chunk with the rope on to the cafeteria roof and pulled it down and measured the length of the rope. Then we came back up and came out to the balcony of the school and threw the wood chunk up to the top of the roof from the balcony then we measured that and dropped it down to the cafeteria roof off the balcony and measured that, then we added all the measurements up and got the total of the building which was 30'*

10". The length of the hall is 92' 0". The hall is longer than the height of the building is.

Another group solved the problem in a different way. They wrote: *We went down into the office and there was a picture of Cornell School. We measured the picture. On the building we got 11¾". On the height of the building we got 4½. So this proves that the hall is longer than the height of the building.*

The variety of methods and units the students used led to an active class discussion that helped reinforce the idea that there are many ways to solve a problem. The activity was also valuable because it provided an opportunity for the children to connect their mathematics learning with their environment. Students need many concrete experiences with measurement throughout the elementary grades.

This group was one of three groups in the class that used the blocks on the outside of the building to measure and compare the two lengths. They reported their answer in inches.

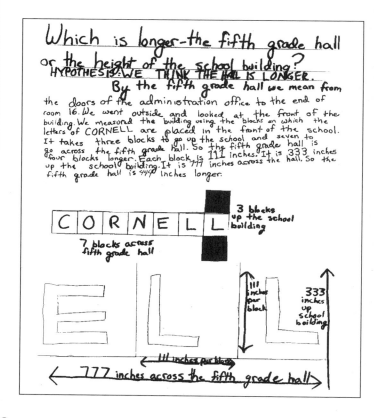

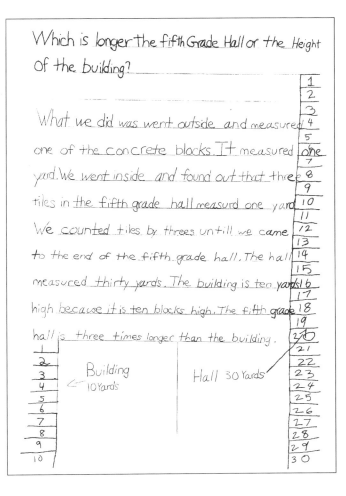

Which is longer the fifth Grade Hall or the Height of the building?

What we did was went outside and measured one of the concrete blocks. It measured one yard. We went inside and found out that three tiles in the fifth grade hall measured one yard. We counted tiles by threes untill we came to the end of the fifth grade hall. The hall measured thirty yards. The building is ten yards high because it is ten blocks high. The fifth grade hall is three times longer than the building.

1
2
3
4
5
6
7
8
9
10

Building
← 10 Yards

Hall 30 Yards

1
2
3
4
5
6
7
8
9
10
11
12
13
14
15
16
17
18
19
20
21
22
23
24
25
26
27
28
29
30

Although this group also used the blocks on the building, they reported their answer in yards.

Which is longer The Fifth Grade Hall or the Height of the Building Do the same in the pictures as you did in the other one but turn your hands until you can fit the height of the school in between your hands.

Go outside and stand facing the fifth grade hall put your hands on the side of your face (see picture) and look at the fifth grade hall Move your hands until you canfit the whole fifth grade hall in betwen your hands. No more and no less.

CORNELL

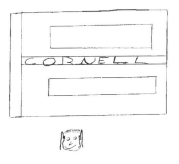

CORNELL

According to our calculation the fifth grade hall is longer then the height of the building.

This group found a way to approximate the distances by using their hands. Their description of what they did begins on the right-hand panel and concludes on the left.

131

GRADE

1
2
3
4
5
6

STRAND
NUMBER
GEOMETRY
MEASUREMENT
STATISTICS
PROBABILITY
PATTERNS AND FUNCTIONS
ALGEBRA
LOGIC

Acrobats, Grandmas, and Ivan

When preparing for a demonstration lesson, Bonnie Tank was looking for a logical reasoning problem to involve fifth graders. In rummaging through my book *Math for Smarty Pants,* I rediscovered "A Mathematical Tug-of-War." The problem seemed appropriate because students are familiar with tug-of-war contests (the context for the problem), and there are many ways to find a solution to the problem. Bonnie presented it to fifth graders in Piedmont, California.

Bonnie began the lesson with a general explanation of what the students would be doing. "I'm going to tell you what happened in the first two rounds of a tug-of-war contest," she told the fifth graders. "Then you'll use the information to figure out what happened in the third round." Bonnie read the story to the class:

Your job in this mathematical contest is to decide who will win the final tug-of-war. The first two rounds give you the information you need.

The First Round.
On one side there are four acrobats who have come down to the ground during the off-season for this special event. They have well-developed arm muscles because of all the

swinging they do, and have proven themselves to be of equal strength. Remember that fact.

On the other side are five neighborhood grandmas, a tugging team that has practiced together for many, many years. They, too, are all equal in strength. Remember that fact also.

In the contest between these two teams, the result is dead even. Neither team can out-tug the other. Remember that too.

The Second Round.

One team is Ivan, the specially trained dog that got his start as a pup when he was taken out for a walk by his owner. Ivan gets pitted against a team made up of two of the grandmas and one acrobat.

Again, it's a draw—an equal pull. Remember that fact.

It's the final tug that you must figure out. It will be between these two teams: Ivan and three of the grandmas on one side, the four acrobats on the other. Can you figure out who will win this tug of war?

One way to solve this problem is to use algebra, a branch of mathematics that uses equations to deal with relationships between quantities. If you haven't learned about algebra yet, you'll have to rely on logical reasoning. Either way it's mathematical thinking you must do. Get a pencil and paper to help you tug on this problem.

Bonnie then asked, "Before you figure out what happened in the third round, would you like to hear the story again?" The students were unanimous in their response. Although they had listened attentively, Bonnie knew that they probably didn't remember the information necessary for solving the problem.

"This time," Bonnie said, "you might want to take notes." She gave the students time to gather pencils and paper and then read the story again, pausing at times for the students to make their notes.

The Students' Work

The students worked in groups of two or three to solve the problem. The consensus was that Ivan and the grandmas would win the third round. However, the ways they reached that conclusion varied greatly.

David and John used a method of substitution. They wrote: *Ivan = 2 grandmas and 1 acrobat. There are already 3 grandmas. Ivan, who is helping them, equals 2 grandmas and 1 acrobat. If you take away Ivan and replace him with 2 grandmas and one acrobat, it will be like round 1 except the grandmas have a acrobat.*

Keith and Andy created "strength points" to arrive at a solution: *Since there are 4 acrobats, out of 100% each of them has 25 strength points. The grandmas had to be equal so each has 20 strength points because there are 5 of them. In the second round, the teams were; 2 G's and 1 A against Ivan. To be equal, Ivan had to have 65 strength points. In the 3rd round, the teams were Ivan and 3 G's against 4 A's. Adding Ivan's and the G's strength points, Ivan and th G's win!*

Keith and Andy assigned "strength points" to the different characters to determine who would win the third round.

A=25   G=20   D=65

20
20
+25
65

20
20
+20
125

Since there are 4 acrobats, out of 100% each of them has 25 strength points. The grandmas had to be equal so each has 20 strength points because there are 5 of them. In the second round, the teams were; 2 G's and 1 A against Ivan. To be equal, Ivan had to have 65 strength points. In the 3rd round, the teams were; Ivan and 3 G's against 4 A's. Adding Ivan's and the G's strength points, Ivan and th G's win!

Kari and Caitlin used fractions to solve the problem.

🐾 = 1   🧓 = 1¼   🐕 = 3¼

Now, say the grandmothers equal 1 unit of work. Each acrobat is stronger than each grandma, so they equal 1¼ units of work. Ivan the dog is equal to 2 grammas and one acrobat. Their units of work equal 3¼ units, so Ivan equals 3¼ units of work. So Ivan and 3 grandmas equal 6¼ units and the acrobats only equal 5. So Ivan and 3 grandmas win!....

Kari and Caitlin used fractions. They wrote: *Now, say the grandmothers equal 1 unit of work. Each acrobat is stronger than each grandma, so they equal 1¼ units of work each. Ivan the dog is equal to 2 grammas and one acrobat. Their units of work equal 3¼ units, so Ivan equals 3¼ units of work. So Ivan and 3 grandmas equal 6¼ units and the acrobats only equal 5. So Ivan and 3 grandmas win!!!!*

Chris, Benny, and Julia also used fractions, but in a different way: *4 acrobats = 5 grandmas which mean that if an acrobat equaled 1 a grandma would equal ⅘. Ivan can take on 2 grandmas and one acrobat. Together that equals 2⅗. 2⅗ (Ivan) + 2⅖ (grandmas) = 5. 4 acrobats together equal 4. That makes Ivan's team stronger.*

Paul and Amelie reasoned with a minimum of numerical calculations. They wrote: *Iven can take on a little more than two acrobats. Three grandmas can take on at least two acrobats. Add a little more than two acrobats and two acrobats, you get more than four acrobats. That means Iven's team has more strength!!*

Having the students present their solutions helped reinforce the idea that a problem can be solved in different ways.

GRADE

1
2
3
4
5
6

STRAND

NUMBER
GEOMETRY
MEASUREMENT
STATISTICS
PROBABILITY
PATTERNS AND FUNCTIONS
ALGEBRA
LOGIC

Tiles in the Bag

This probability lesson gives students experience with making predictions based on a sample and also engages them in thinking about fractions. I taught the lesson to fifth graders in San Francisco, California.

Materials

— Blue, red, and yellow Color Tiles
— One lunch bag

To introduce the lesson, I had the students draw samples from a bag into which I had put 5 blue, 2 red, and 1 yellow tile. I told the children only that I had put 8 Color Tiles in the bag and that they were blue, red, and yellow. I drew three columns on the board, labeling one for each color.

Blue	Red	Yellow

137

I explained to the children that they would draw samples from the bag, and I would record the colors on the board. Many of the children eagerly volunteered to draw samples. I went around the class having each student draw a tile and then replace it in the bag. There was, as there always is with this activity, much cheering. The children cheered for whatever color was chosen. (It seemed that they were more interested in cheering than in what they were cheering for.)

There were 31 children in class that day, and I also drew a tile. The result of the 32 draws was:

Blue	Red	Yellow
ＨＨＴ ＨＨＴ ＨＨＴ ＨＨＴ |||	ＨＨＴ	||||
23	5	4

I asked the children to discuss the results in their groups and answer the following questions:

- Predict how many tiles of each color are in the bag.

- What fraction of the draws are blue?

- What is a more commonplace fraction than $^{23}/_{32}$ that tells about what fraction of the draws were blue?

- Are more or less than $^{3}/_{4}$ of the samples blue?

The Children's Thinking

Three groups predicted 4 blues, 2 reds, and 1 yellow; two groups predicted 5 blues, 2 reds, and 1 yellow; one group predicted 6 blues, 1 red, and 1 yellow; and one group predicted 4 blues, 2 reds, and 2 yellows. I asked the students to explain their reasoning.

Alex explained, "Since there are 8 tiles in the bag, then four tally marks stand for each tile. Then 23 blues is close to 24, so that would be 6 tiles, and 5 reds is close to 4, which should be 1 tile, and 4 yellows is 1 tile."

Jerry said, "We think most are blue, but there are more red tiles than yellow tiles, and that's why we said 5, 2, 1."

Joyce said, "We thought 4, 2, and 2 because we think there are the same number of reds as yellows, and that there could be more than one of each."

I took this opportunity to talk with the class about some probability ideas. First I talked about how sampling is used in real life, offering the situation of how polls are made. David added an example. "It's like when they say that three out of four dentists recommend a toothpaste," he said.

Then I talked about sample size. "Imagine if we had 100 samples instead of 32," I said, "or 800, or even more. The larger your sample, the more reliable the information. It's important to mathematicians to have sample sizes large enough to be useful for making predictions."

I also talked about the students' predictions. "Not everyone can be right," I said. "That's not what's important. What's important is how you reason to make a prediction. I'm interested in your thinking because I know that, without looking in the bag, there's no way to be absolutely sure how many tiles of each color are inside."

Then I told the class that only one group's prediction was correct. The students groaned—but not very loudly.

GRADE

1
2
3
4
5
6

STRAND

NUMBER
GEOMETRY
MEASUREMENT
STATISTICS
PROBABILITY
PATTERNS AND FUNCTIONS
ALGEBRA
LOGIC

Writing Questions from Graphs

Graphs and charts are valuable tools for displaying information so that it's easy to see relationships among the data. It's important that students learn to analyze data and make generalizations. In this lesson, students write questions that can be answered from data the class collected. I taught the lesson to a class of fourth, fifth, and sixth graders in Westport, Connecticut.

Materials

—One sheet of chart paper

To begin this lesson, I asked the students, "Would you rather be the age you are now, younger, or older?"

After an outburst of discussion, I called the students to attention. On a sheet of chart paper, I set up a way for them to record their preferences and had each student put an X in the appropriate place.

What age would you rather be?
Mark with an X.

Younger	X X X
The same age	X X X X X X X X X X X X
Older	X X X X X

In previous lessons, I had modeled how to draw conclusions from data on graphs and given the children opportunities to draw their own conclusions. Also, I had given the students questions to answer based on the data in graphs. In this lesson, I gave them a different task.

After the students had recorded on the graph, I said, "For this graph, you're to work in your groups and write questions that others can answer from the information posted."

After the students had written their questions, I had groups take turns reading aloud one question at a time. Then I gave the class instructions.

"When you hear a question, see if you wrote the same question or a similar one. Decide if the question can be answered from the information on the graph." In this way, I encouraged the students to listen to and think about the questions.

This group asked a variety of questions that required comparing the number of Xs in different categories.

1. Which one was picked the most?
2. What fraction of the class picked younger?
3. How many more people picked older than younger?
4. What fraction of the class picked the same age and younger?
5. If you added the "older" with the "young how much would you get?
6. How many people picked the same age?

It turned out that all of the students' questions could be answered from the given information. However, a different issue arose. Some of the questions had no relationship to the content of the graph. This presented another thinking opportunity for the students: to sort the questions they wrote into two groups—those that did and those that did not relate to the question answered by the graph.

The second question on both of these papers had no relationship to the meaning of the graph's data.

1. What fraction of the class picked the same age? (lowest terms)
2. What would you get if you added the same & the older together and then times it by the younger?
3. How many groups of 2 are there on the graph?

1) How many more people chose the same age over younger?
2) If you plus all the x's on the chart, times it by 10 and divided by 5, what would the answer be?

To end the lesson, I raised one more question. "Would it be a reasonable assignment for you to find solutions to all the questions posed by the groups?"

The students' unanimous response was yes. Solving problems they create themselves helps make students more willing learners. I had the students record and post their questions. Then, for the rest of the lesson, they worked on solving one another's problems.

GRADE		STRAND
1		NUMBER
2		GEOMETRY
3		MEASUREMENT
4		STATISTICS
5		PROBABILITY
6		PATTERNS AND FUNCTIONS
		ALGEBRA
		LOGIC

From the Ceiling to Algebra

Jason, a third grader in Mill Valley, California, inspired a pre-algebra lesson based on ceiling tiles. (See *Math from the Ceiling* on page 93.) I later tried a variation with fifth graders in West Babylon, New York.

Materials

— 10-by-10 grids, one per group of students (See the blackline master on page 174.)

Part of the problem I had presented to third graders was to figure out how many holes there were around the edges of 12-inch-square acoustical tiles, each with a pattern of holes in a square array. With fifth graders, I didn't use a ceiling tile but posed the around-the-edge problem for a 10-by-10 grid.

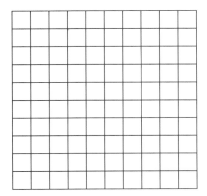

"I have a problem for you to solve," I said, holding up the grid. "I call it the 'Around-the-Edge Problem.' How many squares do you think there are around the edge of this 10-by-10 grid? You could count them, but I'd like you to think about other ways to figure it out. Talk about this in your group and see if you can agree on an answer. Then write about your thinking."

Working in groups of four, the students found five ways to arrive at the answer of 36. As they explained their methods to the class, I translated them to numerical representations on the chalkboard:

1. $(8 \times 4) + 4 = 36$
2. $10 + 10 + 8 + 8 = 36$
3. $(10 \times 4) - 4 = 36$
4. $10 + 9 + 9 + 8 = 36$
5. $9 \times 4 = 36$
6. $100 - 64 = 36$

(The last method was my contribution; I subtracted the number of squares inside the border from the total number of squares in the grid.)

We then tested to see if the methods would work on other grids—a 5-by-5, a 4-by-4, and a 3-by-3. It was easy for the students to see that they did.

"I'm going to write a formula to describe one method," I told the class. "I'll use H to stand for the number of holes on a side and E to stand for the number of holes around the edge. See if you can tell which method it is." I wrote on the board:

$$H + H + (H - 2) + (H - 2) = E$$

It seemed obvious to the students that the formula I wrote described the second method. I then gave the class another problem.

"Your job is to write a formula for each of the other methods," I said. "When you've done this, check that your formulas work for all the grid sizes we tested."

The groups worked for about half an hour. The method that was most difficult for them was the last one—the one I had contributed. The students posted and compared their formulas, which led to a discussion of different algebraic notations.

The activity is rich because it shows that there is more than one way to arrive at a solution. Also, it can be checked concretely by counting around the edge, yet it can also be described abstractly with algebraic formulas.

These students wrote an algebraic formula for each method of solving the around-the-edge problem.

Green Group
Math

1. $4(H-2)+4 = E$

3. $H \times 4 - 4 = E$

4. $H + 2(H-1) + (H-2) = E$

5. $(H-1) \times 4 = E$

6. $H \times H - (H-2)(H-2) = E$

Blue Group

1. $(H-2) \times 4 + 4 = E$

3. $H \times 4 - 4 = E$

4. $H + (H-1) + (H-1) + (H-2) = E$

5. $(H-1) \times 4 = E$

6. $H \times H - (H-2)(H-2) = E$

GRADE

1
2
3
4
5
6

STRAND

NUMBER
GEOMETRY
MEASUREMENT
STATISTICS
PROBABILITY
PATTERNS AND FUNCTIONS
ALGEBRA
LOGIC

The Budgie Problem

The December 1992 issue of *The Oregon Mathematics Teacher (TOMT)* included a problem submitted by Jim O'Keefe from Ontario, Canada. The problem was identified as suitable for grades 8 through 12 and described as one that could be solved "by using a combination of standard methods and a little mathematical intuition." Jan DeLacy thought the problem would be an appropriate challenge for the sixth graders she was teaching in Bellevue, Washington. Cheryl Rectanus later tried it with her fifth graders in Portland, Oregon.

The Problem: A bird collector wants to buy 100 budgies and wants to spend exactly $100. Blue budgies cost $10 each, green budgies cost $3, and yellow budgies cost 50 cents. The collector wants to purchase at least one budgie of each color. How many blue, green, and yellow budgies could he buy?

The article in *TOMT* included an algebraic solution (let x = the number of blue budgies, etc.), and although Jan knew the sixth graders didn't have algebraic skills, she felt they could find other ways to tackle the problem.

"It turned out to be one of the best group/partner interactions I've seen," Jan wrote. "I was thrilled at how they attacked the problem. Only a few hung back saying it was too hard and they didn't know what to do, and as others around them began to try things, even those students got involved. Most used calculators, some used cubes, and some used diagrams and tally marks."

Jan found the students' logic interesting, even when they didn't reach a solution. "I was particularly fascinated by Dorel's approach," she reported. "He found the cost of one budgie of each color—$10 + $3 + $.50 = $13.50—and used the equals key on his calculator to add $13.50 repeatedly until he reached $108. Then he started subtracting birds." Dorel managed to spend $100, but he bought only 21 birds.

This sixth grader's strategy was to investigate possibilities for different numbers of blue budgies.

#	Blue Budgie	money spent after buying blue budgies	Green	Yellow
1	10	$0	0	0
2	9	$10	0	0
3	8	$20		34
4	7	$30		54
5	6	$40		74
6	5	$50	1	94
7	4	$60	1	114
8	3	$70	1	134
9	2	$80	1	154
10	1	$90	1	174

The Lesson with Fifth Graders

When Cheryl Rectanus gave the problem to her fifth graders, she reported, "Some groups used green, blue, and yellow Pattern Blocks to represent the birds, along with play money. Others just used play money but found it wasn't very helpful. Almost every group used calculators and paper and pencil."

After the students had worked on the problem for half of a period, Cheryl interrupted them and asked them to discuss what they knew so far. Several groups discovered that a solution would have to include an even number of yellow budgies. However, Cheryl noted that the students seemed able to pay attention either to buying 100 birds or to spending exactly $100, but not to both.

None of the students reached a solution that first period, but Cheryl had them write about the approaches they had used and the combinations that didn't work.

These fifth graders reported what did and didn't work.

> The Budgie Problem
> This problems doesn't work:
> Yellow-70, Blue-3, Green-5. It
> doesn't work because there is only 78
> budgies. This problem dies not work
> Yellow-80 Blue-30, Green-30 because there is
> only 80 140 birds it is too much. This
> problem doesn't work yellow-75, Green
> 2, blue 23. It doesn't work because
> the yellow, green, and the blue makes
> 100, But all the money makes $157.00
> This also doesn't work yellow-75 blue-
> 2 Green-1. This doesn't work because
> Green, blue and yellow all add up to $3860.
> and in how many budgies, well that adds up
> to 78.

That night, Cheryl organized their information on a database and sorted it in four different ways—by total money spent, by the total number of birds bought, by the number of yellow birds bought, and by the number of green birds bought. She presented the results the next day, and the class looked for trends, noticing which combination of birds came close to a solution.

"Having the information was interesting to the students," Cheryl reported, "but it didn't seem to help them find a solution."

After 45 minutes of work on the second day, one group found a solution. This seemed to motivate the others to continue their search. On the third day, a second group discovered the same solution as the first group. In a class discussion, Cheryl had the students report their approaches and talk about what they learned and how they worked together.

One group wrote: *We approached this problem by playing with the numbers and trying out different combanations. We lerned that this problem is alot eser said than done!*

From another group: *We learned that this problem requires hard thinking, for instance, we had 99 birds and 99 dollars, and we couldn't figure out how to make 100 and 100.*

Another group wrote: *We approached this by taking guesses and finding out if it is right or wrong. We learned that guessing can get you close to the answer.*

Cheryl also asked the students for their opinions about the appropriate grade level for the problem. There was a variety of responses. One group wrote: *We think that the appropriate grade level for this is grade 5 and up because its hard. We don't think younger kids would get it.*

Another wrote: *We think it's 6 grade work because not a lot of people in my class got a 100 birds and a 100 dollars.*

GRADE
1
2
3
4
5
6

STRAND
NUMBER
GEOMETRY
MEASUREMENT
STATISTICS
PROBABILITY
PATTERNS AND FUNCTIONS
ALGEBRA
LOGIC

Probability Tile Games

At the 1989 NCTM annual conference, Julia Szendrei, a math educator from Budapest, Hungary, presented a session on probability. Kris Acquarelli used the ideas with three sixth grade classes in Poway, California.

Materials

— Color Tiles

— Lunch bags

— List of statements (See the blackline master on page 175.)

Kris put 8 Color Tiles in a bag—4 red, 3 green, 1 blue. She listed the contents of the bag on the board and gave each student a sheet with the following statements on it:

1. All 3 tiles are the same color.
2. All the tiles are red.
3. There is a red tile among them.
4. Not all tiles are the same color.
5. There are 2 red tiles among them.
6. Only 1 tile is red; the other 2 tiles are a different color.
7. There is no blue tile among them.
8. There is a green tile among them.
9. There is 1 blue tile.

Kris had each student draw a seven-step game board.

START ○─○─○─○─○─○─○ FINISH

Then she gave the instructions for the first game:

Game 1. Choose one statement. Students in your group take turns drawing a sample of 3 tiles from the bag and revealing the colors to the group. With each draw, you evaluate whether the statement you chose is true for the 3 tiles. If so, mark off one step on your game board. The idea is to reach the last step as quickly as possible.

Kris had the students play several rounds of the game in groups of four, then discuss which statements provided the best strategies.
"Some students asked me about the wording of the clues," Kris reported, "and I simply told them to decide in their groups."
After the students had had a chance to play, Kris asked them to write about which statements they thought were best to choose. She also asked them to write about the statements they felt weren't clear. The students shared their ideas in a class discussion.

The Students' Writing

"In all three classes," Kris wrote, "most students felt that although there were four strong strategies, number 3 was most likely to produce a winner."
Sam believed that statement 3 was one of two best statements. He wrote: *There isn't one best statement there is two. They are: There is a red tile among them (#3) or there is a green tile among them (#8).*

Julia had a different opinion. She wrote: *I think the best choice is number 4 "not all tiles have the same color" because it's very rare that you get all of one color. I think all of the things are clear.*

Sam believed that statements 3 and 8 were the most useful for winning the game.

> There isn't one best statement there is two. They are: There is a red tile among them (#3) or there is a green tile among them (#8)
>
> Those were the colors picked most often
>
> #4 wasn't very clear. It said: not all the tiles have the same color That could mean they are all different colors or it could mean two of the same colors + one different,

Julia's reasoning was unclear.

> I think the best choice is number 4 "not all tiles have the same color" because it's very rare that you get all of one color I think all of the things are clear.

Later, Kris introduced two other games to the students.

Game 2. Pick two statements. After 3 tiles are drawn, exactly one of the statements you chose must be true in order to mark off a step.

Game 3. Choose one statement and then write another one that is different from those given. As with game 2, after 3 tiles are drawn, you mark off a step if exactly one of your statements is true.

Again, Kris asked the students to pick the most useful statements and write about why they were best.

Delia picked statements 3 and 7 as best for game 1, statement 3 for game 2, and statements 3, 5, and 8 for game 3. For game 2, she wrote: *Every time someone played #3 they won because there is 4 reds and 7 because there is only 1 blue.*

Delia found that statement 3 was useful for all three games.

the best stratigies are Game 1
1. number 3, 7
2. Every time someone played #3 they won because there is 4 reds and 7 because there is only 1 blue
3. # 3, 5 and 8 because on #3 and #8 it says There is a red or green tile among them, and you could pick more than one and you did know if there could be more than 1 and #5 says there are 2 red tiles among them, we don't know if there could be more than 2 or just 2.

GRADE
1
2
3
4
5
6

STRAND
NUMBER
GEOMETRY
MEASUREMENT
STATISTICS
PROBABILITY
PATTERNS AND FUNCTIONS
ALGEBRA
LOGIC

Penticubes

Investigating pentominoes is a well-known math activity in which students search for pentominoes by arranging square tiles so that each touches the complete side of at least one other. While Kris Acquarelli was on special assignment in Poway, California, she extended the pentomino exploration with Blanche Gunther's sixth graders. Using interlocking cubes that snap together on all sides, Kris had the students investigate penticubes—three-dimensional shapes made of five cubes each.

Materials

—Multilink or Snap Cubes

—Paper bags (larger than lunch bags), one per group of students

—2-centimeter grid paper (See the blackline master on page 176.)

—Isometric dot paper, optional (See the blackline master on page 177.)

Kris distributed the cubes and asked each student to make a shape by snapping together five cubes.

"Compare the shapes made in your group," she said, "and talk about how they're the same and how they're different. Ignore the colors, and just pay attention to the shapes of the constructions."

The students went to work. Kris had worked with Blanche's class before. She reported, "Students sit together in groups of four, they talk with one another as they work through problems, and they are used to listening to other groups describe their work and thinking."

While the students were working, Kris built three shapes with five cubes each, two that were identical except for the color of the cubes and another that was a mirror image of them.

When Kris called the students back to attention, she asked what they had noticed about their shapes. There was a variety of responses: "Ours were all different." "Some are in just one layer and some have two or three layers." "I think there are a lot of different ones." "Some are simple and some are complicated."

Kris then showed the class the two identical shapes she had made, holding them in different orientations.

"Except for the different colors used," Kris told the class, "I think these two shapes are the same. Can you see why I say that?"

Several students responded. "That can't be." "They don't look the same." "Turn that one around, no, the other way." "Oh, yeah, I see it now." "I don't." "See, they both have an *L*-shape with one sticking up from the short end."

Kris held the shapes so that it was easier to see that both were the same. She then showed the mirror-image construction she had made. "How is this configuration like the other two, and how is it different?" she asked.

Again, several students had ideas. "It has the same *L*." "Yeah, but the other cube isn't sticking up the same." "It would be if you turned it." "No, that doesn't work." "Weird!"

"This shape is a mirror image of the other two," Kris told the class. "With the extra cube on top, the *L*-shapes are reversed."

The Penticube Activity

Kris then introduced the activity. "Work in your groups," she said, "and see how many different configurations of five cubes you can make. Consider shapes that are mirror images of each other to be different. I'll leave these three shapes up here for you to examine if you'd like."

"How many shapes are there?" one student asked.

"I don't know," Kris answered honestly. "I learned recently that there's a commercial set available of these shapes, but I don't know how many come in the set. That gave me the idea of having you find what shapes were possible."

Kris's response satisfied the students, and they were eager to begin. Before they got started, Kris gave a suggestion.

"As you look for shapes," she said, "be sure to organize your group so you can check for duplicates and eliminate those that are the same." The students got right to work.

Kris realized that the students could work on this problem for much longer than the class period would allow. However, she interrupted them when about 15 minutes remained to discuss what they had done.

"How many different shapes have you found?" she asked. The range reported by the groups went from 17 to 35.

"Let's collaborate and see what we know so far," Kris said. "You'll be able to continue your search tomorrow."

Kris then distributed a paper bag to each group. She asked one group to hold up a shape and describe it.

"If your group has this shape," Kris told the rest of the class, "put it in your bag. If not, make one for your bag." There was a busy search as groups rummaged for the shape.

After three rounds, Kris realized that this approach had several problems. It was too time-consuming, students couldn't see one another's shapes well, and there wasn't enough individual participation. She could tell that students were losing interest, and she abandoned the plan.

"Just put all your shapes in your bag," she said, "and you'll get back to work tomorrow."

Additional Explorations

After class, Kris and Blanche met and brain-stormed further explorations. Kris reported, "We wanted students to experience activities that help visual and spatial perception, to use concrete materials to explore geometric concepts, and to communicate their ideas with one another as they problem solve together."

Following are the activities Kris and Blanche developed to use the student-made constructions.

- **Build a Wall.** Using a file folder or notebook, one student hides a penticube and describes it for a partner (or for others in the group) to build. Afterward, students discuss which directions were useful and which were con-fusing or ambiguous.

- **Penticube Jackets.** Using 2-centimeter grid paper, students cut a pattern that can be folded to fit a penticube exactly. (Jackets are nets that fold to cover all faces of the penticube.)

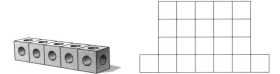

- **More Penticube Jackets.** Students take one penticube and find as many different shaped jackets as possible. (Will the number of possible jackets be the same for all of the penticubes?)

- **Surface Area.** Students compare the surface area of different penticubes and see what they notice about the shapes of penticubes with more and less surface area.

- **Perspective Drawing.** Students practice drawing three-dimensional versions of pen-ticubes. They can use isometric dot paper for these drawings.

- **Building Rectangular Solids.** Students try to put together several identical penticubes or several different penticubes to make rectangular solids. They investigate the sizes and shapes of rectangular solids they can build.

- **Penticube Riddles.** Using 2-centimeter grid paper, students draw top, bottom, and side views of a penticube. They cut out their three drawings, paste them on a tagboard card, and staple the card to a paper bag that holds the actual penticube. Other students try to build the shape using the views drawn. They check their construction by looking in the bag.

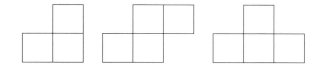

STRAND

NUMBER

GEOMETRY

MEASUREMENT

STATISTICS

PROBABILITY

PATTERNS AND FUNCTIONS

ALGEBRA

LOGIC

Multiplication and Division

In November 1992, David Ott developed a unit on multiplication and division of whole numbers for his sixth graders in San Lorenzo, California. David was interested in having the students solve problems from real-world contexts. The unit consisted of six problems that involved students in arithmetic calculations and required them to gather data, measure, and use geometric ideas.

"The students had a wide range of abilities," David reported. "Some had good instincts and number sense but slow or shaky arithmetic skills. Some had passing arithmetic skills but very little number sense. And while some showed strengths in both number sense and arithmetic, others showed strengths in neither."

Working in groups of four, students were to choose three of the six problems in the unit, solve them, and present two of their solutions to the class. David directed the students to put each solution on a separate sheet of paper and asked them to show all of their work. He also told them that all group members had to understand their group's work and contribute to group reports.

Following are the directions for four of the problems in David's unit. (The other two problems related to previous work the students had done.)

■ **Replacing Floor Tiles.** Figure out the number of floor tiles needed to tile the floor of our classroom. Then calculate the number of floor tiles needed for our wing and for all the classrooms in the school.

- **Stacking Chairs.** If we stacked all of our chairs on top of one another, how high would the stack reach?

- **Head to Heels.** Figure out the length of your group if all of you were to lie heel to head. Then use that information to approximate the length of all the students in our class lying heel to head.

- **Filling the Room with Tables.** Figure out the maximum number of tables that could completely fill the classroom floor area.

Solving the Problems

David reported that the problems engaged the students, and all were involved in solving the problems and preparing and presenting reports.

Students' solutions to the problems were quite different. For example, for "Replacing Floor Tiles," students had to decide how to deal with places where whole tiles weren't needed. Could some tiles be cut and each part used, or would whole tiles be necessary and the unused portions discarded? In "Stacking Chairs," students measured the chairs with differing degrees of precision. Also, some groups included the teacher's chair and some didn't. Answers varied for "Head to Heels" because each group used the heights of its members to approximate the length of the whole class laid end to end.

For "Head to Heels," these students used the heights in their own group to estimate the heights of the rest of the students.

Head to heels

Raul is 5'1, Jenny is 4'11, Miguel is 5'4 and amanda is 4'11. 9th is 12.

Raul = 5×12 = 60" +1" = 61"
Jenny = 4×12 = 48" +11" = 59"
Miguel = 5×12 = 60" +4" = 64"
Amanda = 4×12 = 48" +11" = 59"

$$61 + 59 + 64 + 59 = 243"$$

$$243 \times 7 = 1701$$

There are 7 table groups 4 people at each. 28 people in the class. (We evened the number 29 to 28.)

The height of all the people at our table is 243".

The estimated height of the class is 1701" by our height.

GRADE
1
2
3
4
5
6

STRAND
NUMBER
GEOMETRY
MEASUREMENT
STATISTICS
PROBABILITY
PATTERNS AND FUNCTIONS
ALGEBRA
LOGIC

Guess Our Number

In this riddle activity, students combine their number sense and logical reasoning abilities to write mathematical riddles and clues. Cathy Humphreys taught this lesson to sixth graders in San Jose, California.

To introduce the activity, Cathy gave the class a riddle to solve. "I am thinking of a number," she said. "See if you can figure it out from these clues." Cathy had written the clues on an overhead transparency. She showed the first two clues to the class.

Clue 1. The number is less than 30.
Clue 2. It is a multiple of 3.

"Talk in your groups about what you know from the clues," she told the class.

After just a few moments, the students reported the numbers that fit these clues: 3, 6, 9, 12, 15, 18, 21, 24, and 27.

"I know one more number that fits these clues," Cathy said. The students were stumped, so Cathy reminded them about zero and added it to the list. Then she showed the next clue.

Clue 3. The number is odd.

Groups huddled together and quickly eliminated the even numbers and agreed that the possibilities now were 3, 9, 15, 21, and 27. Cathy then gave the fourth clue.

Clue 4. The number is not a square number.

"So it can't be 9," Jon blurted out. The others agreed. Cathy displayed the last clue.

Clue 5. The sum of the digits is 6.

It was now obvious to the students that the only possible answer was 15.

"I'm going to give you another set of clues," Cathy then told the class. "This time, I'll show you all the clues at once. Work in your groups to solve the riddle."

Clue 1. The number has two digits.
Clue 2. It is a factor of 60.
Clue 3. The number is not a multiple of 10.
Clue 4. The number is not prime.

Cathy's previous experience had taught her that two errors were typical when students wrote their own riddles: Clues sometimes led to more than one possible answer, and riddles sometimes included redundant clues. To address these possible pitfalls, Cathy purposely included both of them in her second riddle. Both 12 and 15 were possible solutions, and clue 4 was unnecessary.

Two groups arrived at the answer of 12, three got 15, and two groups discovered that both numbers were possible.

"Then my riddle is incomplete," Cathy said when the class agreed that two answers were plausible.

"Which one is right?" Kelly asked.

"The number I was thinking of was 15," Cathy responded. "In your groups, think of a clue that would make 15 the only possible answer."

The groups came up with several suggestions: "The number is odd." "The number is a multiple of 5." "The number isn't even." "If you add the digits, you get 6."

Cathy then said, "My riddle was incomplete, but I also included a clue that wasn't necessary at all."

"Oh, yeah," Nathan said, "you didn't need to say the number wasn't prime. We already knew that."

"How did you know?" Cathy asked.

Tami answered. "It couldn't be 2, 3, or 5 because you said it had to have two digits, and those were the only possible numbers that were prime."

"A clue that's unnecessary is called a redundant clue," Cathy told the class. She wrote the word *redundant* on the overhead.

Cathy then had the students work in pairs to write their own riddles. "Be sure your clues lead to only one answer," she cautioned, "and check to make sure you don't have any redundant clues."

These students wrote complete riddles without redundant clues.

Clue1: we are thinking of a number less than 20.
Clue2: It's a multiple of 2.
Clue3: It's Not Square, It's not prime.
Clue4: Ore Number has six factors.
Clue5: Are Number is higher than twelve.

We are thinking of a number

clue 1: Our number is less than 40
clue 2: Our number is an odd number
clue 3: Our number is not a square number
clue 4: Our number is not prime
clue 5: Our number is not a multiple of 5
clue 6: Our number is a factor of 165

GRADE		STRAND
1		NUMBER
2		**GEOMETRY**
3		MEASUREMENT
4		STATISTICS
5		PROBABILITY
6		PATTERNS AND FUNCTIONS
		ALGEBRA
		LOGIC

What Is a Polygon?—A Geoboard Lesson

Students often first encounter the word *polygon* in a textbook definition usually followed by several pictorial representations. The idea of what a polygon is isn't complicated, but the word is not commonly used outside of the math classroom, so students often have trouble remembering what it means. Cathy Humphreys developed this lesson to help her students in San Jose, California, learn what polygons are.

Materials

— Geoboards, one per student
— Rubber bands

Cathy had planned to use geoboards to teach area. When she asked her students to make a polygon on their geoboards, she was met with blank stares.

"What's a polygon?" the students wanted to know.

Rather than continue the lesson she had planned, Cathy decided to provide an opportunity for the students to learn about polygons. She gave the class the following direction. "Use just one rubber band and make any shape you'd like on your geoboard."

Once the students had done this, Cathy asked 12 of them to prop their geoboards on the chalkboard tray, so everyone in the class could see their shapes. She sorted the geoboards into two sets.

159

"All of the shapes on the left are polygons," Cathy explained. She continued, "None of the shapes on the right are polygons. Use this information and discuss in your groups what you think a polygon is."

These shapes are polygons.

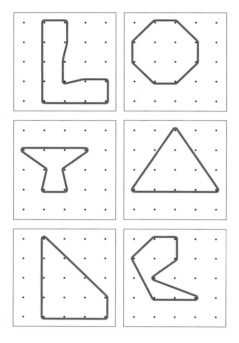

These shapes are *not* polygons.

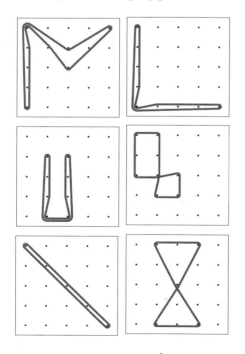

Students discussed their ideas and presented them to the class. Cathy then had the students whose geoboards were not on the chalkboard tray add them to the correct sets, explaining why they were or were not polygons. Finally, students wrote definitions of the word *polygon* and read them to one another.

Note: This lesson, taught to fifth graders, appears on the geoboard videotape in the "Mathematics with Manipulatives" series. (See the Bibliography on page 179.)

Fifth graders wrote these definitions of polygons.

> a polygon is a shape with no sides touching each other. It also has to be closed.
>
> example

> A polygon is a mini-sided figure with space inside it without any lines touching or crossing it.

> a polygon is any kind of shape that is completly open in the inside and has no crosses in it and is connected

GRADE

1
2
3
4
5
6

STRAND

NUMBER
GEOMETRY
MEASUREMENT
STATISTICS
PROBABILITY
PATTERNS AND FUNCTIONS
ALGEBRA
LOGIC

When Is the Cup Half Full?

My dad was a one-and-a-half-cup-of-coffee man. The cup of coffee he enjoyed after dinner was never quite enough. When offered a refill, he always replied with the same request, "Just half a cup, please."

Over the years, no matter how much coffee was poured into his cup for that second serving, it earned a comment.

"Look at that, the waiter must need glasses!" was one standard. I'm not sure that my dad ever felt that he was properly served half a cup of coffee.

More recently, six of us were having dinner out and a friend asked for half a cup of coffee when offered a refill. The waitress filled her cup. This time it was I who couldn't resist a comment.

"Do you think your cup is half full now?" I asked. The cup was a standard, rounded cup, much wider at the top than at the bottom.

Everyone at the table looked at me. They peered into the cup, then looked at me again, then peered into the cup again.

"Is this one of your math teacher questions?" someone asked.

A discussion began about where the halfway mark would be on the cup. The discussion became animated and began to get rowdy. It occurred to me that this might be an interesting question to raise with students. The following week, I brought the problem to a class of sixth graders in Mill Valley, California.

Materials

— Plastic glasses that are wider at the top than at the bottom, one per pair of students

— Dried beans or rice

— Measuring cup, 1 cup or larger, at least one

— Measuring spoons

For this lesson, I wanted the students to engage in two activities: predict at what level the plastic glass would be half full and design a procedure for finding the halfway mark.

I organized the class into pairs; there were 11 pairs and 1 group of three. I gave each group a plastic glass and explained the activity.

"After you and your partner discuss and mark where you think the halfway point might be," I said to the class, "I'd like you to design a procedure that you could use to find it. Please write your procedure clearly enough so others can use it."

Most students eyeballed the glass to predict where the halfway point was. One pair, however, took careful measurements of the diameter of the top, the diameter of the bottom, and the weight of the glass. They felt sure that the halfway mark could be calculated from these measurements. But they were stumped as how to do so, and they finally made a guess.

As students finished their work, I first checked that they had written their procedures clearly. Then I gave them two choices—either use their procedure to find the actual halfway mark or design an alternative procedure. In this way, all students stayed engaged until every pair had completed at least one procedure. This took just about 15 minutes. I then called the class to attention for a discussion.

"How many different procedures do you think we'll find from the 12 groups?" I asked. Their predictions ranged from three to nine, with most feeling there would be four or five different methods. Students then read their procedures. We discussed whether each one would work and whether it differed from the others suggested.

Several groups made use of the information "10 oz.," which was stamped on the bottom of

the glass. However, their methods differed. I pointed out to the class that these methods worked only when you knew the capacity of the containers.

These students used the 10-ounce capacity of the glass to develop procedures for finding the halfway mark.

Method for finding half-way mark

1. Since the cup is 10 oz, you take 5 oz of oil and 5 oz of vinigar.
2. Take each liquid first pour the vinigar and then oil.
3. Wait for the liquids to settle and where they are divided is where the half-way mark is.

where they divided | oil | —mark
vinigar

How to test for the halfway mark

Scientifically it was a guess. But we did know one thing that the top was larger than the bottom, so the halfway mark would be higher. Like Craig said the top of the cup has more space.

Procedure

A simple way is to fill the cup with five ounces of water. And there's your answer

Four pairs suggested procedures that used beans. Two suggested filling the container and counting the beans into two equal piles, one suggested using a measuring cup to find half the beans, and the other wanted to use a tablespoon to count scoops of beans. The class decided that these procedures fit into two categories, one for counting and one for measuring.

This pair suggested a five-step procedure using beans.

> 1st fill the cup with beans to the top
> 2nd dump all the beans out
> 3rd count them into eqaul parts
> 4th put half of the beans in the cup
> 5th and make the mark

In all, the students agreed that they had found seven different procedures. Determining the categories for classifying their procedures was a valuable thinking opportunity.

An Afternote

I organized this experience lesson differently when I tried it with other classes. I brought in an assortment of about a dozen containers—plastic glasses of different sizes; Styrofoam and paper drinking cups; and empty jars and bottles of unusual shapes, such as those used for salad dressing and liquid detergent. I labeled them A, B, C, and so on.

First, I had groups decide how many centimeters up from the bottom they thought the halfway mark would be on each container. Then I asked them to write one procedure that could be used to find the halfway marks of all of the containers. After groups reported and discussed their procedures, each group applied two different procedures to each of two containers. They posted the distances up from the bottom to the halfway

marks on each container so that students could compare these with their original predictions.

This problem-solving lesson always engages students and provides for lively discussions.

BLACKLINE
MASTERS

Geoboard Dot Paper

From 50 Problem-Solving Lessons ©1996 Math Solutions Publications

Shapes for Exploring Halves

From *50 Problem-Solving Lessons* ©1996 Math Solutions Publications

Roll for $1.00

You need: A partner or small group
One die
Pennies (about 30)
Dimes (about 20)

1. Each person takes a turn rolling one die.

2. On each turn, all players use the number rolled.

3. Each player takes as many pennies OR dimes as
    the number rolled. A player may not take both
    pennies and dimes on the same turn.

4. Each player puts pennies in the Pennies column
    and dimes in the Dimes column.

5. When a player has 10 or more pennies, he or she
    MUST exchange 10 pennies for a dime. Put the dime
    in any box in the Dimes column.

6. Players who go over $1.00 are out of the game and
    must wait for the next round.

7. The game is over after seven rolls. The winner is the player
    who has the closest to but not more than $1.00.

From 50 Problem-Solving Lessons ©1996 Math Solutions Publications

Calculator Explorations

PLUS PATTERNS

1. Press **2 + 2 =**
   You should have 4 on the display.
   Now press = again and again and again.
   What pattern of numbers appears?
2. Press **3 + 2 = = = = =** . . .
   What pattern appears?
3. Press **2 + 3 = = = = =** . . .
   What pattern appears?
4. Try other numbers. Write about what you discover.

MINUS PATTERNS

1. Press **20 – 2 = = =** . . . until you get to zero.
2. Start with other numbers and then press **– 2 = = =** . . .
   What can you discover about numbers that get to
   zero and those that do not?
3. Try other combinations of "starting" and "minus" numbers—
   for example,

   15 – 4 = = = . . .   **10 – 3 = = =** . . .
   15 – 3 = = = . . .   **11 – 6 = = =** . . .

   What can you learn about pairs of numbers that do or
   do not get to zero?

DIVISION PATTERNS

1. Press **8 ÷ 4 =**
   You should have 2 on the display.
2. Press **8 ÷ 3 =**
   You should get 2.6666666.
3. Try other division examples. Before pressing =, predict
   whether the answer will be a whole number (like 2, 3, 5, or 11)
   or a decimal number (like 2.6666666, 1.25, 3.5, or 0.375).
   Write about what you discover.

From *50 Problem-Solving Lessons* ©1996 Math Solutions Publications

Calculators and the Education of Youth

National Council of Teachers of Mathematics Position Statement

Developed by the NCTM's major committees, influenced by the deliberations of the Delegate Assembly, and approved by the Board of Directors, position statements are intended to guide discussion and influence decisions affecting school mathematics. The Council grants permission for them to be copied for distribution and used whenever they can be helpful in promoting better mathematics education.

Calculators are widely used at home and in the workplace. Increased use of calculators in school will ensure that students' experiences in mathematics will match the realities of every day life, develop their reasoning skills, and promote the understanding and application of mathematics. The National Council of Teachers of Mathematics therefore recommends the integration of the calculator into the school mathematics program at all grade levels in classwork, homework, and evaluation.

Instruction with calculators will extend the understanding of mathematics and will allow all students access to rich, problem-solving experiences. This instruction must develop students' ability to know how and when to use a calculator. Skill in estimation and the ability to decide if the solution to a problem is reasonable and essential adjuncts to the effective use of the calculator.

Evaluation must be in alignment with normal, everyday use of calculators in the classroom. Testing instruments that measure students' understanding of mathematics and its applications must include calculator use. As the availability of calculators increases and the technology improves, testing instruments and evaluation practices must be continually upgraded to reflect these changes. The National Council of Teachers of Mathematics recommends that all students use calculators to—

- explore and experiment with mathematical ideas such as patterns, numerical and algebraic properties, and functions;
- develop and reinforce skills such as estimation, computation, graphing, and analyzing data;
- focus on problem-solving processes rather than the computations associated with problems;
- perform the tedious computations that often develop when working with real data in problem situations;
- gain access to mathematical ideas and experiences that go beyond those levels limited by traditional paper-and-pencil computation.

The National Council of Teachers of Mathematics also recommends that every mathematics teacher at every level promote the use of

calculators to enhance mathematics instruction by—

- modeling the use of calculators in a variety of situations;
- using calculators in computation, problem solving, concept development, pattern recognition, data analysis, and graphing;
- incorporating the use of calculators in testing mathematical skills and concepts;
- keeping current with the state-of-the-art technology appropriate for the grade level being taught:
- exploring and developing new ways to use calculators to support instruction and assessment.

The National Council of Teachers of Mathematics also recommends that—

- school districts conduct staff development programs that enhance teachers' understanding of the use of appropriate state-of-the-art calculators in the classroom;
- teacher preparation institutions develop preservice and in-service programs that use a variety of calculators, including graphing calculators, at all levels of the curriculum;
- educators responsible for selecting curriculum materials make choices that reflect and support the use of calculators in the classroom;
- publishers, authors, and test and competition writers integrate the use of calculators at all levels of mathematics;
- mathematics educators inform students, parents, administrators, and school boards about the research that shows the advantages of including calculators as an everyday tool for the student of mathematics.

Research and experience have clearly demonstrated the potential of calculators to enhance students' learning in mathematics. The cognitive gain in number sense, conceptual development, and visualization can empower and motivate students to engage in true mathematical problem solving at a level previously denied to all but the most talented. The calculator is an essential tool for all students of mathematics.

171

The Game of Leftovers

You need: A partner
One die
15 Color Tiles
One cup to hold the tiles
Six paper plates or 3-inch paper squares ("plates")

1. Take turns. On your turn, roll the die, take that number of paper plates or squares, and divide the tiles among them. Keep any leftover tiles.

2. Both players record the math sentence that describes what happened.

   For example: 15 ÷ 4 = 3 R3

   In front of each sentence write the initial of the person who rolled the die.

3. Return the tiles on the plates to the cup before the next player takes a turn.

4. Play until all the tiles are gone. Then figure your scores by counting how many tiles each of you has. The winner is the player with the most leftovers. Add your scores to make sure that they total the 15 tiles you started with.

5. When you finish a game, look at each of your sentences with a remainder of zero (R0). Write on the class chart each sentence with R0 that isn't already posted.

From *50 Problem-Solving Lessons* ©1996 Math Solutions Publications

The Firehouse Problem

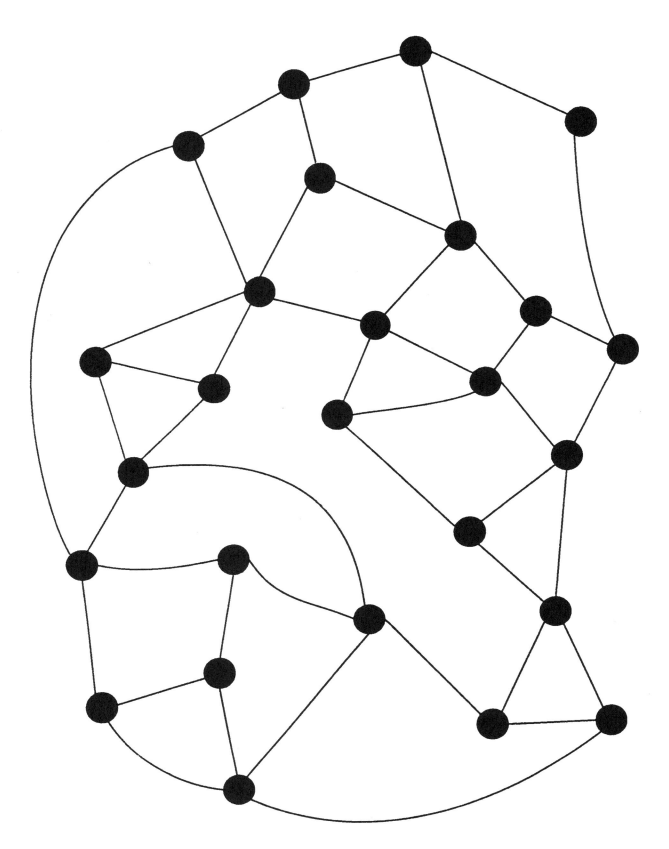

10-by-10 Grids

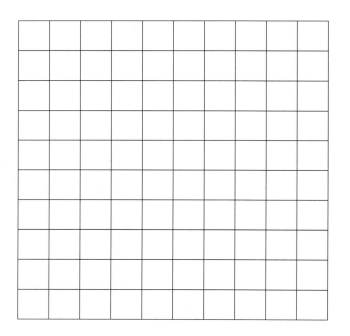

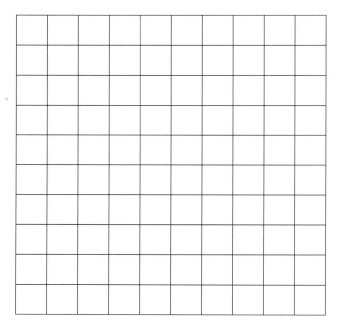

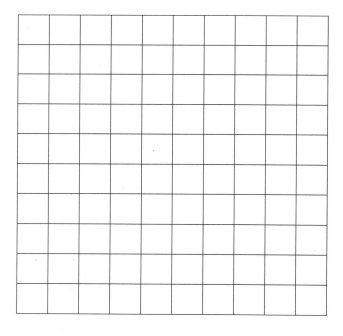

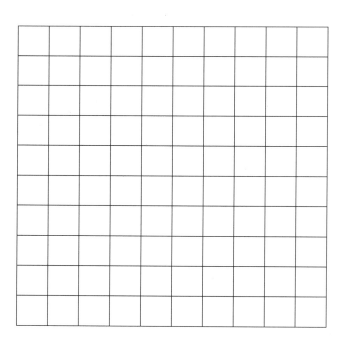

174

Probability Tile Game Statements

1. All 3 tiles are the same color.

2. All the tiles are red.

3. There is a red tile among them.

4. Not all tiles are the same color.

5. There are 2 red tiles among them.

6. Only 1 tile is red; the other 2 tiles are a different color.

7. There is no blue tile among them.

8. There is a green tile among them.

9. There is 1 blue tile.

From *50 Problem-Solving Lessons* ©1996 Math Solutions Publications

2-Centimeter Grid Paper

From *50 Problem-Solving Lessons* ©1996 Math Solutions Publications

Isometric Dot Paper

177

Bibliography

Burns, Marilyn. *A Collection of Math Lessons From Grades 3 Through 6*. Math Solutions Publications, 1987.

_____. *Math By All Means: Probability, Grades 3–4*. Math Solutions Publications, 1995.

_____. *Math for Smarty Pants*. Little, Brown and Company, 1982.

Burns, Marilyn, and Bonnie Tank. *A Collection of Math Lessons From Grades 1 Through 3*. Math Solutions Publications, 1988.

Casey, Nancy. "The Whole Language Connection," *Washington Mathematics,* Washington State Mathematics Council. 1991.

Kaye, Peggy. *Games for Math*. Pantheon Books, 1988.

National Council of Teachers of Mathematics. *Curriculum and Evaluation Standards for School Mathematics*. NCTM, 1989.

Nozaki, Akihiro, and Mitsumasa Anno. *Anno's Magic Hat Tricks*. Philomel Books, 1985.

Ohanian, Susan and Marilyn Burns. *Math By All Means: Division, Grades 3–4*. Math Solutions Publications, 1995.

O'Keefe, Jim. "Non-Standard Word Problems," *The Oregon Mathematics Teacher (TOMT)*, December 1992, pp. 14–15.

Rice, Eve. *Peter's Pockets*. Illustrated by Nancy Winslow Parker. Greenwillow Books, 1989.

Sheffield, Stephanie. *Math and Literature (K–3), Book Two*. Math Solutions Publications, 1995.

Index

Using GNU Fortran

For GCC version 4.3.3

(GCC)

The gfortran team

ISBN 1441412662

Printed in America

Published & distributed under the terms of the GNU Free Documentation Licence by SoHoBooks

http://www.gnu.org
http://gcc.gnu.org/onlinedocs/

Published by the Free Software Foundation
51 Franklin Street, Fifth Floor
Boston, MA 02110-1301, USA

Short Contents

Table of Contents

7 Intrinsic Modules 163

Contributing 167

GNU General Public License 171

GNU Free Documentation License 183

Funding Free Software 191

Option Index 193

Keyword Index 195

1 Introduction

This manual documents the use of `gfortran`, the GNU Fortran compiler. You can find in this manual how to invoke `gfortran`, as well as its features and incompatibilities.

The GNU Fortran compiler front end was designed initially as a free replacement for, or alternative to, the unix `f95` command; `gfortran` is the command you'll use to invoke the compiler.

1.1 About GNU Fortran

The GNU Fortran compiler is still in an early state of development. It can generate code for most constructs and expressions, but much work remains to be done.

When the GNU Fortran compiler is finished, it will do everything you expect from any decent compiler:

- Read a user's program, stored in a file and containing instructions written in Fortran 77, Fortran 90, Fortran 95 or Fortran 2003. This file contains *source code*.

- Translate the user's program into instructions a computer can carry out more quickly than it takes to translate the instructions in the first place. The result after compilation of a program is *machine code*, code designed to be efficiently translated and processed by a machine such as your computer. Humans usually aren't as good writing machine code as they are at writing Fortran (or C++, Ada, or Java), because is easy to make tiny mistakes writing machine code.

- Provide the user with information about the reasons why the compiler is unable to create a binary from the source code. Usually this will be the case if the source code is flawed. When writing Fortran, it is easy to make big mistakes. The Fortran 90 requires that the compiler can point out mistakes to the user. An incorrect usage of the language causes an *error message*.

  The compiler will also attempt to diagnose cases where the user's program contains a correct usage of the language, but instructs the computer to do something questionable. This kind of diagnostics message is called a *warning message*.

- Provide optional information about the translation passes from the source code to machine code. This can help a user of the compiler to find the cause of certain bugs which may not be obvious in the source code, but may be more easily found at a lower level compiler output. It also helps developers to find bugs in the compiler itself.

- Provide information in the generated machine code that can make it easier to find bugs in the program (using a debugging tool, called a *debugger*, such as the GNU Debugger `gdb`).

- Locate and gather machine code already generated to perform actions requested by statements in the user's program. This machine code is organized into *modules* and is located and *linked* to the user program.

The GNU Fortran compiler consists of several components:

- A version of the `gcc` command (which also might be installed as the system's `cc` command) that also understands and accepts Fortran source code. The `gcc` command is the *driver* program for all the languages in the GNU Compiler Collection (GCC); With gcc, you can compile the source code of any language for which a front end is available in GCC.

- The gfortran command itself, which also might be installed as the system's f95 command. gfortran is just another driver program, but specifically for the Fortran compiler only. The difference with gcc is that gfortran will automatically link the correct libraries to your program.

- A collection of run-time libraries. These libraries contain the machine code needed to support capabilities of the Fortran language that are not directly provided by the machine code generated by the gfortran compilation phase, such as intrinsic functions and subroutines, and routines for interaction with files and the operating system.

- The Fortran compiler itself, (f951). This is the GNU Fortran parser and code generator, linked to and interfaced with the GCC backend library. f951 "translates" the source code to assembler code. You would typically not use this program directly; instead, the gcc or gfortran driver programs will call it for you.

1.2 GNU Fortran and GCC

GNU Fortran is a part of GCC, the *GNU Compiler Collection*. GCC consists of a collection of front ends for various languages, which translate the source code into a language-independent form called *GENERIC*. This is then processed by a common middle end which provides optimization, and then passed to one of a collection of back ends which generate code for different computer architectures and operating systems.

Functionally, this is implemented with a driver program (gcc) which provides the command-line interface for the compiler. It calls the relevant compiler front-end program (e.g., f951 for Fortran) for each file in the source code, and then calls the assembler and linker as appropriate to produce the compiled output. In a copy of GCC which has been compiled with Fortran language support enabled, gcc will recognize files with '.f', '.for', '.ftn', '.f90', '.f95', and '.f03' extensions as Fortran source code, and compile it accordingly. A gfortran driver program is also provided, which is identical to gcc except that it automatically links the Fortran runtime libraries into the compiled program.

Source files with '.f', '.for', '.fpp', '.ftn', '.F', '.FOR', '.FPP', and '.FTN' extensions are treated as fixed form. Source files with '.f90', '.f95', '.f03', '.F90', '.F95', and '.F03' extensions are treated as free form. The capitalized versions of either form are run through preprocessing. Source files with the lower case '.fpp' extension are also run through preprocessing.

This manual specifically documents the Fortran front end, which handles the programming language's syntax and semantics. The aspects of GCC which relate to the optimization passes and the back-end code generation are documented in the GCC manual; see Section "Introduction" in *Using the GNU Compiler Collection (GCC)*. The two manuals together provide a complete reference for the GNU Fortran compiler.

1.3 Preprocessing and conditional compilation

Many Fortran compilers including GNU Fortran allow passing the source code through a C preprocessor (CPP; sometimes also called the Fortran preprocessor, FPP) to allow for conditional compilation. In the case of GNU Fortran, this is the GNU C Preprocessor in the traditional mode. On systems with case-preserving file names, the preprocessor is automatically invoked if the file extension is .F, .FOR, .FTN, .F90, .F95 or .F03; otherwise use for fixed-format code the option -x f77-cpp-input and for free-format code -x f95-cpp-input. Invocation of the preprocessor can be suppressed using -x f77 or -x f95.

If the GNU Fortran invoked the preprocessor, __GFORTRAN__ is defined and __GNUC__, __GNUC_MINOR__ and __GNUC_PATCHLEVEL__ can be used to determine the version of the compiler. See Section "Overview" in *The C Preprocessor* for details.

While CPP is the de-facto standard for preprocessing Fortran code, Part 3 of the Fortran 95 standard (ISO/IEC 1539-3:1998) defines Conditional Compilation, which is not widely used and not directly supported by the GNU Fortran compiler. You can use the program coco to preprocess such files (http://users.erols.com/dnagle/coco.html).

1.4 GNU Fortran and G77

The GNU Fortran compiler is the successor to g77, the Fortran 77 front end included in GCC prior to version 4. It is an entirely new program that has been designed to provide Fortran 95 support and extensibility for future Fortran language standards, as well as providing backwards compatibility for Fortran 77 and nearly all of the GNU language extensions supported by g77.

1.5 Project Status

> As soon as gfortran can parse all of the statements correctly, it will be in the "larva" state. When we generate code, the "puppa" state. When gfortran is done, we'll see if it will be a beautiful butterfly, or just a big bug....
>
> –Andy Vaught, April 2000

The start of the GNU Fortran 95 project was announced on the GCC homepage in March 18, 2000 (even though Andy had already been working on it for a while, of course).

The GNU Fortran compiler is able to compile nearly all standard-compliant Fortran 95, Fortran 90, and Fortran 77 programs, including a number of standard and non-standard extensions, and can be used on real-world programs. In particular, the supported extensions include OpenMP, Cray-style pointers, and several Fortran 2003 features such as enumeration, stream I/O, and some of the enhancements to allocatable array support from TR 15581. However, it is still under development and has a few remaining rough edges.

At present, the GNU Fortran compiler passes the NIST Fortran 77 Test Suite, and produces acceptable results on the LAPACK Test Suite. It also provides respectable performance on the Polyhedron Fortran compiler benchmarks and the Livermore Fortran Kernels test. It has been used to compile a number of large real-world programs, including the HIRLAM weather-forecasting code and the Tonto quantum chemistry package; see http://gcc.gnu.org/wiki/GfortranApps for an extended list.

Among other things, the GNU Fortran compiler is intended as a replacement for G77. At this point, nearly all programs that could be compiled with G77 can be compiled with GNU Fortran, although there are a few minor known regressions.

The primary work remaining to be done on GNU Fortran falls into three categories: bug fixing (primarily regarding the treatment of invalid code and providing useful error messages), improving the compiler optimizations and the performance of compiled code, and extending the compiler to support future standards—in particular, Fortran 2003.

1.6 Standards

The GNU Fortran compiler implements ISO/IEC 1539:1997 (Fortran 95). As such, it can also compile essentially all standard-compliant Fortran 90 and Fortran 77 programs. It also supports the ISO/IEC TR-15581 enhancements to allocatable arrays, and the OpenMP Application Program Interface v2.5 specification.

In the future, the GNU Fortran compiler may also support other standard variants of and extensions to the Fortran language. These include ISO/IEC 1539-1:2004 (Fortran 2003).

Part I: Invoking GNU Fortran

2 GNU Fortran Command Options

The `gfortran` command supports all the options supported by the `gcc` command. Only options specific to GNU Fortran are documented here.

See Section "GCC Command Options" in *Using the GNU Compiler Collection (GCC)*, for information on the non-Fortran-specific aspects of the `gcc` command (and, therefore, the `gfortran` command).

All GCC and GNU Fortran options are accepted both by **gfortran** and by **gcc** (as well as any other drivers built at the same time, such as **g++**), since adding GNU Fortran to the GCC distribution enables acceptance of GNU Fortran options by all of the relevant drivers.

In some cases, options have positive and negative forms; the negative form of '`-ffoo`' would be '`-fno-foo`'. This manual documents only one of these two forms, whichever one is not the default.

2.1 Option summary

Here is a summary of all the options specific to GNU Fortran, grouped by type. Explanations are in the following sections.

Fortran Language Options

See Section 2.2 [Options controlling Fortran dialect], page 8.

```
-fall-intrinsics -ffree-form -fno-fixed-form
-fdollar-ok -fimplicit-none -fmax-identifier-length
-std=std -fd-lines-as-code -fd-lines-as-comments
-ffixed-line-length-n -ffixed-line-length-none
-ffree-line-length-n -ffree-line-length-none
-fdefault-double-8 -fdefault-integer-8 -fdefault-real-8
-fcray-pointer -fopenmp -fno-range-check -fbackslash -fmodule-private
```

Error and Warning Options

See Section 2.3 [Options to request or suppress errors and warnings], page 10.

```
-fmax-errors=n
-fsyntax-only -pedantic -pedantic-errors
-Wall -Waliasing -Wampersand -Wcharacter-truncation -Wconversion
-Wimplicit-interface -Wline-truncation -Wnonstd-intrinsics -Wsurprising
-Wno-tabs -Wunderflow -Wunused-parameter
```

Debugging Options

See Section 2.4 [Options for debugging your program or GNU Fortran], page 12.

```
-fdump-parse-tree -ffpe-trap=list
-fdump-core -fbacktrace
```

Directory Options

See Section 2.5 [Options for directory search], page 13.

```
-Idir -Jdir -Mdir -fintrinsic-modules-path dir
```

Link Options

See Section 2.6 [Options for influencing the linking step], page 13.

```
-static-libgfortran
```

Runtime Options

See Section 2.7 [Options for influencing runtime behavior], page 14.

```
-fconvert=conversion  -frecord-marker=length
-fmax-subrecord-length=length  -fsign-zero
```

Code Generation Options

See Section 2.8 [Options for code generation conventions], page 14.

```
-fno-automatic  -ff2c  -fno-underscoring  -fsecond-underscore
-fbounds-check  -fmax-stack-var-size=n
-fpack-derived  -frepack-arrays  -fshort-enums  -fexternal-blas
-fblas-matmul-limit=n  -frecursive  -finit-local-zero
-finit-integer=n  -finit-real=<zero|inf|-inf|nan>
-finit-logical=<true|false>  -finit-character=n
```

2.2 Options controlling Fortran dialect

The following options control the details of the Fortran dialect accepted by the compiler:

`-ffree-form`
`-ffixed-form`

Specify the layout used by the source file. The free form layout was introduced in Fortran 90. Fixed form was traditionally used in older Fortran programs. When neither option is specified, the source form is determined by the file extension.

`-fall-intrinsics`

Accept all of the intrinsic procedures provided in libgfortran without regard to the setting of '-std'. In particular, this option can be quite useful with '-std=f95'. Additionally, gfortran will ignore '-Wnonstd-intrinsics'.

`-fd-lines-as-code`
`-fd-lines-as-comments`

Enable special treatment for lines beginning with d or D in fixed form sources. If the '-fd-lines-as-code' option is given they are treated as if the first column contained a blank. If the '-fd-lines-as-comments' option is given, they are treated as comment lines.

`-fdefault-double-8`

Set the DOUBLE PRECISION type to an 8 byte wide type.

`-fdefault-integer-8`

Set the default integer and logical types to an 8 byte wide type. Do nothing if this is already the default.

`-fdefault-real-8`

Set the default real type to an 8 byte wide type. Do nothing if this is already the default.

`-fdollar-ok`

Allow '$' as a valid character in a symbol name.

`-fbackslash`

Change the interpretation of backslashes in string literals from a single backslash character to "C-style" escape characters. The following combinations are expanded \a, \b, \f, \n, \r, \t, \v, \\, and \0 to the ASCII characters alert, backspace, form feed, newline, carriage return, horizontal tab, vertical practices, but not all. However, improvements to GNU Fortran in this area are welcome.

This should be used in conjunction with '-std=f95' or '-std=f2003'.

-pedantic-errors
    Like '-pedantic', except that errors are produced rather than warnings.

-Wall   Enables commonly used warning options pertaining to usage that we recommend avoiding and that we believe are easy to avoid. This currently includes '-Waliasing', '-Wampersand', '-Wsurprising', '-Wnonstd-intrinsics', '-Wno-tabs', and '-Wline-truncation'.

-Waliasing
    Warn about possible aliasing of dummy arguments. Specifically, it warns if the same actual argument is associated with a dummy argument with INTENT(IN) and a dummy argument with INTENT(OUT) in a call with an explicit interface.

    The following example will trigger the warning.

```
interface
  subroutine bar(a,b)
    integer, intent(in) :: a
    integer, intent(out) :: b
  end subroutine
end interface
integer :: a

call bar(a,a)
```

-Wampersand
    Warn about missing ampersand in continued character constants. The warning is given with '-Wampersand', '-pedantic', '-std=f95', and '-std=f2003'. Note: With no ampersand given in a continued character constant, GNU Fortran assumes continuation at the first non-comment, non-whitespace character after the ampersand that initiated the continuation.

-Wcharacter-truncation
    Warn when a character assignment will truncate the assigned string.

-Wconversion
    Warn about implicit conversions between different types.

-Wimplicit-interface
    Warn if a procedure is called without an explicit interface. Note this only checks that an explicit interface is present. It does not check that the declared interfaces are consistent across program units.

-Wnonstd-intrinsics
    Warn if the user tries to use an intrinsic that does not belong to the standard the user has chosen via the '-std' option.

-Wsurprising
    Produce a warning when "suspicious" code constructs are encountered. While technically legal these usually indicate that an error has been made.

    This currently produces a warning under the following circumstances:

- An INTEGER SELECT construct has a CASE that can never be matched as its lower value is greater than its upper value.

- A LOGICAL SELECT construct has three CASE statements.

- A TRANSFER specifies a source that is shorter than the destination.

-Wtabs   By default, tabs are accepted as whitespace, but tabs are not members of the Fortran Character Set. For continuation lines, a tab followed by a digit between 1 and 9 is supported. '-Wno-tabs' will cause a warning to be issued if a tab is encountered. Note, '-Wno-tabs' is active for '-pedantic', '-std=f95', '-std=f2003', and '-Wall'.

-Wunderflow

Produce a warning when numerical constant expressions are encountered, which yield an UNDERFLOW during compilation.

-Wunused-parameter

Contrary to gcc's meaning of '-Wunused-parameter', gfortran's implementation of this option does not warn about unused dummy arguments, but about unused PARAMETER values. '-Wunused-parameter' is not included in '-Wall' but is implied by '-Wall -Wextra'.

-Werror   Turns all warnings into errors.

See Section "Options to Request or Suppress Errors and Warnings" in *Using the GNU Compiler Collection (GCC)*, for information on more options offered by the GBE shared by gfortran, gcc and other GNU compilers.

Some of these have no effect when compiling programs written in Fortran.

2.4 Options for debugging your program or GNU Fortran

GNU Fortran has various special options that are used for debugging either your program or the GNU Fortran compiler.

-fdump-parse-tree

Output the internal parse tree before starting code generation. Only really useful for debugging the GNU Fortran compiler itself.

-ffpe-trap=*list*

Specify a list of IEEE exceptions when a Floating Point Exception (FPE) should be raised. On most systems, this will result in a SIGFPE signal being sent and the program being interrupted, producing a core file useful for debugging. *list* is a (possibly empty) comma-separated list of the following IEEE exceptions: 'invalid' (invalid floating point operation, such as SQRT(-1.0)), 'zero' (division by zero), 'overflow' (overflow in a floating point operation), 'underflow' (underflow in a floating point operation), 'precision' (loss of precision during operation) and 'denormal' (operation produced a denormal value).

Some of the routines in the Fortran runtime library, like 'CPU_TIME', are likely to to trigger floating point exceptions when ffpe-trap=precision is used. For this reason, the use of ffpe-trap=precision is not recommended.

`-fbacktrace`
> Specify that, when a runtime error is encountered or a deadly signal is emitted (segmentation fault, illegal instruction, bus error or floating-point exception), the Fortran runtime library should output a backtrace of the error. This option only has influence for compilation of the Fortran main program.

`-fdump-core`
> Request that a core-dump file is written to disk when a runtime error is encountered on systems that support core dumps. This option is only effective for the compilation of the Fortran main program.

See Section "Options for Debugging Your Program or GCC" in *Using the GNU Compiler Collection (GCC)*, for more information on debugging options.

2.5 Options for directory search

These options affect how GNU Fortran searches for files specified by the INCLUDE directive and where it searches for previously compiled modules.

It also affects the search paths used by `cpp` when used to preprocess Fortran source.

`-Idir`
> These affect interpretation of the INCLUDE directive (as well as of the `#include` directive of the `cpp` preprocessor).
>
> Also note that the general behavior of '-I' and INCLUDE is pretty much the same as of '-I' with `#include` in the `cpp` preprocessor, with regard to looking for 'header.gcc' files and other such things.
>
> This path is also used to search for '.mod' files when previously compiled modules are required by a USE statement.
>
> See Section "Options for Directory Search" in *Using the GNU Compiler Collection (GCC)*, for information on the '-I' option.

`-Mdir`

`-Jdir`
> This option specifies where to put '.mod' files for compiled modules. It is also added to the list of directories to searched by an USE statement.
>
> The default is the current directory.
>
> '-J' is an alias for '-M' to avoid conflicts with existing GCC options.

`-fintrinsic-modules-path dir`
> This option specifies the location of pre-compiled intrinsic modules, if they are not in the default location expected by the compiler.

2.6 Influencing the linking step

These options come into play when the compiler links object files into an executable output file. They are meaningless if the compiler is not doing a link step.

`-static-libgfortran`
> On systems that provide 'libgfortran' as a shared and a static library, this option forces the use of the static version. If no shared version of 'libgfortran' was built when the compiler was configured, this option has no effect.

2.7 Influencing runtime behavior

These options affect the runtime behavior of programs compiled with GNU Fortran.

`-fconvert=conversion`

> Specify the representation of data for unformatted files. Valid values for conversion are: 'native', the default; 'swap', swap between big- and little-endian; 'big-endian', use big-endian representation for unformatted files; 'little-endian', use little-endian representation for unformatted files.
>
> *This option has an effect only when used in the main program. The* CONVERT *specifier and the GFORTRAN_CONVERT_UNIT environment variable override the default specified by '-fconvert'.*

`-frecord-marker=length`

> Specify the length of record markers for unformatted files. Valid values for length are 4 and 8. Default is 4. *This is different from previous versions of* gfortran, which specified a default record marker length of 8 on most systems. If you want to read or write files compatible with earlier versions of gfortran, use '-frecord-marker=8'.

`-fmax-subrecord-length=length`

> Specify the maximum length for a subrecord. The maximum permitted value for length is 2147483639, which is also the default. Only really useful for use by the gfortran testsuite.

`-fsign-zero`

> When writing zero values, show the negative sign if the sign bit is set. fno-sign-zero does not print the negative sign of zero values for compatibility with F77. Default behavior is to show the negative sign.

2.8 Options for code generation conventions

These machine-independent options control the interface conventions used in code generation.

Most of them have both positive and negative forms; the negative form of '-ffoo' would be '-fno-foo'. In the table below, only one of the forms is listed—the one which is not the default. You can figure out the other form by either removing 'no-' or adding it.

`-fno-automatic`

> Treat each program unit (except those marked as RECURSIVE) as if the SAVE statement were specified for every local variable and array referenced in it. Does not affect common blocks. (Some Fortran compilers provide this option under the name '-static' or '-save'.) The default, which is '-fautomatic', uses the stack for local variables smaller than the value given by '-fmax-stack-var-size'. Use the option '-frecursive' to use no static memory.

`-ff2c`   Generate code designed to be compatible with code generated by g77 and f2c.

> The calling conventions used by g77 (originally implemented in f2c) require functions that return type default REAL to actually return the C type double, and functions that return type COMPLEX to return the values via an extra

argument in the calling sequence that points to where to store the return value. Under the default GNU calling conventions, such functions simply return their results as they would in GNU C—default `REAL` functions return the C type `float`, and `COMPLEX` functions return the GNU C type `complex`. Additionally, this option implies the '-fsecond-underscore' option, unless '-fno-second-underscore' is explicitly requested.

This does not affect the generation of code that interfaces with the `libgfortran` library.

Caution: It is not a good idea to mix Fortran code compiled with '-ff2c' with code compiled with the default '-fno-f2c' calling conventions as, calling `COMPLEX` or default `REAL` functions between program parts which were compiled with different calling conventions will break at execution time.

Caution: This will break code which passes intrinsic functions of type default `REAL` or `COMPLEX` as actual arguments, as the library implementations use the '-fno-f2c' calling conventions.

-fno-underscoring

Do not transform names of entities specified in the Fortran source file by appending underscores to them.

With '-funderscoring' in effect, GNU Fortran appends one underscore to external names with no underscores. This is done to ensure compatibility with code produced by many UNIX Fortran compilers.

Caution: The default behavior of GNU Fortran is incompatible with f2c and g77, please use the '-ff2c' option if you want object files compiled with GNU Fortran to be compatible with object code created with these tools.

Use of '-fno-underscoring' is not recommended unless you are experimenting with issues such as integration of GNU Fortran into existing system environments (vis-à-vis existing libraries, tools, and so on).

For example, with '-funderscoring', and assuming other defaults like '-fcase-lower' and that `j()` and `max_count()` are external functions while `my_var` and `lvar` are local variables, a statement like

```
I = J() + MAX_COUNT (MY_VAR, LVAR)
```

is implemented as something akin to:

```
i = j_() + max_count__(&my_var__, &lvar);
```

With '-fno-underscoring', the same statement is implemented as:

```
i = j() + max_count(&my_var, &lvar);
```

Use of '-fno-underscoring' allows direct specification of user-defined names while debugging and when interfacing GNU Fortran code with other languages.

Note that just because the names match does *not* mean that the interface implemented by GNU Fortran for an external name matches the interface implemented by some other language for that same name. That is, getting code produced by GNU Fortran to link to code produced by some other compiler using this or any other method can be only a small part of the overall solution—getting the code generated by both compilers to agree on issues other than

naming can require significant effort, and, unlike naming disagreements, linkers
normally cannot detect disagreements in these other areas.

Also, note that with '-fno-underscoring', the lack of appended underscores in-
troduces the very real possibility that a user-defined external name will conflict
with a name in a system library, which could make finding unresolved-reference
bugs quite difficult in some cases—they might occur at program run time, and
show up only as buggy behavior at run time.

In future versions of GNU Fortran we hope to improve naming and linking
issues so that debugging always involves using the names as they appear in the
source, even if the names as seen by the linker are mangled to prevent accidental
linking between procedures with incompatible interfaces.

-fsecond-underscore

By default, GNU Fortran appends an underscore to external names. If this
option is used GNU Fortran appends two underscores to names with underscores
and one underscore to external names with no underscores. GNU Fortran also
appends two underscores to internal names with underscores to avoid naming
collisions with external names.

This option has no effect if '-fno-underscoring' is in effect. It is implied by
the '-ff2c' option.

Otherwise, with this option, an external name such as MAX_COUNT is implemented as a reference to the link-time external symbol max_count__, instead
of max_count_. This is required for compatibility with g77 and f2c, and is
implied by use of the '-ff2c' option.

-fbounds-check

Enable generation of run-time checks for array subscripts and against the declared minimum and maximum values. It also checks array indices for assumed
and deferred shape arrays against the actual allocated bounds.

Some checks require that '-fbounds-check' is set for the compilation of the
main program.

In the future this may also include other forms of checking, e.g., checking substring references.

-fmax-stack-var-size=n

This option specifies the size in bytes of the largest array that will be put on
the stack; if the size is exceeded static memory is used (except in procedures
marked as RECURSIVE). Use the option '-frecursive' to allow for recursive
procedures which do not have a RECURSIVE attribute or for parallel programs.
Use '-fno-automatic' to never use the stack.

This option currently only affects local arrays declared with constant bounds,
and may not apply to all character variables. Future versions of GNU Fortran
may improve this behavior.

The default value for n is 32768.

-fpack-derived

> This option tells GNU Fortran to pack derived type members as closely as possible. Code compiled with this option is likely to be incompatible with code compiled without this option, and may execute slower.

-frepack-arrays

> In some circumstances GNU Fortran may pass assumed shape array sections via a descriptor describing a noncontiguous area of memory. This option adds code to the function prologue to repack the data into a contiguous block at runtime.

> This should result in faster accesses to the array. However it can introduce significant overhead to the function call, especially when the passed data is noncontiguous.

-fshort-enums

> This option is provided for interoperability with C code that was compiled with the '-fshort-enums' option. It will make GNU Fortran choose the smallest INTEGER kind a given enumerator set will fit in, and give all its enumerators this kind.

-fexternal-blas

> This option will make gfortran generate calls to BLAS functions for some matrix operations like MATMUL, instead of using our own algorithms, if the size of the matrices involved is larger than a given limit (see '-fblas-matmul-limit'). This may be profitable if an optimized vendor BLAS library is available. The BLAS library will have to be specified at link time.

-fblas-matmul-limit=n

> Only significant when '-fexternal-blas' is in effect. Matrix multiplication of matrices with size larger than (or equal to) n will be performed by calls to BLAS functions, while others will be handled by gfortran internal algorithms. If the matrices involved are not square, the size comparison is performed using the geometric mean of the dimensions of the argument and result matrices.

> The default value for n is 30.

-frecursive

> Allow indirect recursion by forcing all local arrays to be allocated on the stack. This flag cannot be used together with '-fmax-stack-var-size=' or '-fno-automatic'.

-finit-local-zero
-finit-integer=n
-finit-real=<zero|inf|-inf|nan>
-finit-logical=<true|false>
-finit-character=n

> The '-finit-local-zero' option instructs the compiler to initialize local INTEGER, REAL, and COMPLEX variables to zero, LOGICAL variables to false, and CHARACTER variables to a string of null bytes. Finer-grained initialization options are provided by the '-finit-integer=n', '-finit-real=<zero|inf|-inf|nan>' (which also initializes the real and imaginary parts of local COMPLEX

variables), '`-finit-logical=<true|false>`', and '`-finit-character=n`' (where *n* is an ASCII character value) options. These options do not initialize components of derived type variables, nor do they initialize variables that appear in an `EQUIVALENCE` statement. (This limitation may be removed in future releases).

Note that the '`-finit-real=nan`' option initializes `REAL` and `COMPLEX` variables with a quiet NaN.

See Section "Options for Code Generation Conventions" in *Using the GNU Compiler Collection (GCC)*, for information on more options offered by the GBE shared by `gfortran`, `gcc`, and other GNU compilers.

2.9 Environment variables affecting `gfortran`

The `gfortran` compiler currently does not make use of any environment variables to control its operation above and beyond those that affect the operation of `gcc`.

See Section "Environment Variables Affecting GCC" in *Using the GNU Compiler Collection (GCC)*, for information on environment variables.

See Chapter 3 [Runtime], page 19, for environment variables that affect the run-time behavior of programs compiled with GNU Fortran.

3 Runtime: Influencing runtime behavior with environment variables

The behavior of the `gfortran` can be influenced by environment variables.

Malformed environment variables are silently ignored.

3.1 GFORTRAN_STDIN_UNIT—Unit number for standard input

This environment variable can be used to select the unit number preconnected to standard input. This must be a positive integer. The default value is 5.

3.2 GFORTRAN_STDOUT_UNIT—Unit number for standard output

This environment variable can be used to select the unit number preconnected to standard output. This must be a positive integer. The default value is 6.

3.3 GFORTRAN_STDERR_UNIT—Unit number for standard error

This environment variable can be used to select the unit number preconnected to standard error. This must be a positive integer. The default value is 0.

3.4 GFORTRAN_USE_STDERR—Send library output to standard error

This environment variable controls where library output is sent. If the first letter is 'y', 'Y' or '1', standard error is used. If the first letter is 'n', 'N' or '0', standard output is used.

3.5 GFORTRAN_TMPDIR—Directory for scratch files

This environment variable controls where scratch files are created. If this environment variable is missing, GNU Fortran searches for the environment variable TMP. If this is also missing, the default is '/tmp'.

3.6 GFORTRAN_UNBUFFERED_ALL—Don't buffer I/O on all units

This environment variable controls whether all I/O is unbuffered. If the first letter is 'y', 'Y' or '1', all I/O is unbuffered. This will slow down small sequential reads and writes. If the first letter is 'n', 'N' or '0', I/O is buffered. This is the default.

3.7 GFORTRAN_UNBUFFERED_PRECONNECTED—Don't buffer I/O on preconnected units

The environment variable named GFORTRAN_UNBUFFERED_PRECONNECTED controls whether I/O on a preconnected unit (i.e STDOUT or STDERR) is unbuffered. If the first letter is 'y', 'Y' or '1', I/O is unbuffered. This will slow down small sequential reads and writes. If the first letter is 'n', 'N' or '0', I/O is buffered. This is the default.

3.8 GFORTRAN_SHOW_LOCUS—Show location for runtime errors

If the first letter is 'y', 'Y' or '1', filename and line numbers for runtime errors are printed. If the first letter is 'n', 'N' or '0', don't print filename and line numbers for runtime errors. The default is to print the location.

3.9 GFORTRAN_OPTIONAL_PLUS—Print leading + where permitted

If the first letter is 'y', 'Y' or '1', a plus sign is printed where permitted by the Fortran standard. If the first letter is 'n', 'N' or '0', a plus sign is not printed in most cases. Default is not to print plus signs.

3.10 GFORTRAN_DEFAULT_RECL—Default record length for new files

This environment variable specifies the default record length, in bytes, for files which are opened without a RECL tag in the OPEN statement. This must be a positive integer. The default value is 1073741824 bytes (1 GB).

3.11 GFORTRAN_LIST_SEPARATOR—Separator for list output

This environment variable specifies the separator when writing list-directed output. It may contain any number of spaces and at most one comma. If you specify this on the command line, be sure to quote spaces, as in

```
$ GFORTRAN_LIST_SEPARATOR=' , ' ./a.out
```

when a.out is the compiled Fortran program that you want to run. Default is a single space.

3.12 GFORTRAN_CONVERT_UNIT—Set endianness for unformatted I/O

By setting the GFORTRAN_CONVERT_UNIT variable, it is possible to change the representation of data for unformatted files. The syntax for the GFORTRAN_CONVERT_UNIT variable is:

```
GFORTRAN_CONVERT_UNIT: mode | mode ';' exception | exception ;
mode: 'native' | 'swap' | 'big_endian' | 'little_endian' ;
exception: mode ':' unit_list | unit_list ;
unit_list: unit_spec | unit_list unit_spec ;
unit_spec: INTEGER | INTEGER '-' INTEGER ;
```

The variable consists of an optional default mode, followed by a list of optional exceptions, which are separated by semicolons from the preceding default and each other. Each exception consists of a format and a comma-separated list of units. Valid values for the modes are the same as for the CONVERT specifier:

NATIVE Use the native format. This is the default.

SWAP Swap between little- and big-endian.

LITTLE_ENDIAN Use the little-endian format for unformatted files.

BIG_ENDIAN Use the big-endian format for unformatted files.

A missing mode for an exception is taken to mean BIG_ENDIAN. Examples of values for GFORTRAN_CONVERT_UNIT are:

'big_endian' Do all unformatted I/O in big_endian mode.

'little_endian;native:10-20,25' Do all unformatted I/O in little_endian mode, except for units 10 to 20 and 25, which are in native format.

'10-20' Units 10 to 20 are big-endian, the rest is native.

Setting the environment variables should be done on the command line or via the `export` command for `sh`-compatible shells and via `setenv` for `csh`-compatible shells.

Example for `sh`:

```
$ gfortran foo.f90
$ GFORTRAN_CONVERT_UNIT='big_endian;native:10-20' ./a.out
```

Example code for `csh`:

```
% gfortran foo.f90
% setenv GFORTRAN_CONVERT_UNIT 'big_endian;native:10-20'
% ./a.out
```

Using anything but the native representation for unformatted data carries a significant speed overhead. If speed in this area matters to you, it is best if you use this only for data that needs to be portable.

See Section 5.1.14 [CONVERT specifier], page 33, for an alternative way to specify the data representation for unformatted files. See Section 2.7 [Runtime Options], page 14, for setting a default data representation for the whole program. The `CONVERT` specifier overrides the '`-fconvert`' compile options.

Note that the values specified via the GFORTRAN_CONVERT_UNIT environment variable will override the CONVERT specifier in the open statement. This is to give control over data formats to users who do not have the source code of their program available.

3.13 GFORTRAN_ERROR_DUMPCORE—Dump core on run-time errors

If the `GFORTRAN_ERROR_DUMPCORE` variable is set to 'y', 'Y' or '1' (only the first letter is relevant) then library run-time errors cause core dumps. To disable the core dumps, set the variable to 'n', 'N', '0'. Default is not to core dump unless the '`-fdump-core`' compile option was used.

3.14 GFORTRAN_ERROR_BACKTRACE—Show backtrace on run-time errors

If the `GFORTRAN_ERROR_BACKTRACE` variable is set to 'y', 'Y' or '1' (only the first letter is relevant) then a backtrace is printed when a run-time error occurs. To disable the backtracing, set the variable to 'n', 'N', '0'. Default is not to print a backtrace unless the '`-fbacktrace`' compile option was used.

Part II: Language Reference

4 Fortran 2003 Status

Although GNU Fortran focuses on implementing the Fortran 95 standard for the time being, a few Fortran 2003 features are currently available.

- Intrinsics `command_argument_count`, `get_command`, `get_command_argument`, `get_environment_variable`, and `move_alloc`.
- Array constructors using square brackets. That is, `[...]` rather than `(/.../)`.
- `FLUSH` statement.
- `IOMSG=` specifier for I/O statements.
- Support for the declaration of enumeration constants via the `ENUM` and `ENUMERATOR` statements. Interoperability with `gcc` is guaranteed also for the case where the `-fshort-enums` command line option is given.
- TR 15581:
  - `ALLOCATABLE` dummy arguments.
  - `ALLOCATABLE` function results
  - `ALLOCATABLE` components of derived types
- The `OPEN` statement supports the `ACCESS='STREAM'` specifier, allowing I/O without any record structure.
- Namelist input/output for internal files.
- The `PROTECTED` statement and attribute.
- The `VALUE` statement and attribute.
- The `VOLATILE` statement and attribute.
- The `IMPORT` statement, allowing to import host-associated derived types.
- `USE` statement with `INTRINSIC` and `NON_INTRINSIC` attribute; supported intrinsic modules: `ISO_FORTRAN_ENV`, `OMP_LIB` and `OMP_LIB_KINDS`.
- Renaming of operators in the `USE` statement.
- Interoperability with C (ISO C Bindings)
- BOZ as argument of INT, REAL, DBLE and CMPLX.

5 Extensions

The two sections below detail the extensions to standard Fortran that are implemented in GNU Fortran, as well as some of the popular or historically important extensions that are not (or not yet) implemented. For the latter case, we explain the alternatives available to GNU Fortran users, including replacement by standard-conforming code or GNU extensions.

5.1 Extensions implemented in GNU Fortran

GNU Fortran implements a number of extensions over standard Fortran. This chapter contains information on their syntax and meaning. There are currently two categories of GNU Fortran extensions, those that provide functionality beyond that provided by any standard, and those that are supported by GNU Fortran purely for backward compatibility with legacy compilers. By default, '-std=gnu' allows the compiler to accept both types of extensions, but to warn about the use of the latter. Specifying either '-std=f95' or '-std=f2003' disables both types of extensions, and '-std=legacy' allows both without warning.

5.1.1 Old-style kind specifications

GNU Fortran allows old-style kind specifications in declarations. These look like:

```
TYPESPEC*size x,y,z
```

where TYPESPEC is a basic type (INTEGER, REAL, etc.), and where size is a byte count corresponding to the storage size of a valid kind for that type. (For COMPLEX variables, size is the total size of the real and imaginary parts.) The statement then declares x, y and z to be of type TYPESPEC with the appropriate kind. This is equivalent to the standard-conforming declaration

```
TYPESPEC(k) x,y,z
```

where k is equal to size for most types, but is equal to size/2 for the COMPLEX type.

5.1.2 Old-style variable initialization

GNU Fortran allows old-style initialization of variables of the form:

```
INTEGER i/1/,j/2/
REAL x(2,2) /3*0.,1./
```

The syntax for the initializers is as for the DATA statement, but unlike in a DATA statement, an initializer only applies to the variable immediately preceding the initialization. In other words, something like INTEGER I,J/2,3/ is not valid. This style of initialization is only allowed in declarations without double colons (::); the double colons were introduced in Fortran 90, which also introduced a standard syntax for initializing variables in type declarations.

Examples of standard-conforming code equivalent to the above example are:

```
! Fortran 90
    INTEGER :: i = 1, j = 2
    REAL :: x(2,2) = RESHAPE((/0.,0.,0.,1./),SHAPE(x))
! Fortran 77
    INTEGER i, j
    REAL x(2,2)
    DATA i/1/, j/2/, x/3*0.,1./
```

Note that variables which are explicitly initialized in declarations or in **DATA** statements automatically acquire the **SAVE** attribute.

5.1.3 Extensions to namelist

GNU Fortran fully supports the Fortran 95 standard for namelist I/O including array qualifiers, substrings and fully qualified derived types. The output from a namelist write is compatible with namelist read. The output has all names in upper case and indentation to column 1 after the namelist name. Two extensions are permitted:

Old-style use of '$' instead of '&'

```
$MYNML
 X(:)%Y(2) = 1.0 2.0 3.0
 CH(1:4) = "abcd"
$END
```

It should be noted that the default terminator is '/' rather than '&END'.

Querying of the namelist when inputting from stdin. After at least one space, entering '?' sends to stdout the namelist name and the names of the variables in the namelist:

```
 ?

&mynml
 x
 x%y
 ch
&end
```

Entering '=?' outputs the namelist to stdout, as if WRITE(*,NML = mynml) had been called:

```
 =?

&MYNML
 X(1)%Y=  0.000000     ,  1.000000     ,  0.000000     ,
 X(2)%Y=  0.000000     ,  2.000000     ,  0.000000     ,
 X(3)%Y=  0.000000     ,  3.000000     ,  0.000000     ,
 CH=abcd,  /
```

To aid this dialog, when input is from stdin, errors send their messages to stderr and execution continues, even if **IOSTAT** is set.

PRINT namelist is permitted. This causes an error if '-std=f95' is used.

```
PROGRAM test_print
  REAL, dimension (4)  ::  x = (/1.0, 2.0, 3.0, 4.0/)
  NAMELIST /mynml/ x
  PRINT mynml
END PROGRAM test_print
```

Expanded namelist reads are permitted. This causes an error if '-std=f95' is used. In the following example, the first element of the array will be given the value 0.00 and the two succeeding elements will be given the values 1.00 and 2.00.

```
&MYNML
 X(1,1) = 0.00 , 1.00 , 2.00
 /
```

5.1.4 X format descriptor without count field

To support legacy codes, GNU Fortran permits the count field of the X edit descriptor in FORMAT statements to be omitted. When omitted, the count is implicitly assumed to be one.

```
      PRINT 10, 2, 3
10    FORMAT (I1, X, I1)
```

5.1.5 Commas in FORMAT specifications

To support legacy codes, GNU Fortran allows the comma separator to be omitted immediately before and after character string edit descriptors in FORMAT statements.

```
      PRINT 10, 2, 3
10    FORMAT ('FOO='I1' BAR='I2)
```

5.1.6 Missing period in FORMAT specifications

To support legacy codes, GNU Fortran allows missing periods in format specifications if and only if '-std=legacy' is given on the command line. This is considered non-conforming code and is discouraged.

```
      REAL :: value
      READ(*,10) value
10    FORMAT ('F4')
```

5.1.7 I/O item lists

To support legacy codes, GNU Fortran allows the input item list of the READ statement, and the output item lists of the WRITE and PRINT statements, to start with a comma.

5.1.8 BOZ literal constants

Besides decimal constants, Fortran also supports binary (b), octal (o) and hexadecimal (z) integer constants. The syntax is: 'prefix quote digits quote', were the prefix is either b, o or z, quote is either ' or " and the digits are for binary 0 or 1, for octal between 0 and 7, and for hexadecimal between 0 and F. (Example: b'01011101'.)

Up to Fortran 95, BOZ literals were only allowed to initialize integer variables in DATA statements. Since Fortran 2003 BOZ literals are also allowed as argument of REAL, DBLE, INT and CMPLX; the result is the same as if the integer BOZ literal had been converted by TRANSFER to, respectively, real, double precision, integer or complex. As GNU Fortran extension the intrinsic procedures FLOAT, DFLOAT, COMPLEX and DCMPLX are treated alike.

As an extension, GNU Fortran allows hexadecimal BOZ literal constants to be specified using the X prefix, in addition to the standard Z prefix. The BOZ literal can also be specified by adding a suffix to the string, for example, Z'ABC' and 'ABC'Z are equivalent.

Furthermore, GNU Fortran allows using BOZ literal constants outside DATA statements and the four intrinsic functions allowed by Fortran 2003. In DATA statements, in direct assignments, where the right-hand side only contains a BOZ literal constant, and for old-style initializers of the form integer i /o'0173'/, the constant is transferred as if TRANSFER had been used; for COMPLEX numbers, only the real part is initialized unless CMPLX is used. In all other cases, the BOZ literal constant is converted to an INTEGER value with the largest decimal representation. This value is then converted numerically to the type and kind of the variable in question. (For instance real :: r = b'0000001' + 1 initializes r with 2.0.) As different compilers implement the extension differently, one should be careful when doing bitwise initialization of non-integer variables.

Note that initializing an `INTEGER` variable with a statement such as `DATA i/Z'FFFFFFFF'/` will give an integer overflow error rather than the desired result of −1 when `i` is a 32-bit integer on a system that supports 64-bit integers. The '-fno-range-check' option can be used as a workaround for legacy code that initializes integers in this manner.

5.1.9 Real array indices

As an extension, GNU Fortran allows the use of `REAL` expressions or variables as array indices.

5.1.10 Unary operators

As an extension, GNU Fortran allows unary plus and unary minus operators to appear as the second operand of binary arithmetic operators without the need for parenthesis.

```
X = Y * -Z
```

5.1.11 Implicitly convert `LOGICAL` and `INTEGER` values

As an extension for backwards compatibility with other compilers, GNU Fortran allows the implicit conversion of `LOGICAL` values to `INTEGER` values and vice versa. When converting from a `LOGICAL` to an `INTEGER`, `.FALSE.` is interpreted as zero, and `.TRUE.` is interpreted as one. When converting from `INTEGER` to `LOGICAL`, the value zero is interpreted as `.FALSE.` and any nonzero value is interpreted as `.TRUE.`.

```
LOGICAL :: l
l = 1
INTEGER :: i
i = .TRUE.
```

However, there is no implicit conversion of `INTEGER` values in `if`-statements, nor of `LOGICAL` or `INTEGER` values in I/O operations.

5.1.12 Hollerith constants support

GNU Fortran supports Hollerith constants in assignments, function arguments, and `DATA` and `ASSIGN` statements. A Hollerith constant is written as a string of characters preceded by an integer constant indicating the character count, and the letter `H` or `h`, and stored in bytewise fashion in a numeric (`INTEGER`, `REAL`, or `complex`) or `LOGICAL` variable. The constant will be padded or truncated to fit the size of the variable in which it is stored.

Examples of valid uses of Hollerith constants:

```
complex*16 x(2)
data x /16Habcdefghijklmnop, 16Hqrstuvwxyz012345/
x(1) = 16HABCDEFGHIJKLMNOP
call foo (4h abc)
```

Invalid Hollerith constants examples:

```
integer*4 a
a = 8H12345678 ! Valid, but the Hollerith constant will be truncated.
a = 0H         ! At least one character is needed.
```

In general, Hollerith constants were used to provide a rudimentary facility for handling character strings in early Fortran compilers, prior to the introduction of `CHARACTER` variables in Fortran 77; in those cases, the standard-compliant equivalent is to convert the program to use proper character strings. On occasion, there may be a case where the intent is specifically to initialize a numeric variable with a given byte sequence. In these cases, the same result can be obtained by using the TRANSFER statement, as in this example.

```
INTEGER(KIND=4) :: a
a = TRANSFER ("abcd", a)      ! equivalent to: a = 4Habcd
```

5.1.13 Cray pointers

Cray pointers are part of a non-standard extension that provides a C-like pointer in Fortran. This is accomplished through a pair of variables: an integer "pointer" that holds a memory address, and a "pointee" that is used to dereference the pointer.

Pointer/pointee pairs are declared in statements of the form:

```
pointer ( <pointer> , <pointee> )
```

or,

```
pointer ( <pointer1> , <pointee1> ), ( <pointer2> , <pointee2> ), ...
```

The pointer is an integer that is intended to hold a memory address. The pointee may be an array or scalar. A pointee can be an assumed size array—that is, the last dimension may be left unspecified by using a * in place of a value—but a pointee cannot be an assumed shape array. No space is allocated for the pointee.

The pointee may have its type declared before or after the pointer statement, and its array specification (if any) may be declared before, during, or after the pointer statement. The pointer may be declared as an integer prior to the pointer statement. However, some machines have default integer sizes that are different than the size of a pointer, and so the following code is not portable:

```
integer ipt
pointer (ipt, iarr)
```

If a pointer is declared with a kind that is too small, the compiler will issue a warning; the resulting binary will probably not work correctly, because the memory addresses stored in the pointers may be truncated. It is safer to omit the first line of the above example; if explicit declaration of ipt's type is omitted, then the compiler will ensure that ipt is an integer variable large enough to hold a pointer.

Pointer arithmetic is valid with Cray pointers, but it is not the same as C pointer arithmetic. Cray pointers are just ordinary integers, so the user is responsible for determining how many bytes to add to a pointer in order to increment it. Consider the following example:

```
real target(10)
real pointee(10)
pointer (ipt, pointee)
ipt = loc (target)
ipt = ipt + 1
```

The last statement does not set ipt to the address of target(1), as it would in C pointer arithmetic. Adding 1 to ipt just adds one byte to the address stored in ipt.

Any expression involving the pointee will be translated to use the value stored in the pointer as the base address.

To get the address of elements, this extension provides an intrinsic function LOC(). The LOC() function is equivalent to the & operator in C, except the address is cast to an integer type:

```
real ar(10)
pointer(ipt, arpte(10))
real arpte
ipt = loc(ar)   ! Makes arpte is an alias for ar
arpte(1) = 1.0 ! Sets ar(1) to 1.0
```

The pointer can also be set by a call to the `MALLOC` intrinsic (see Section 6.141 [MALLOC], page 116).

Cray pointees often are used to alias an existing variable. For example:

```
integer target(10)
integer iarr(10)
pointer (ipt, iarr)
ipt = loc(target)
```

As long as `ipt` remains unchanged, `iarr` is now an alias for `target`. The optimizer, however, will not detect this aliasing, so it is unsafe to use `iarr` and `target` simultaneously. Using a pointee in any way that violates the Fortran aliasing rules or assumptions is illegal. It is the user's responsibility to avoid doing this; the compiler works under the assumption that no such aliasing occurs.

Cray pointers will work correctly when there is no aliasing (i.e., when they are used to access a dynamically allocated block of memory), and also in any routine where a pointee is used, but any variable with which it shares storage is not used. Code that violates these rules may not run as the user intends. This is not a bug in the optimizer; any code that violates the aliasing rules is illegal. (Note that this is not unique to GNU Fortran; any Fortran compiler that supports Cray pointers will "incorrectly" optimize code with illegal aliasing.)

There are a number of restrictions on the attributes that can be applied to Cray pointers and pointees. Pointees may not have the `ALLOCATABLE`, `INTENT`, `OPTIONAL`, `DUMMY`, `TARGET`, `INTRINSIC`, or `POINTER` attributes. Pointers may not have the `DIMENSION`, `POINTER`, `TARGET`, `ALLOCATABLE`, `EXTERNAL`, or `INTRINSIC` attributes. Pointees may not occur in more than one pointer statement. A pointee cannot be a pointer. Pointees cannot occur in equivalence, common, or data statements.

A Cray pointer may also point to a function or a subroutine. For example, the following excerpt is valid:

```
implicit none
external sub
pointer (subptr,subpte)
external subpte
subptr = loc(sub)
call subpte()
[...]
subroutine sub
[...]
end subroutine sub
```

A pointer may be modified during the course of a program, and this will change the location to which the pointee refers. However, when pointees are passed as arguments, they are treated as ordinary variables in the invoked function. Subsequent changes to the pointer will not change the base address of the array that was passed.

5.1.14 CONVERT specifier

GNU Fortran allows the conversion of unformatted data between little- and big-endian representation to facilitate moving of data between different systems. The conversion can be indicated with the `CONVERT` specifier on the `OPEN` statement. See Section 3.12 [GFOR-TRAN_CONVERT_UNIT], page 20, for an alternative way of specifying the data format via an environment variable.

Valid values for `CONVERT` are:

`CONVERT='NATIVE'` Use the native format. This is the default.

`CONVERT='SWAP'` Swap between little- and big-endian.

`CONVERT='LITTLE_ENDIAN'` Use the little-endian representation for unformatted files.

`CONVERT='BIG_ENDIAN'` Use the big-endian representation for unformatted files.

Using the option could look like this:

```
open(file='big.dat',form='unformatted',access='sequential', &
     convert='big_endian')
```

The value of the conversion can be queried by using `INQUIRE(CONVERT=ch)`. The values returned are `'BIG_ENDIAN'` and `'LITTLE_ENDIAN'`.

`CONVERT` works between big- and little-endian for `INTEGER` values of all supported kinds and for `REAL` on IEEE systems of kinds 4 and 8. Conversion between different "extended double" types on different architectures such as m68k and x86_64, which GNU Fortran supports as `REAL(KIND=10)` and `REAL(KIND=16)`, will probably not work.

Note that the values specified via the GFORTRAN_CONVERT_UNIT environment variable will override the CONVERT specifier in the open statement. This is to give control over data formats to users who do not have the source code of their program available.

Using anything but the native representation for unformatted data carries a significant speed overhead. If speed in this area matters to you, it is best if you use this only for data that needs to be portable.

5.1.15 OpenMP

OpenMP (Open Multi-Processing) is an application programming interface (API) that supports multi-platform shared memory multiprocessing programming in C/C++ and Fortran on many architectures, including Unix and Microsoft Windows platforms. It consists of a set of compiler directives, library routines, and environment variables that influence run-time behavior.

GNU Fortran strives to be compatible to the OpenMP Application Program Interface v2.5.

To enable the processing of the OpenMP directive `!$omp` in free-form source code; the `c$omp`, `*$omp` and `!$omp` directives in fixed form; the `!$` conditional compilation sentinels in free form; and the `c$`, `*$` and `!$` sentinels in fixed form, `gfortran` needs to be invoked with the '`-fopenmp`'. This also arranges for automatic linking of the GNU OpenMP runtime library Section "libgomp" in *GNU OpenMP runtime library*.

The OpenMP Fortran runtime library routines are provided both in a form of a Fortran 90 module named `omp_lib` and in a form of a Fortran `include` file named '`omp_lib.h`'.

An example of a parallelized loop taken from Appendix A.1 of the OpenMP Application Program Interface v2.5:

```
SUBROUTINE A1(N, A, B)
  INTEGER I, N
  REAL B(N), A(N)
!$OMP PARALLEL DO !I is private by default
  DO I=2,N
    B(I) = (A(I) + A(I-1)) / 2.0
  ENDDO
!$OMP END PARALLEL DO
END SUBROUTINE A1
```

Please note:

- '-fopenmp' implies '-frecursive', i.e. all local arrays will be allocated on the stack. When porting existing code to OpenMP, this may lead to surprising results, especially to segmentation faults if the stacksize is limited.

- On glibc-based systems, OpenMP enabled applications can not be statically linked due to limitations of the underlying pthreads-implementation. It might be possible to get a working solution if -Wl,--whole-archive -lpthread -Wl,--no-whole-archive is added to the command line. However, this is not supported by gcc and thus not recommended.

5.1.16 Argument list functions %VAL, %REF and %LOC

GNU Fortran supports argument list functions %VAL, %REF and %LOC statements, for backward compatibility with g77. It is recommended that these should be used only for code that is accessing facilities outside of GNU Fortran, such as operating system or windowing facilities. It is best to constrain such uses to isolated portions of a program–portions that deal specifically and exclusively with low-level, system-dependent facilities. Such portions might well provide a portable interface for use by the program as a whole, but are themselves not portable, and should be thoroughly tested each time they are rebuilt using a new compiler or version of a compiler.

%VAL passes a scalar argument by value, %REF passes it by reference and %LOC passes its memory location. Since gfortran already passes scalar arguments by reference, %REF is in effect a do-nothing. %LOC has the same effect as a fortran pointer.

An example of passing an argument by value to a C subroutine foo.:

```
C
C prototype      void foo_ (float x);
C
      external foo
      real*4 x
      x = 3.14159
      call foo (%VAL (x))
      end
```

For details refer to the g77 manual http://gcc.gnu.org/onlinedocs/gcc-3.4.6/g77/index.htm

Also, the gfortran testsuite c_by_val.f and its partner c_by_val.c are worth a look.

5.2 Extensions not implemented in GNU Fortran

The long history of the Fortran language, its wide use and broad userbase, the large number of different compiler vendors and the lack of some features crucial to users in the first standards have lead to the existence of an important number of extensions to the language. While some of the most useful or popular extensions are supported by the GNU Fortran compiler, not all existing extensions are supported. This section aims at listing these extensions and offering advice on how best make code that uses them running with the GNU Fortran compiler.

5.2.1 STRUCTURE and RECORD

Structures are user-defined aggregate data types; this functionality was standardized in Fortran 90 with an different syntax, under the name of "derived types". Here is an example of code using the non portable structure syntax:

```
! Declaring a structure named ''item'' and containing three fields:
! an integer ID, an description string and a floating-point price.
STRUCTURE /item/
  INTEGER id
  CHARACTER(LEN=200) description
  REAL price
END STRUCTURE

! Define two variables, an single record of type ''item''
! named ''pear'', and an array of items named ''store_catalog''
RECORD /item/ pear, store_catalog(100)

! We can directly access the fields of both variables
pear.id = 92316
pear.description = "juicy D'Anjou pear"
pear.price = 0.15
store_catalog(7).id = 7831
store_catalog(7).description = "milk bottle"
store_catalog(7).price = 1.2

! We can also manipulates the whole structure
store_catalog(12) = pear
print *, store_catalog(12)
```

This code can easily be rewritten in the Fortran 90 syntax as following:

```
! ''STRUCTURE /name/ ... END STRUCTURE'' becomes
! ''TYPE name ... END TYPE''
TYPE item
  INTEGER id
  CHARACTER(LEN=200) description
  REAL price
END TYPE

! ''RECORD /name/ variable'' becomes ''TYPE(name) variable''
TYPE(item) pear, store_catalog(100)

! Instead of using a dot (.) to access fields of a record, the
! standard syntax uses a percent sign (%)
pear%id = 92316
```

```
pear%description = "juicy D'Anjou pear"
pear%price = 0.15
store_catalog(7)%id = 7831
store_catalog(7)%description = "milk bottle"
store_catalog(7)%price = 1.2

! Assignments of a whole variable don't change
store_catalog(12) = pear
print *, store_catalog(12)
```

5.2.2 ENCODE and DECODE statements

GNU Fortran doesn't support the ENCODE and DECODE statements. These statements are best replaced by READ and WRITE statements involving internal files (CHARACTER variables and arrays), which have been part of the Fortran standard since Fortran 77. For example, replace a code fragment like

```
      INTEGER*1 LINE(80)
      REAL A, B, C
c     ... Code that sets LINE
      DECODE (80, 9000, LINE) A, B, C
 9000 FORMAT (1X, 3(F10.5))
```

with the following:

```
      CHARACTER(LEN=80) LINE
      REAL A, B, C
c     ... Code that sets LINE
      READ (UNIT=LINE, FMT=9000) A, B, C
 9000 FORMAT (1X, 3(F10.5))
```

Similarly, replace a code fragment like

```
      INTEGER*1 LINE(80)
      REAL A, B, C
c     ... Code that sets A, B and C
      ENCODE (80, 9000, LINE) A, B, C
 9000 FORMAT (1X, 'OUTPUT IS ', 3(F10.5))
```

with the following:

```
      INTEGER*1 LINE(80)
      REAL A, B, C
c     ... Code that sets A, B and C
      WRITE (UNIT=LINE, FMT=9000) A, B, C
 9000 FORMAT (1X, 'OUTPUT IS ', 3(F10.5))
```

6 Intrinsic Procedures

6.1 Introduction to intrinsic procedures

The intrinsic procedures provided by GNU Fortran include all of the intrinsic procedures required by the Fortran 95 standard, a set of intrinsic procedures for backwards compatibility with G77, and a small selection of intrinsic procedures from the Fortran 2003 standard. Any conflict between a description here and a description in either the Fortran 95 standard or the Fortran 2003 standard is unintentional, and the standard(s) should be considered authoritative.

The enumeration of the `KIND` type parameter is processor defined in the Fortran 95 standard. GNU Fortran defines the default integer type and default real type by `INTEGER(KIND=4)` and `REAL(KIND=4)`, respectively. The standard mandates that both data types shall have another kind, which have more precision. On typical target architectures supported by **gfortran**, this kind type parameter is `KIND=8`. Hence, `REAL(KIND=8)` and `DOUBLE PRECISION` are equivalent. In the description of generic intrinsic procedures, the kind type parameter will be specified by `KIND=*`, and in the description of specific names for an intrinsic procedure the kind type parameter will be explicitly given (e.g., `REAL(KIND=4)` or `REAL(KIND=8)`). Finally, for brevity the optional `KIND=` syntax will be omitted.

Many of the intrinsic procedures take one or more optional arguments. This document follows the convention used in the Fortran 95 standard, and denotes such arguments by square brackets.

GNU Fortran offers the '-std=f95' and '-std=gnu' options, which can be used to restrict the set of intrinsic procedures to a given standard. By default, **gfortran** sets the '-std=gnu' option, and so all intrinsic procedures described here are accepted. There is one caveat. For a select group of intrinsic procedures, **g77** implemented both a function and a subroutine. Both classes have been implemented in **gfortran** for backwards compatibility with **g77**. It is noted here that these functions and subroutines cannot be intermixed in a given subprogram. In the descriptions that follow, the applicable standard for each intrinsic procedure is noted.

6.2 ABORT — Abort the program

Description:

> `ABORT` causes immediate termination of the program. On operating systems that support a core dump, `ABORT` will produce a core dump, which is suitable for debugging purposes.

Standard: GNU extension

Class: Subroutine

Syntax: `CALL ABORT`

Return value:

> Does not return.

Example:

```
program test_abort
  integer :: i = 1, j = 2
  if (i /= j) call abort
end program test_abort
```

See also: Section 6.66 [EXIT], page 77, Section 6.121 [KILL], page 106

6.3 ABS — Absolute value

Description:

ABS(X) computes the absolute value of X.

Standard: F77 and later, has overloads that are GNU extensions

Class: Elemental function

Syntax: RESULT = ABS(X)

Arguments:

X   The type of the argument shall be an INTEGER(*), REAL(*), or COMPLEX(*).

Return value:

The return value is of the same type and kind as the argument except the return value is REAL(*) for a COMPLEX(*) argument.

Example:

```
program test_abs
  integer :: i = -1
  real :: x = -1.e0
  complex :: z = (-1.e0,0.e0)
  i = abs(i)
  x = abs(x)
  x = abs(z)
end program test_abs
```

Specific names:

Name	Argument	Return type	Standard
CABS(Z)	COMPLEX(4) Z	REAL(4)	F77 and later
DABS(X)	REAL(8) X	REAL(8)	F77 and later
IABS(I)	INTEGER(4) I	INTEGER(4)	F77 and later
ZABS(Z)	COMPLEX(8) Z	COMPLEX(8)	GNU extension
CDABS(Z)	COMPLEX(8) Z	COMPLEX(8)	GNU extension

6.4 ACCESS — Checks file access modes

Description:

ACCESS(NAME, MODE) checks whether the file *NAME* exists, is readable, writable or executable. Except for the executable check, ACCESS can be replaced by Fortran 95's INQUIRE.

Standard: GNU extension

Class: Inquiry function

Syntax: RESULT = ACCESS(NAME, MODE)

Arguments:

NAME	Scalar `CHARACTER` with the file name. Tailing blank are ignored unless the character `achar(0)` is present, then all characters up to and excluding `achar(0)` are used as file name.
MODE	Scalar `CHARACTER` with the file access mode, may be any concatenation of `"r"` (readable), `"w"` (writable) and `"x"` (executable), or `" "` to check for existence.

Return value:

Returns a scalar `INTEGER`, which is 0 if the file is accessible in the given mode; otherwise or if an invalid argument has been given for `MODE` the value 1 is returned.

Example:

```
program access_test
  implicit none
  character(len=*), parameter :: file  = 'test.dat'
  character(len=*), parameter :: file2 = 'test.dat  '//achar(0)
  if(access(file,' ') == 0) print *, trim(file),' is exists'
  if(access(file,'r') == 0) print *, trim(file),' is readable'
  if(access(file,'w') == 0) print *, trim(file),' is writable'
  if(access(file,'x') == 0) print *, trim(file),' is executable'
  if(access(file2,'rwx') == 0) &
    print *, trim(file2),' is readable, writable and executable'
end program access_test
```

Specific names:
See also:

6.5 ACHAR — Character in ASCII collating sequence

Description:

`ACHAR(I)` returns the character located at position `I` in the ASCII collating sequence.

Standard: F77 and later

Class: Elemental function

Syntax: `RESULT = ACHAR(I)`

Arguments:

I	The type shall be `INTEGER(*)`.

Return value:

The return value is of type `CHARACTER` with a length of one. The kind type parameter is the same as `KIND('A')`.

Example:

```
program test_achar
  character c
  c = achar(32)
end program test_achar
```

Note: See Section 6.104 [ICHAR], page 97 for a discussion of converting between numerical values and formatted string representations.

See also: Section 6.38 [CHAR], page 59, Section 6.98 [IACHAR], page 94, Section 6.104
[ICHAR], page 97

6.6 ACOS — Arccosine function

Description:
ACOS(X) computes the arccosine of *X* (inverse of COS(X)).

Standard: F77 and later

Class: Elemental function

Syntax: RESULT = ACOS(X)

Arguments:
X   The type shall be REAL(*) with a magnitude that is less than
                        one.

Return value:
The return value is of type REAL(*) and it lies in the range $0 \leq acos(x) \leq \pi$.
The kind type parameter is the same as *X*.

Example:
```
program test_acos
  real(8) :: x = 0.866_8
  x = acos(x)
end program test_acos
```

Specific names:

Name	Argument	Return type	Standard
DACOS(X)	REAL(8) X	REAL(8)	F77 and later

See also: Inverse function: Section 6.45 [COS], page 63

6.7 ACOSH — Hyperbolic arccosine function

Description:
ACOSH(X) computes the hyperbolic arccosine of *X* (inverse of COSH(X)).

Standard: GNU extension

Class: Elemental function

Syntax: RESULT = ACOSH(X)

Arguments:
X   The type shall be REAL(*) with a magnitude that is greater
                        or equal to one.

Return value:
The return value is of type REAL(*) and it lies in the range $0 \leq acosh(x) \leq \infty$.

Example:
```
PROGRAM test_acosh
  REAL(8), DIMENSION(3) :: x = (/ 1.0, 2.0, 3.0 /)
  WRITE (*,*) ACOSH(x)
END PROGRAM
```

Specific names:

Name	Argument	Return type	Standard
DACOSH(X)	REAL(8) X	REAL(8)	GNU extension

See also: Inverse function: Section 6.46 [COSH], page 64

6.8 ADJUSTL — Left adjust a string

Description:

ADJUSTL(STR) will left adjust a string by removing leading spaces. Spaces are inserted at the end of the string as needed.

Standard: F95 and later

Class: Elemental function

Syntax: RESULT = ADJUSTL(STR)

Arguments:

STR   The type shall be CHARACTER.

Return value:

The return value is of type CHARACTER where leading spaces are removed and the same number of spaces are inserted on the end of *STR*.

Example:

```
program test_adjustl
  character(len=20) :: str = '   gfortran'
  str = adjustl(str)
  print *, str
end program test_adjustl
```

See also: Section 6.9 [ADJUSTR], page 41, Section 6.213 [TRIM], page 157

6.9 ADJUSTR — Right adjust a string

Description:

ADJUSTR(STR) will right adjust a string by removing trailing spaces. Spaces are inserted at the start of the string as needed.

Standard: F95 and later

Class: Elemental function

Syntax: RESULT = ADJUSTR(STR)

Arguments:

STR   The type shall be CHARACTER.

Return value:

The return value is of type CHARACTER where trailing spaces are removed and the same number of spaces are inserted at the start of *STR*.

Example:

```
program test_adjustr
  character(len=20) :: str = 'gfortran'
  str = adjustr(str)
  print *, str
end program test_adjustr
```

See also: Section 6.8 [ADJUSTL], page 41, Section 6.213 [TRIM], page 157

6.10 AIMAG — Imaginary part of complex number

Description:

AIMAG(Z) yields the imaginary part of complex argument Z. The IMAG(Z) and IMAGPART(Z) intrinsic functions are provided for compatibility with g77, and their use in new code is strongly discouraged.

Standard: F77 and later, has overloads that are GNU extensions

Class: Elemental function

Syntax: RESULT = AIMAG(Z)

Arguments:

Z   The type of the argument shall be COMPLEX(*).

Return value:

The return value is of type real with the kind type parameter of the argument.

Example:

```
program test_aimag
  complex(4) z4
  complex(8) z8
  z4 = cmplx(1.e0_4, 0.e0_4)
  z8 = cmplx(0.e0_8, 1.e0_8)
  print *, aimag(z4), dimag(z8)
end program test_aimag
```

Specific names:

Name	Argument	Return type	Standard
DIMAG(Z)	COMPLEX(8) Z	REAL(8)	GNU extension
IMAG(Z)	COMPLEX(*) Z	REAL(*)	GNU extension
IMAGPART(Z)	COMPLEX(*) Z	REAL(*)	GNU extension

6.11 AINT — Truncate to a whole number

Description:

AINT(X [, KIND]) truncates its argument to a whole number.

Standard: F77 and later

Class: Elemental function

Syntax: RESULT = AINT(X [, KIND])

Arguments:

X   The type of the argument shall be REAL(*).
KIND   (Optional) An INTEGER(*) initialization expression indicating the kind parameter of the result.

Return value:

The return value is of type real with the kind type parameter of the argument if the optional *KIND* is absent; otherwise, the kind type parameter will be given by *KIND*. If the magnitude of X is less than one, then `AINT(X)` returns zero. If the magnitude is equal to or greater than one, then it returns the largest whole number that does not exceed its magnitude. The sign is the same as the sign of X.

Example:

```
program test_aint
  real(4) x4
  real(8) x8
  x4 = 1.234E0_4
  x8 = 4.321_8
  print *, aint(x4), dint(x8)
  x8 = aint(x4,8)
end program test_aint
```

Specific names:

Name	Argument	Return type	Standard
DINT(X)	REAL(8) X	REAL(8)	F77 and later

6.12 ALARM — Execute a routine after a given delay

Description:

`ALARM(SECONDS, HANDLER [, STATUS])` causes external subroutine *HANDLER* to be executed after a delay of *SECONDS* by using `alarm(2)` to set up a signal and `signal(2)` to catch it. If *STATUS* is supplied, it will be returned with the number of seconds remaining until any previously scheduled alarm was due to be delivered, or zero if there was no previously scheduled alarm.

Standard: GNU extension

Class: Subroutine

Syntax: `CALL ALARM(SECONDS, HANDLER [, STATUS])`

Arguments:

SECONDS	The type of the argument shall be a scalar `INTEGER`. It is `INTENT(IN)`.
HANDLER	Signal handler (`INTEGER FUNCTION` or `SUBROUTINE`) or dummy/global `INTEGER` scalar. The scalar values may be either `SIG_IGN=1` to ignore the alarm generated or `SIG_DFL=0` to set the default action. It is `INTENT(IN)`.
STATUS	(Optional) *STATUS* shall be a scalar variable of the default `INTEGER` kind. It is `INTENT(OUT)`.

Example:

```
program test_alarm
  external handler_print
  integer i
  call alarm (3, handler_print, i)
  print *, i
```

```
        call sleep(10)
        end program test_alarm
```

This will cause the external routine *handler_print* to be called after 3 seconds.

6.13 ALL —— All values in *MASK* along *DIM* are true

Description:

ALL(MASK [, DIM]) determines if all the values are true in *MASK* in the array along dimension *DIM*.

Standard: F95 and later

Class: Transformational function

Syntax: RESULT = ALL(MASK [, DIM])

Arguments:

MASK	The type of the argument shall be LOGICAL(*) and it shall not be scalar.
DIM	(Optional) *DIM* shall be a scalar integer with a value that lies between one and the rank of *MASK*.

Return value:

ALL(MASK) returns a scalar value of type LOGICAL(*) where the kind type parameter is the same as the kind type parameter of *MASK*. If *DIM* is present, then ALL(MASK, DIM) returns an array with the rank of *MASK* minus 1. The shape is determined from the shape of *MASK* where the *DIM* dimension is elided.

(A)   ALL(MASK) is true if all elements of *MASK* are true. It also is true if *MASK* has zero size; otherwise, it is false.

(B)   If the rank of *MASK* is one, then ALL(MASK,DIM) is equivalent to ALL(MASK). If the rank is greater than one, then ALL(MASK,DIM) is determined by applying ALL to the array sections.

Example:

```
program test_all
  logical l
  l = all((/.true., .true., .true./))
  print *, l
  call section
  contains
    subroutine section
      integer a(2,3), b(2,3)
      a = 1
      b = 1
      b(2,2) = 2
      print *, all(a .eq. b, 1)
      print *, all(a .eq. b, 2)
    end subroutine section
end program test_all
```

6.14 ALLOCATED — Status of an allocatable entity

Description:

ALLOCATED(X) checks the status of whether X is allocated.

Standard: F95 and later

Class: Inquiry function

Syntax: RESULT = ALLOCATED(X)

Arguments:

X The argument shall be an ALLOCATABLE array.

Return value:

The return value is a scalar LOGICAL with the default logical kind type parameter. If X is allocated, ALLOCATED(X) is .TRUE.; otherwise, it returns .FALSE.

Example:

```
program test_allocated
  integer :: i = 4
  real(4), allocatable :: x(:)
  if (allocated(x) .eqv. .false.) allocate(x(i))
end program test_allocated
```

6.15 AND — Bitwise logical AND

Description:

Bitwise logical AND.

This intrinsic routine is provided for backwards compatibility with GNU Fortran 77. For integer arguments, programmers should consider the use of the Section 6.99 [IAND], page 95 intrinsic defined by the Fortran standard.

Standard: GNU extension

Class: Function

Syntax: RESULT = AND(I, J)

Arguments:

I The type shall be either INTEGER(*) or LOGICAL.
J The type shall be either INTEGER(*) or LOGICAL.

Return value:

The return type is either INTEGER(*) or LOGICAL after cross-promotion of the arguments.

Example:

```
PROGRAM test_and
  LOGICAL :: T = .TRUE., F = .FALSE.
  INTEGER :: a, b
  DATA a / Z'F' /, b / Z'3' /

  WRITE (*,*) AND(T, T), AND(T, F), AND(F, T), AND(F, F)
  WRITE (*,*) AND(a, b)
END PROGRAM
```

See also: F95 elemental function: Section 6.99 [IAND], page 95

6.16 ANINT — Nearest whole number

Description:

ANINT(X [, KIND]) rounds its argument to the nearest whole number.

Standard: F77 and later

Class: Elemental function

Syntax: RESULT = ANINT(X [, KIND])

Arguments:

X	The type of the argument shall be REAL(*).
KIND	(Optional) An INTEGER(*) initialization expression indicating the kind parameter of the result.

Return value:

The return value is of type real with the kind type parameter of the argument if the optional *KIND* is absent; otherwise, the kind type parameter will be given by *KIND*. If *X* is greater than zero, then ANINT(X) returns AINT(X+0.5). If *X* is less than or equal to zero, then it returns AINT(X-0.5).

Example:

```
program test_anint
  real(4) x4
  real(8) x8
  x4 = 1.234E0_4
  x8 = 4.321_8
  print *, anint(x4), dnint(x8)
  x8 = anint(x4,8)
end program test_anint
```

Specific names:

Name	Argument	Return type	Standard
DNINT(X)	REAL(8) X	REAL(8)	F77 and later

6.17 ANY — Any value in *MASK* along *DIM* is true

Description:

ANY(MASK [, DIM]) determines if any of the values in the logical array *MASK* along dimension *DIM* are .TRUE..

Standard: F95 and later

Class: Transformational function

Syntax: RESULT = ANY(MASK [, DIM])

Arguments:

MASK	The type of the argument shall be LOGICAL(*) and it shall not be scalar.
DIM	(Optional) *DIM* shall be a scalar integer with a value that lies between one and the rank of *MASK*.

Return value:

ANY(MASK) returns a scalar value of type LOGICAL(*) where the kind type parameter is the same as the kind type parameter of *MASK*. If *DIM* is present, then ANY(MASK, DIM) returns an array with the rank of *MASK* minus 1. The shape is determined from the shape of *MASK* where the *DIM* dimension is elided.

(A)   ANY(MASK) is true if any element of *MASK* is true; otherwise, it is false. It also is false if *MASK* has zero size.

(B)   If the rank of *MASK* is one, then ANY(MASK,DIM) is equivalent to ANY(MASK). If the rank is greater than one, then ANY(MASK,DIM) is determined by applying ANY to the array sections.

Example:

```
program test_any
  logical l
  l = any((/.true., .true., .true./))
  print *, l
  call section
  contains
    subroutine section
      integer a(2,3), b(2,3)
      a = 1
      b = 1
      b(2,2) = 2
      print *, any(a .eq. b, 1)
      print *, any(a .eq. b, 2)
    end subroutine section
end program test_any
```

6.18 ASIN — Arcsine function

Description:

ASIN(X) computes the arcsine of its *X* (inverse of SIN(X)).

Standard: F77 and later

Class: Elemental function

Syntax: RESULT = ASIN(X)

Arguments:

X   The type shall be REAL(*), and a magnitude that is less than one.

Return value:

The return value is of type REAL(*) and it lies in the range $-\pi/2 \leq \mathrm{asin}(x) \leq \pi/2$. The kind type parameter is the same as *X*.

Example:

```
program test_asin
  real(8) :: x = 0.866_8
  x = asin(x)
end program test_asin
```

Specific names:

Name	Argument	Return type	Standard
DASIN(X)	REAL(8) X	REAL(8)	F77 and later

See also: Inverse function: Section 6.191 [SIN], page 144

6.19 ASINH — Hyperbolic arcsine function

Description:

ASINH(X) computes the hyperbolic arcsine of X (inverse of SINH(X)).

Standard: GNU extension

Class: Elemental function

Syntax: RESULT = ASINH(X)

Arguments:

X The type shall be REAL(*), with X a real number.

Return value:

The return value is of type REAL(*) and it lies in the range $-\infty \leq \mathrm{asinh}(x) \leq \infty$.

Example:

```
PROGRAM test_asinh
  REAL(8), DIMENSION(3) :: x = (/ -1.0, 0.0, 1.0 /)
  WRITE (*,*) ASINH(x)
END PROGRAM
```

Specific names:

Name	Argument	Return type	Standard
DASINH(X)	REAL(8) X	REAL(8)	GNU extension.

See also: Inverse function: Section 6.192 [SINH], page 145

6.20 ASSOCIATED — Status of a pointer or pointer/target pair

Description:

ASSOCIATED(PTR [, TGT]) determines the status of the pointer PTR or if PTR is associated with the target TGT.

Standard: F95 and later

Class: Inquiry function

Syntax: RESULT = ASSOCIATED(PTR [, TGT])

Arguments:

PTR PTR shall have the POINTER attribute and it can be of any type.

TGT (Optional) TGT shall be a POINTER or a TARGET. It must have the same type, kind type parameter, and array rank as PTR.

The status of neither PTR nor TGT can be undefined.

Return value:

> ASSOCIATED(PTR) returns a scalar value of type LOGICAL(4). There are several cases:
>
> (A) If the optional *TGT* is not present, then ASSOCIATED(PTR)
> > is true if *PTR* is associated with a target; otherwise, it returns false.
>
> (B) If *TGT* is present and a scalar target, the result is true if
> > *TGT* is not a 0 sized storage sequence and the target associated with *PTR* occupies the same storage units. If *PTR* is disassociated, then the result is false.
>
> (C) If *TGT* is present and an array target, the result is true if
> > *TGT* and *PTR* have the same shape, are not 0 sized arrays, are arrays whose elements are not 0 sized storage sequences, and *TGT* and *PTR* occupy the same storage units in array element order. As in case(B), the result is false, if *PTR* is disassociated.
>
> (D) If *TGT* is present and an scalar pointer, the result is true if
> > target associated with *PTR* and the target associated with *TGT* are not 0 sized storage sequences and occupy the same storage units. The result is false, if either *TGT* or *PTR* is disassociated.
>
> (E) If *TGT* is present and an array pointer, the result is true if
> > target associated with *PTR* and the target associated with *TGT* have the same shape, are not 0 sized arrays, are arrays whose elements are not 0 sized storage sequences, and *TGT* and *PTR* occupy the same storage units in array element order. The result is false, if either *TGT* or *PTR* is disassociated.

Example:

```
program test_associated
  implicit none
  real, target  :: tgt(2) = (/1., 2./)
  real, pointer :: ptr(:)
  ptr => tgt
  if (associated(ptr)     .eqv. .false.) call abort
  if (associated(ptr,tgt) .eqv. .false.) call abort
end program test_associated
```

See also: Section 6.162 [NULL], page 128

6.21 ATAN — Arctangent function

Description:

> ATAN(X) computes the arctangent of *X*.

Standard: F77 and later

Class: Elemental function

Syntax: RESULT = ATAN(X)

Arguments:

> X   The type shall be REAL(*).

Return value:

> The return value is of type `REAL(*)` and it lies in the range $-\pi/2 \le atan(x) \le \pi/2$.

Example:

```
program test_atan
  real(8) :: x = 2.866_8
  x = atan(x)
end program test_atan
```

Specific names:

Name	Argument	Return type	Standard
DATAN(X)	REAL(8) X	REAL(8)	F77 and later

See also: Inverse function: Section 6.206 [TAN], page 153

6.22 ATAN2 — Arctangent function

Description:

> `ATAN2(Y,X)` computes the arctangent of the complex number $X + iY$.

Standard: F77 and later

Class: Elemental function

Syntax: `RESULT = ATAN2(Y,X)`

Arguments:

Y	The type shall be `REAL(*)`.
X	The type and kind type parameter shall be the same as Y. If Y is zero, then X must be nonzero.

Return value:

> The return value has the same type and kind type parameter as Y. It is the principal value of the complex number $X + iY$. If X is nonzero, then it lies in the range $-\pi \le atan(x) \le \pi$. The sign is positive if Y is positive. If Y is zero, then the return value is zero if X is positive and π if X is negative. Finally, if X is zero, then the magnitude of the result is $\pi/2$.

Example:

```
program test_atan2
  real(4) :: x = 1.e0_4, y = 0.5e0_4
  x = atan2(y,x)
end program test_atan2
```

Specific names:

Name	Argument	Return type	Standard
DATAN2(X)	REAL(8) X	REAL(8)	F77 and later

6.23 ATANH — Hyperbolic arctangent function

Description:

> `ATANH(X)` computes the hyperbolic arctangent of X (inverse of `TANH(X)`).

Standard: GNU extension

Class: Elemental function

Syntax: `RESULT = ATANH(X)`

Arguments:

      X   The type shall be `REAL(*)` with a magnitude that is less than
                            or equal to one.

Return value:

      The return value is of type `REAL(*)` and it lies in the range $-\infty \le \mathrm{atanh}(x) \le \infty$.

Example:

```
PROGRAM test_atanh
  REAL, DIMENSION(3) :: x = (/ -1.0, 0.0, 1.0 /)
  WRITE (*,*) ATANH(x)
END PROGRAM
```

Specific names:

Name	Argument	Return type	Standard
DATANH(X)	REAL(8) X	REAL(8)	GNU extension

See also: Inverse function: Section 6.207 [TANH], page 153

6.24 `BESJ0` — Bessel function of the first kind of order 0

Description:

      `BESJ0(X)` computes the Bessel function of the first kind of order 0 of *X*.

Standard: GNU extension

Class: Elemental function

Syntax: `RESULT = BESJ0(X)`

Arguments:

      X   The type shall be `REAL(*)`, and it shall be scalar.

Return value:

      The return value is of type `REAL(*)` and it lies in the range $-0.4027... \le Bessel(0, x) \le 1$.

Example:

```
program test_besj0
  real(8) :: x = 0.0_8
  x = besj0(x)
end program test_besj0
```

Specific names:

Name	Argument	Return type	Standard
DBESJ0(X)	REAL(8) X	REAL(8)	GNU extension

6.25 BESJ1 — Bessel function of the first kind of order 1

Description:

BESJ1(X) computes the Bessel function of the first kind of order 1 of X.

Standard: GNU extension

Class: Elemental function

Syntax: `RESULT = BESJ1(X)`

Arguments:

X   The type shall be REAL(*), and it shall be scalar.

Return value:

The return value is of type REAL(*) and it lies in the range $-0.5818... \leq Bessel(0, x) \leq 0.5818$.

Example:

```
program test_besj1
  real(8) :: x = 1.0_8
  x = besj1(x)
end program test_besj1
```

Specific names:

Name	Argument	Return type	Standard
DBESJ1(X)	REAL(8) X	REAL(8)	GNU extension

6.26 BESJN — Bessel function of the first kind

Description:

BESJN(N, X) computes the Bessel function of the first kind of order N of X.

If both arguments are arrays, their ranks and shapes shall conform.

Standard: GNU extension

Class: Elemental function

Syntax: `RESULT = BESJN(N, X)`

Arguments:

N   Shall be a scalar or an array of type INTEGER(*).
X   Shall be a scalar or an array of type REAL(*).

Return value:

The return value is a scalar of type REAL(*).

Example:

```
program test_besjn
  real(8) :: x = 1.0_8
  x = besjn(5,x)
end program test_besjn
```

Specific names:

Name	Argument	Return type	Standard
DBESJN(X)	INTEGER(*) N REAL(8) X	REAL(8)	GNU extension

6.27 BESY0 — Bessel function of the second kind of order 0

Description:

BESY0(X) computes the Bessel function of the second kind of order 0 of X.

Standard: GNU extension

Class: Elemental function

Syntax: RESULT = BESY0(X)

Arguments:

X   The type shall be REAL(*), and it shall be scalar.

Return value:

The return value is a scalar of type REAL(*).

Example:

```
program test_besy0
  real(8) :: x = 0.0_8
  x = besy0(x)
end program test_besy0
```

Specific names:

Name	Argument	Return type	Standard
DBESY0(X)	REAL(8) X	REAL(8)	GNU extension

6.28 BESY1 — Bessel function of the second kind of order 1

Description:

BESY1(X) computes the Bessel function of the second kind of order 1 of X.

Standard: GNU extension

Class: Elemental function

Syntax: RESULT = BESY1(X)

Arguments:

X   The type shall be REAL(*), and it shall be scalar.

Return value:

The return value is a scalar of type REAL(*).

Example:

```
program test_besy1
  real(8) :: x = 1.0_8
  x = besy1(x)
end program test_besy1
```

Specific names:

Name	Argument	Return type	Standard
DBESY1(X)	REAL(8) X	REAL(8)	GNU extension

6.29 `BESYN` — Bessel function of the second kind

Description:

> `BESYN(N, X)` computes the Bessel function of the second kind of order N of X.
>
> If both arguments are arrays, their ranks and shapes shall conform.

Standard: GNU extension

Class: Elemental function

Syntax: `RESULT = BESYN(N, X)`

Arguments:

N	Shall be a scalar or an array of type `INTEGER(*)`.
X	Shall be a scalar or an array of type `REAL(*)`.

Return value:

> The return value is a scalar of type `REAL(*)`.

Example:

```
program test_besyn
  real(8) :: x = 1.0_8
  x = besyn(5,x)
end program test_besyn
```

Specific names:

Name	Argument	Return type	Standard
DBESYN(N,X)	INTEGER(*) N REAL(8) X	REAL(8)	GNU extension

6.30 `BIT_SIZE` — Bit size inquiry function

Description:

> `BIT_SIZE(I)` returns the number of bits (integer precision plus sign bit) represented by the type of I.

Standard: F95 and later

Class: Inquiry function

Syntax: `RESULT = BIT_SIZE(I)`

Arguments:

I	The type shall be `INTEGER(*)`.

Return value:

> The return value is of type `INTEGER(*)`

Example:

```
program test_bit_size
    integer :: i = 123
    integer :: size
    size = bit_size(i)
    print *, size
end program test_bit_size
```

6.31 BTEST — Bit test function

Description:

BTEST(I,POS) returns logical .TRUE. if the bit at *POS* in *I* is set.

Standard: F95 and later

Class: Elemental function

Syntax: RESULT = BTEST(I, POS)

Arguments:

I	The type shall be INTEGER(*).
POS	The type shall be INTEGER(*).

Return value:

The return value is of type LOGICAL

Example:

```
program test_btest
    integer :: i = 32768 + 1024 + 64
    integer :: pos
    logical :: bool
    do pos=0,16
        bool = btest(i, pos)
        print *, pos, bool
    end do
end program test_btest
```

6.32 C_ASSOCIATED — Status of a C pointer

Description:

C_ASSOICATED(c_prt1[, c_ptr2]) determines the status of the C pointer *c_ptr1* or if *c_ptr1* is associated with the target *c_ptr2*.

Standard: F2003 and later

Class: Inquiry function

Syntax: RESULT = C_ASSOICATED(c_prt1[, c_ptr2])

Arguments:

c_ptr1	Scalar of the type C_PTR or C_FUNPTR.
c_ptr2	(Optional) Scalar of the same type as *c_ptr1*.

Return value:

The return value is of type LOGICAL; it is .false. if either *c_ptr1* is a C NULL pointer or if *c_ptr1* and *c_ptr2* point to different addresses.

Example:

```
subroutine association_test(a,b)
  use iso_c_binding, only: c_associated, c_loc, c_ptr
  implicit none
  real, pointer :: a
  type(c_ptr) :: b
  if(c_associated(b, c_loc(a))) &
     stop 'b and a do not point to same target'
end subroutine association_test
```

See also: Section 6.36 [C_LOC], page 58, Section 6.33 [C_FUNLOC], page 56

6.33 C_FUNLOC — Obtain the C address of a procedure

Description:
C_FUNLOC(x) determines the C address of the argument.

Standard: F2003 and later

Class: Inquiry function

Syntax: RESULT = C_FUNLOC(x)

Arguments:
x   Interoperable function or pointer to such function.

Return value:
The return value is of type C_FUNPTR and contains the C address of the argument.

Example:

```
module x
  use iso_c_binding
  implicit none
contains
  subroutine sub(a) bind(c)
    real(c_float) :: a
    a = sqrt(a)+5.0
  end subroutine sub
end module x
program main
  use iso_c_binding
  use x
  implicit none
  interface
    subroutine my_routine(p) bind(c,name='myC_func')
      import :: c_funptr
      type(c_funptr), intent(in) :: p
    end subroutine
  end interface
  call my_routine(c_funloc(sub))
end program main
```

See also: Section 6.32 [C_ASSOCIATED], page 55, Section 6.36 [C_LOC], page 58, Section 6.35 [C_F_POINTER], page 57, Section 6.34 [C_F_PROCPOINTER], page 56

6.34 C_F_PROCPOINTER — Convert C into Fortran procedure pointer

Description:
C_F_PROCPOINTER(cptr, fptr) Assign the target of the C function pointer *cptr* to the Fortran procedure pointer *fptr*.

Note: Due to the currently lacking support of procedure pointers in GNU Fortran this function is not fully operable.

Standard: F2003 and later

Class: Subroutine

Syntax: CALL C_F_PROCPOINTER(cptr, fptr)

Arguments:

cptr	scalar of the type C_FUNPTR. It is INTENT(IN).
fptr	procedure pointer interoperable with *cptr*. It is INTENT(OUT).

Example:

```
program main
  use iso_c_binding
  implicit none
  abstract interface
    function func(a)
      import :: c_float
      real(c_float), intent(in) :: a
      real(c_float) :: func
    end function
  end interface
  interface
    function getIterFunc() bind(c,name="getIterFunc")
      import :: c_funptr
      type(c_funptr) :: getIterFunc
    end function
  end interface
  type(c_funptr) :: cfunptr
  procedure(func), pointer :: myFunc
  cfunptr = getIterFunc()
  call c_f_procpointer(cfunptr, myFunc)
end program main
```

See also: Section 6.36 [C_LOC], page 58, Section 6.35 [C_F_POINTER], page 57

6.35 C_F_POINTER — Convert C into Fortran pointer

Description:

C_F_POINTER(cptr, fptr[, shape]) Assign the target the C pointer *cptr* to
the Fortran pointer *fptr* and specify its shape.

Standard: F2003 and later

Class: Subroutine

Syntax: CALL C_F_POINTER(cptr, fptr[, shape])

Arguments:

cptr	scalar of the type C_PTR. It is INTENT(IN).
fptr	pointer interoperable with *cptr*. It is INTENT(OUT).
shape	(Optional) Rank-one array of type INTEGER with INTENT(IN). It shall be present if and only if *fptr* is an array. The size must be equal to the rank of *fptr*.

Example:

```
program main
  use iso_c_binding
```

```
implicit none
interface
  subroutine my_routine(p) bind(c,name='myC_func')
    import :: c_ptr
    type(c_ptr), intent(out) :: p
  end subroutine
end interface
type(c_ptr) :: cptr
real,pointer :: a(:)
call my_routine(cptr)
call c_f_pointer(cptr, a, [12])
end program main
```

See also: Section 6.36 [C_LOC], page 58, Section 6.34 [C_F_PROCPOINTER], page 56

6.36 C_LOC — Obtain the C address of an object

Description:

C_LOC(x) determines the C address of the argument.

Standard: F2003 and later

Class: Inquiry function

Syntax: RESULT = C_LOC(x)

Arguments:

x   Associated scalar pointer or interoperable scalar or allocated
                       allocatable variable with TARGET attribute.

Return value:

The return value is of type C_PTR and contains the C address of the argument.

Example:

```
subroutine association_test(a,b)
  use iso_c_binding, only: c_associated, c_loc, c_ptr
  implicit none
  real, pointer :: a
  type(c_ptr) :: b
  if(c_associated(b, c_loc(a))) &
      stop 'b and a do not point to same target'
end subroutine association_test
```

See also: Section 6.32 [C_ASSOCIATED], page 55, Section 6.33 [C_FUNLOC], page 56,
             Section 6.35 [C_F_POINTER], page 57, Section 6.34 [C_F_PROCPOINTER],
             page 56

6.37 CEILING — Integer ceiling function

Description:

CEILING(X) returns the least integer greater than or equal to X.

Standard: F95 and later

Class: Elemental function

Syntax: RESULT = CEILING(X [, KIND])

Arguments:

X	The type shall be `REAL(*)`.
KIND	(Optional) An `INTEGER(*)` initialization expression indicating the kind parameter of the result.

Return value:

The return value is of type `INTEGER(KIND)`

Example:

```
program test_ceiling
    real :: x = 63.29
    real :: y = -63.59
    print *, ceiling(x) ! returns 64
    print *, ceiling(y) ! returns -63
end program test_ceiling
```

See also: Section 6.73 [FLOOR], page 81, Section 6.160 [NINT], page 127

6.38 CHAR — Character conversion function

Description:

CHAR(I [, KIND]) returns the character represented by the integer *I*.

Standard: F77 and later

Class: Elemental function

Syntax: `RESULT = CHAR(I [, KIND])`

Arguments:

I	The type shall be `INTEGER(*)`.
KIND	(Optional) An `INTEGER(*)` initialization expression indicating the kind parameter of the result.

Return value:

The return value is of type `CHARACTER(1)`

Example:

```
program test_char
    integer :: i = 74
    character(1) :: c
    c = char(i)
    print *, i, c ! returns 'J'
end program test_char
```

Note: See Section 6.104 [ICHAR], page 97 for a discussion of converting between numerical values and formatted string representations.

See also: Section 6.5 [ACHAR], page 39, Section 6.98 [IACHAR], page 94, Section 6.104 [ICHAR], page 97

6.39 CHDIR — Change working directory

Description:

Change current working directory to a specified path.

This intrinsic is provided in both subroutine and function forms; however, only one form can be used in any given program unit.

Standard: GNU extension

Class: Subroutine, function

Syntax:

```
CALL CHDIR(NAME [, STATUS])
STATUS = CHDIR(NAME)
```

Arguments:

NAME   The type shall be `CHARACTER(*)` and shall specify a valid path within the file system.

STATUS   (Optional) `INTEGER` status flag of the default kind. Returns 0 on success, and a system specific and nonzero error code otherwise.

Example:

```
PROGRAM test_chdir
  CHARACTER(len=255) :: path
  CALL getcwd(path)
  WRITE(*,*) TRIM(path)
  CALL chdir("/tmp")
  CALL getcwd(path)
  WRITE(*,*) TRIM(path)
END PROGRAM
```

See also: Section 6.88 [GETCWD], page 90

6.40 CHMOD — Change access permissions of files

Description:

CHMOD changes the permissions of a file. This function invokes `/bin/chmod` and might therefore not work on all platforms.

This intrinsic is provided in both subroutine and function forms; however, only one form can be used in any given program unit.

Standard: GNU extension

Class: Subroutine, function

Syntax:

```
CALL CHMOD(NAME, MODE[, STATUS])
STATUS = CHMOD(NAME, MODE)
```

Arguments:

NAME   Scalar `CHARACTER` with the file name. Trailing blanks are ignored unless the character `achar(0)` is present, then all characters up to and excluding `achar(0)` are used as the file name.

MODE   Scalar `CHARACTER` giving the file permission. *MODE* uses the same syntax as the *MODE* argument of `/bin/chmod`.

STATUS   (optional) scalar `INTEGER`, which is 0 on success and nonzero otherwise.

Return value:

In either syntax, *STATUS* is set to 0 on success and nonzero otherwise.

Example: CHMOD as subroutine

```
program chmod_test
  implicit none
  integer :: status
  call chmod('test.dat','u+x',status)
  print *, 'Status: ', status
end program chmod_test
```

CHMOD as function:

```
program chmod_test
  implicit none
  integer :: status
  status = chmod('test.dat','u+x')
  print *, 'Status: ', status
end program chmod_test
```

6.41 CMPLX — Complex conversion function

Description:

CMPLX(X [, Y [, KIND]]) returns a complex number where X is converted to the real component. If Y is present it is converted to the imaginary component. If Y is not present then the imaginary component is set to 0.0. If X is complex then Y must not be present.

Standard: F77 and later

Class: Elemental function

Syntax: RESULT = CMPLX(X [, Y [, KIND]])

Arguments:

X	The type may be INTEGER(*), REAL(*), or COMPLEX(*).
Y	(Optional; only allowed if X is not COMPLEX(*).) May be INTEGER(*) or REAL(*).
KIND	(Optional) An INTEGER(*) initialization expression indicating the kind parameter of the result.

Return value:

The return value is of COMPLEX type, with a kind equal to *KIND* if it is specified. If *KIND* is not specified, the result is of the default COMPLEX kind, regardless of the kinds of X and Y.

Example:

```
program test_cmplx
    integer :: i = 42
    real :: x = 3.14
    complex :: z
    z = cmplx(i, x)
    print *, z, cmplx(x)
end program test_cmplx
```

See also: Section 6.43 [COMPLEX], page 62

6.42 COMMAND_ARGUMENT_COUNT — Get number of command line arguments

Description:

COMMAND_ARGUMENT_COUNT() returns the number of arguments passed on the command line when the containing program was invoked.

Standard: F2003

Class: Inquiry function

Syntax: RESULT = COMMAND_ARGUMENT_COUNT()

Arguments:

None

Return value:

The return value is of type INTEGER(4)

Example:

```
program test_command_argument_count
    integer :: count
    count = command_argument_count()
    print *, count
end program test_command_argument_count
```

See also: Section 6.86 [GET_COMMAND], page 89, Section 6.87 [GET_COMMAND_ARGUMENT] page 89

6.43 COMPLEX — Complex conversion function

Description:

COMPLEX(X, Y) returns a complex number where X is converted to the real component and Y is converted to the imaginary component.

Standard: GNU extension

Class: Elemental function

Syntax: RESULT = COMPLEX(X, Y)

Arguments:

X	The type may be INTEGER(*) or REAL(*).
Y	The type may be INTEGER(*) or REAL(*).

Return value:

If X and Y are both of INTEGER type, then the return value is of default COMPLEX type.

If X and Y are of REAL type, or one is of REAL type and one is of INTEGER type, then the return value is of COMPLEX type with a kind equal to that of the REAL argument with the highest precision.

Example:

```
program test_complex
    integer :: i = 42
    real :: x = 3.14
    print *, complex(i, x)
end program test_complex
```

See also: Section 6.41 [CMPLX], page 61

6.44 `CONJG` — Complex conjugate function

Description:

CONJG(Z) returns the conjugate of Z. If Z is (x, y) then the result is (x, -y)

Standard: F77 and later, has overloads that are GNU extensions

Class: Elemental function

Syntax: Z = CONJG(Z)

Arguments:

Z   The type shall be COMPLEX(*).

Return value:

The return value is of type COMPLEX(*).

Example:

```
program test_conjg
    complex :: z = (2.0, 3.0)
    complex(8) :: dz = (2.71_8, -3.14_8)
    z= conjg(z)
    print *, z
    dz = dconjg(dz)
    print *, dz
end program test_conjg
```

Specific names:

Name	Argument	Return type	Standard
DCONJG(Z)	COMPLEX(8) Z	COMPLEX(8)	GNU extension

6.45 `COS` — Cosine function

Description:

COS(X) computes the cosine of X.

Standard: F77 and later, has overloads that are GNU extensions

Class: Elemental function

Syntax: RESULT = COS(X)

Arguments:

X   The type shall be REAL(*) or COMPLEX(*).

Return value:

The return value is of type REAL(*) and it lies in the range $-1 \leq \cos(x) \leq 1$.
The kind type parameter is the same as X.

Example:

```
program test_cos
  real :: x = 0.0
  x = cos(x)
end program test_cos
```

Specific names:

Name	Argument	Return type	Standard
DCOS(X)	REAL(8) X	REAL(8)	F77 and later
CCOS(X)	COMPLEX(4) X	COMPLEX(4)	F77 and later
ZCOS(X)	COMPLEX(8) X	COMPLEX(8)	GNU extension
CDCOS(X)	COMPLEX(8) X	COMPLEX(8)	GNU extension

See also: Inverse function: Section 6.6 [ACOS], page 40

6.46 COSH — Hyperbolic cosine function

Description:
COSH(X) computes the hyperbolic cosine of X.

Standard: F77 and later

Class: Elemental function

Syntax: X = COSH(X)

Arguments:
X   The type shall be REAL(*).

Return value:
The return value is of type REAL(*) and it is positive $(\cosh(x) \geq 0$.

Example:
```
program test_cosh
  real(8) :: x = 1.0_8
  x = cosh(x)
end program test_cosh
```

Specific names:

Name	Argument	Return type	Standard
DCOSH(X)	REAL(8) X	REAL(8)	F77 and later

See also: Inverse function: Section 6.7 [ACOSH], page 40

6.47 COUNT — Count function

Description:
COUNT(MASK [, DIM [, KIND]]) counts the number of .TRUE. elements of *MASK* along the dimension of *DIM*. If *DIM* is omitted it is taken to be 1. *DIM* is a scaler of type INTEGER in the range of $1/leqDIM/leqn)$ where n is the rank of *MASK*.

Standard: F95 and later

Class: Transformational function

Syntax: RESULT = COUNT(MASK [, DIM [, KIND]])

Arguments:
MASK   The type shall be LOGICAL.
DIM   (Optional) The type shall be INTEGER.
KIND   (Optional) An INTEGER initialization expression indicating the kind parameter of the result.

Return value:

> The return value is of type `INTEGER` and of kind *KIND*. If *KIND* is absent, the return value is of default integer kind. The result has a rank equal to that of *MASK*.

Example:

```
program test_count
    integer, dimension(2,3) :: a, b
    logical, dimension(2,3) :: mask
    a = reshape( (/ 1, 2, 3, 4, 5, 6 /), (/ 2, 3 /))
    b = reshape( (/ 0, 7, 3, 4, 5, 8 /), (/ 2, 3 /))
    print '(3i3)', a(1,:)
    print '(3i3)', a(2,:)
    print *
    print '(3i3)', b(1,:)
    print '(3i3)', b(2,:)
    print *
    mask = a.ne.b
    print '(3l3)', mask(1,:)
    print '(3l3)', mask(2,:)
    print *
    print '(3i3)', count(mask)
    print *
    print '(3i3)', count(mask, 1)
    print *
    print '(3i3)', count(mask, 2)
end program test_count
```

6.48 `CPU_TIME` —— CPU elapsed time in seconds

Description:

> Returns a `REAL(*)` value representing the elapsed CPU time in seconds. This is useful for testing segments of code to determine execution time.
>
> If a time source is available, time will be reported with microsecond resolution. If no time source is available, *TIME* is set to `-1.0`.
>
> Note that *TIME* may contain a, system dependent, arbitrary offset and may not start with `0.0`. For `CPU_TIME`, the absolute value is meaningless, only differences between subsequent calls to this subroutine, as shown in the example below, should be used.

Standard: F95 and later

Class: Subroutine

Syntax: `CALL CPU_TIME(TIME)`

Arguments:

> *TIME*   The type shall be `REAL(*)` with `INTENT(OUT)`.

Return value:

> None

Example:

```
program test_cpu_time
    real :: start, finish
```

```
              call cpu_time(start)
                  ! put code to test here
              call cpu_time(finish)
              print '("Time = ",f6.3," seconds.")',finish-start
          end program test_cpu_time
```

See also: Section 6.205 [SYSTEM_CLOCK], page 152, Section 6.51 [DATE_AND_TIME],
page 67

6.49 CSHIFT — Circular shift elements of an array

Description:

CSHIFT(ARRAY, SHIFT [, DIM]) performs a circular shift on elements of *AR-RAY* along the dimension of *DIM*. If *DIM* is omitted it is taken to be **1**. *DIM* is a scaler of type **INTEGER** in the range of $1/leqDIM/leqn$) where n is the rank of *ARRAY*. If the rank of *ARRAY* is one, then all elements of *ARRAY* are shifted by *SHIFT* places. If rank is greater than one, then all complete rank one sections of *ARRAY* along the given dimension are shifted. Elements shifted out one end of each rank one section are shifted back in the other end.

Standard: F95 and later

Class: Transformational function

Syntax: RESULT = CSHIFT(ARRAY, SHIFT [, DIM])

Arguments:

ARRAY	Shall be an array of any type.
SHIFT	The type shall be **INTEGER**.
DIM	The type shall be **INTEGER**.

Return value:

Returns an array of same type and rank as the *ARRAY* argument.

Example:

```
          program test_cshift
              integer, dimension(3,3) :: a
              a = reshape( (/ 1, 2, 3, 4, 5, 6, 7, 8, 9 /), (/ 3, 3 /))
              print '(3i3)', a(1,:)
              print '(3i3)', a(2,:)
              print '(3i3)', a(3,:)
              a = cshift(a, SHIFT=(/1, 2, -1/), DIM=2)
              print *
              print '(3i3)', a(1,:)
              print '(3i3)', a(2,:)
              print '(3i3)', a(3,:)
          end program test_cshift
```

6.50 CTIME — Convert a time into a string

Description:

CTIME converts a system time value, such as returned by TIME8(), to a string of the form 'Sat Aug 19 18:13:14 1995'.

This intrinsic is provided in both subroutine and function forms; however, only one form can be used in any given program unit.

Standard: GNU extension

Class: Subroutine, function

Syntax:

```
CALL CTIME(TIME, RESULT).
RESULT = CTIME(TIME), (not recommended).
```

Arguments:

TIME	The type shall be of type INTEGER(KIND=8).
RESULT	The type shall be of type CHARACTER.

Return value:

The converted date and time as a string.

Example:

```
program test_ctime
    integer(8) :: i
    character(len=30) :: date
    i = time8()

    ! Do something, main part of the program

    call ctime(i,date)
    print *, 'Program was started on ', date
end program test_ctime
```

See Also: Section 6.95 [GMTIME], page 93, Section 6.140 [LTIME], page 116, Section 6.208 [TIME], page 154, Section 6.209 [TIME8], page 155

6.51 DATE_AND_TIME — Date and time subroutine

Description:

DATE_AND_TIME(DATE, TIME, ZONE, VALUES) gets the corresponding date and time information from the real-time system clock. *DATE* is INTENT(OUT) and has form ccyymmdd. *TIME* is INTENT(OUT) and has form hhmmss.sss. *ZONE* is INTENT(OUT) and has form (+-)hhmm, representing the difference with respect to Coordinated Universal Time (UTC). Unavailable time and date parameters return blanks.

VALUES is INTENT(OUT) and provides the following:

VALUE(1):	The year
VALUE(2):	The month
VALUE(3):	The day of the month
VALUE(4):	Time difference with UTC in minutes
VALUE(5):	The hour of the day
VALUE(6):	The minutes of the hour
VALUE(7):	The seconds of the minute
VALUE(8):	The milliseconds of the second

Standard: F95 and later

Class: Subroutine

Syntax: `CALL DATE_AND_TIME([DATE, TIME, ZONE, VALUES])`

Arguments:

DATE	(Optional) The type shall be `CHARACTER(8)` or larger.
TIME	(Optional) The type shall be `CHARACTER(10)` or larger.
ZONE	(Optional) The type shall be `CHARACTER(5)` or larger.
VALUES	(Optional) The type shall be `INTEGER(8)`.

Return value:

None

Example:

```
program test_time_and_date
    character(8)  :: date
    character(10) :: time
    character(5)  :: zone
    integer,dimension(8) :: values
    ! using keyword arguments
    call date_and_time(date,time,zone,values)
    call date_and_time(DATE=date,ZONE=zone)
    call date_and_time(TIME=time)
    call date_and_time(VALUES=values)
    print '(a,2x,a,2x,a)', date, time, zone
    print '(8i5))', values
end program test_time_and_date
```

See also: Section 6.48 [CPU_TIME], page 65, Section 6.205 [SYSTEM_CLOCK], page 152

6.52 `DBLE` — Double conversion function

Description:

`DBLE(X)` Converts X to double precision real type.

Standard: F77 and later

Class: Elemental function

Syntax: `RESULT = DBLE(X)`

Arguments:

X	The type shall be `INTEGER(*)`, `REAL(*)`, or `COMPLEX(*)`.

Return value:

The return value is of type double precision real.

Example:

```
program test_dble
    real    :: x = 2.18
    integer :: i = 5
    complex :: z = (2.3,1.14)
    print *, dble(x), dble(i), dble(z)
end program test_dble
```

See also: Section 6.54 [DFLOAT], page 69, Section 6.70 [FLOAT], page 79, Section 6.175 [REAL], page 135

6.53 `DCMPLX` — Double complex conversion function

Description:

DCMPLX(X [,Y]) returns a double complex number where X is converted to the real component. If Y is present it is converted to the imaginary component. If Y is not present then the imaginary component is set to 0.0. If X is complex then Y must not be present.

Standard: GNU extension

Class: Elemental function

Syntax: RESULT = DCMPLX(X [, Y])

Arguments:

X	The type may be INTEGER(*), REAL(*), or COMPLEX(*).
Y	(Optional if X is not COMPLEX(*).) May be INTEGER(*) or REAL(*).

Return value:

The return value is of type COMPLEX(8)

Example:

```
program test_dcmplx
    integer :: i = 42
    real :: x = 3.14
    complex :: z
    z = cmplx(i, x)
    print *, dcmplx(i)
    print *, dcmplx(x)
    print *, dcmplx(z)
    print *, dcmplx(x,i)
end program test_dcmplx
```

6.54 `DFLOAT` — Double conversion function

Description:

DFLOAT(X) Converts X to double precision real type.

Standard: GNU extension

Class: Elemental function

Syntax: RESULT = DFLOAT(X)

Arguments:

X	The type shall be INTEGER(*).

Return value:

The return value is of type double precision real.

Example:

```
program test_dfloat
    integer :: i = 5
    print *, dfloat(i)
end program test_dfloat
```

See also: Section 6.52 [DBLE], page 68, Section 6.70 [FLOAT], page 79, Section 6.175 [REAL], page 135

6.55 `DIGITS` — Significant digits function

Description:

DIGITS(X) returns the number of significant digits of the internal model representation of *X*. For example, on a system using a 32-bit floating point representation, a default real number would likely return 24.

Standard: F95 and later

Class: Inquiry function

Syntax: RESULT = DIGITS(X)

Arguments:

X   The type may be `INTEGER(*)` or `REAL(*)`.

Return value:

The return value is of type `INTEGER`.

Example:

```
program test_digits
    integer :: i = 12345
    real :: x = 3.143
    real(8) :: y = 2.33
    print *, digits(i)
    print *, digits(x)
    print *, digits(y)
end program test_digits
```

6.56 `DIM` — Positive difference

Description:

DIM(X,Y) returns the difference X-Y if the result is positive; otherwise returns zero.

Standard: F77 and later

Class: Elemental function

Syntax: RESULT = DIM(X, Y)

Arguments:

X   The type shall be `INTEGER(*)` or `REAL(*)`
Y   The type shall be the same type and kind as *X*.

Return value:

The return value is of type `INTEGER(*)` or `REAL(*)`.

Example:

```
program test_dim
    integer :: i
    real(8) :: x
    i = dim(4, 15)
    x = dim(4.345_8, 2.111_8)
    print *, i
    print *, x
end program test_dim
```

Specific names:

Name	Argument	Return type	Standard
IDIM(X,Y)	INTEGER(4) X,Y	INTEGER(4)	F77 and later
DDIM(X,Y)	REAL(8) X,Y	REAL(8)	F77 and later

6.57 DOT_PRODUCT — Dot product function

Description:

DOT_PRODUCT(X,Y) computes the dot product multiplication of two vectors X and Y. The two vectors may be either numeric or logical and must be arrays of rank one and of equal size. If the vectors are INTEGER(*) or REAL(*), the result is SUM(X*Y). If the vectors are COMPLEX(*), the result is SUM(CONJG(X)*Y). If the vectors are LOGICAL, the result is ANY(X.AND.Y).

Standard: F95 and later

Class: Transformational function

Syntax: RESULT = DOT_PRODUCT(X, Y)

Arguments:

X	The type shall be numeric or LOGICAL, rank 1.
Y	The type shall be numeric or LOGICAL, rank 1.

Return value:

If the arguments are numeric, the return value is a scaler of numeric type, INTEGER(*), REAL(*), or COMPLEX(*). If the arguments are LOGICAL, the return value is .TRUE. or .FALSE..

Example:

```
program test_dot_prod
    integer, dimension(3) :: a, b
    a = (/ 1, 2, 3 /)
    b = (/ 4, 5, 6 /)
    print '(3i3)', a
    print *
    print '(3i3)', b
    print *
    print *, dot_product(a,b)
end program test_dot_prod
```

6.58 DPROD — Double product function

Description:

DPROD(X,Y) returns the product X*Y.

Standard: F77 and later

Class: Elemental function

Syntax: RESULT = DPROD(X, Y)

Arguments:

X	The type shall be REAL.
Y	The type shall be REAL.

Return value:
> The return value is of type `REAL(8)`.

Example:

```
program test_dprod
    real :: x = 5.2
    real :: y = 2.3
    real(8) :: d
    d = dprod(x,y)
    print *, d
end program test_dprod
```

6.59 DREAL — Double real part function

Description:
> `DREAL(Z)` returns the real part of complex variable *Z*.

Standard: GNU extension

Class: Elemental function

Syntax: `RESULT = DREAL(Z)`

Arguments:
> *Z*   The type shall be `COMPLEX(8)`.

Return value:
> The return value is of type `REAL(8)`.

Example:

```
program test_dreal
    complex(8) :: z = (1.3_8,7.2_8)
    print *, dreal(z)
end program test_dreal
```

See also: Section 6.10 [AIMAG], page 42

6.60 DTIME — Execution time subroutine (or function)

Description:
> `DTIME(TARRAY, RESULT)` initially returns the number of seconds of runtime since the start of the process's execution in *RESULT. TARRAY* returns the user and system components of this time in `TARRAY(1)` and `TARRAY(2)` respectively. *RESULT* is equal to `TARRAY(1)` + `TARRAY(2)`.
>
> Subsequent invocations of `DTIME` return values accumulated since the previous invocation.
>
> On some systems, the underlying timings are represented using types with sufficiently small limits that overflows (wrap around) are possible, such as 32-bit types. Therefore, the values returned by this intrinsic might be, or become, negative, or numerically less than previous values, during a single run of the compiled program.
>
> Please note, that this implementation is thread safe if used within OpenMP directives, i. e. its state will be consistent while called from multiple threads.

However, if `DTIME` is called from multiple threads, the result is still the time since the last invocation. This may not give the intended results. If possible, use `CPU_TIME` instead.

This intrinsic is provided in both subroutine and function forms; however, only one form can be used in any given program unit.

TARRAY and *RESULT* are `INTENT(OUT)` and provide the following:

TARRAY(1):	User time in seconds.
TARRAY(2):	System time in seconds.
RESULT:	Run time since start in seconds.

Standard: GNU extension

Class: Subroutine, function

Syntax:

```
CALL DTIME(TARRAY, RESULT).
RESULT = DTIME(TARRAY), (not recommended).
```

Arguments:

TARRAY	The type shall be `REAL`, `DIMENSION(2)`.
RESULT	The type shall be `REAL`.

Return value:

Elapsed time in seconds since the last invocation or since the start of program execution if not called before.

Example:

```
program test_dtime
    integer(8) :: i, j
    real, dimension(2) :: tarray
    real :: result
    call dtime(tarray, result)
    print *, result
    print *, tarray(1)
    print *, tarray(2)
    do i=1,100000000    ! Just a delay
        j = i * i - i
    end do
    call dtime(tarray, result)
    print *, result
    print *, tarray(1)
    print *, tarray(2)
end program test_dtime
```

See also: Section 6.48 [CPU_TIME], page 65

6.61 EOSHIFT — End-off shift elements of an array

Description:

`EOSHIFT(ARRAY, SHIFT[,BOUNDARY, DIM])` performs an end-off shift on elements of *ARRAY* along the dimension of *DIM*. If *DIM* is omitted it is taken to be 1. *DIM* is a scaler of type `INTEGER` in the range of $1/leqDIM/leqn$) where n is the rank of *ARRAY*. If the rank of *ARRAY* is one, then all elements of

ARRAY are shifted by *SHIFT* places. If rank is greater than one, then all complete rank one sections of *ARRAY* along the given dimension are shifted. Elements shifted out one end of each rank one section are dropped. If *BOUNDARY* is present then the corresponding value of from *BOUNDARY* is copied back in the other end. If *BOUNDARY* is not present then the following are copied in depending on the type of *ARRAY*.

Array Type	Boundary Value
Numeric	0 of the type and kind of *ARRAY*.
Logical	.FALSE..
Character(*len*)	*len* blanks.

Standard: F95 and later

Class: Transformational function

Syntax: `RESULT = EOSHIFT(ARRAY, SHIFT [, BOUNDARY, DIM])`

Arguments:

ARRAY	May be any type, not scaler.
SHIFT	The type shall be INTEGER.
BOUNDARY	Same type as *ARRAY*.
DIM	The type shall be INTEGER.

Return value:
Returns an array of same type and rank as the *ARRAY* argument.

Example:

```
program test_eoshift
    integer, dimension(3,3) :: a
    a = reshape( (/ 1, 2, 3, 4, 5, 6, 7, 8, 9 /), (/ 3, 3 /))
    print '(3i3)', a(1,:)
    print '(3i3)', a(2,:)
    print '(3i3)', a(3,:)
    a = EOSHIFT(a, SHIFT=(/1, 2, 1/), BOUNDARY=-5, DIM=2)
    print *
    print '(3i3)', a(1,:)
    print '(3i3)', a(2,:)
    print '(3i3)', a(3,:)
end program test_eoshift
```

6.62 EPSILON — Epsilon function

Description:
EPSILON(X) returns a nearly negligible number relative to 1.

Standard: F95 and later

Class: Inquiry function

Syntax: `RESULT = EPSILON(X)`

Arguments:

X	The type shall be REAL(*).

Return value:
The return value is of same type as the argument.

Example:

```
program test_epsilon
    real :: x = 3.143
    real(8) :: y = 2.33
    print *, EPSILON(x)
    print *, EPSILON(y)
end program test_epsilon
```

6.63 ERF — Error function

Description:

ERF(X) computes the error function of *X*.

Standard: GNU Extension

Class: Elemental function

Syntax: RESULT = ERF(X)

Arguments:

X   The type shall be REAL(*), and it shall be scalar.

Return value:

The return value is a scalar of type REAL(*) and it is positive $(-1 \leq erf(x) \leq 1$.

Example:

```
program test_erf
  real(8) :: x = 0.17_8
  x = erf(x)
end program test_erf
```

Specific names:

Name	Argument	Return type	Standard
DERF(X)	REAL(8) X	REAL(8)	GNU extension

6.64 ERFC — Error function

Description:

ERFC(X) computes the complementary error function of *X*.

Standard: GNU extension

Class: Elemental function

Syntax: RESULT = ERFC(X)

Arguments:

X   The type shall be REAL(*), and it shall be scalar.

Return value:

The return value is a scalar of type REAL(*) and it is positive $(0 \leq erfc(x) \leq 2$.

Example:

```
program test_erfc
  real(8) :: x = 0.17_8
  x = erfc(x)
end program test_erfc
```

Specific names:

Name	Argument	Return type	Standard
DERFC(X)	REAL(8) X	REAL(8)	GNU extension

6.65 ETIME — Execution time subroutine (or function)

Description:

ETIME(TARRAY, RESULT) returns the number of seconds of runtime since the start of the process's execution in *RESULT*. *TARRAY* returns the user and system components of this time in TARRAY(1) and TARRAY(2) respectively. *RESULT* is equal to TARRAY(1) + TARRAY(2).

On some systems, the underlying timings are represented using types with sufficiently small limits that overflows (wrap around) are possible, such as 32-bit types. Therefore, the values returned by this intrinsic might be, or become, negative, or numerically less than previous values, during a single run of the compiled program.

This intrinsic is provided in both subroutine and function forms; however, only one form can be used in any given program unit.

TARRAY and *RESULT* are INTENT(OUT) and provide the following:

TARRAY(1):	User time in seconds.
TARRAY(2):	System time in seconds.
RESULT:	Run time since start in seconds.

Standard: GNU extension

Class: Subroutine, function

Syntax:

CALL ETIME(TARRAY, RESULT).
RESULT = ETIME(TARRAY), (not recommended).

Arguments:

TARRAY	The type shall be REAL, DIMENSION(2).
RESULT	The type shall be REAL.

Return value:

Elapsed time in seconds since the start of program execution.

Example:

```
program test_etime
    integer(8) :: i, j
    real, dimension(2) :: tarray
    real :: result
    call ETIME(tarray, result)
    print *, result
    print *, tarray(1)
    print *, tarray(2)
    do i=1,100000000    ! Just a delay
        j = i * i - i
    end do
    call ETIME(tarray, result)
    print *, result
```

```
      print *, tarray(1)
      print *, tarray(2)
    end program test_etime
```

See also: Section 6.48 [CPU_TIME], page 65

6.66 `EXIT` — Exit the program with status.

Description:

> `EXIT` causes immediate termination of the program with status. If status is omitted it returns the canonical *success* for the system. All Fortran I/O units are closed.

Standard: GNU extension

Class: Subroutine

Syntax: `CALL EXIT([STATUS])`

Arguments:

> *STATUS*   Shall be an `INTEGER` of the default kind.

Return value:

> `STATUS` is passed to the parent process on exit.

Example:

```
    program test_exit
      integer :: STATUS = 0
      print *, 'This program is going to exit.'
      call EXIT(STATUS)
    end program test_exit
```

See also: Section 6.2 [ABORT], page 37, Section 6.121 [KILL], page 106

6.67 `EXP` — Exponential function

Description:

> `EXP(X)` computes the base e exponential of X.

Standard: F77 and later, has overloads that are GNU extensions

Class: Elemental function

Syntax: `RESULT = EXP(X)`

Arguments:

> *X*   The type shall be `REAL(*)` or `COMPLEX(*)`.

Return value:

> The return value has same type and kind as *X*.

Example:

```
    program test_exp
      real :: x = 1.0
      x = exp(x)
    end program test_exp
```

Specific names:

Name	Argument	Return type	Standard
DEXP(X)	REAL(8) X	REAL(8)	F77 and later
CEXP(X)	COMPLEX(4) X	COMPLEX(4)	F77 and later
ZEXP(X)	COMPLEX(8) X	COMPLEX(8)	GNU extension
CDEXP(X)	COMPLEX(8) X	COMPLEX(8)	GNU extension

6.68 EXPONENT — **Exponent function**

Description:

EXPONENT(X) returns the value of the exponent part of X. If X is zero the value returned is zero.

Standard: F95 and later

Class: Elemental function

Syntax: RESULT = EXPONENT(X)

Arguments:

X   The type shall be REAL(*).

Return value:

The return value is of type default INTEGER.

Example:

```
program test_exponent
  real :: x = 1.0
  integer :: i
  i = exponent(x)
  print *, i
  print *, exponent(0.0)
end program test_exponent
```

6.69 FDATE — **Get the current time as a string**

Description:

FDATE(DATE) returns the current date (using the same format as CTIME) in *DATE*. It is equivalent to CALL CTIME(DATE, TIME()).

This intrinsic is provided in both subroutine and function forms; however, only one form can be used in any given program unit.

DATE is an INTENT(OUT) CHARACTER variable.

Standard: GNU extension

Class: Subroutine, function

Syntax:

CALL FDATE(DATE).
DATE = FDATE(), (not recommended).

Arguments:

DATE   The type shall be of type CHARACTER.

Return value:

> The current date as a string.

Example:

```
program test_fdate
    integer(8) :: i, j
    character(len=30) :: date
    call fdate(date)
    print *, 'Program started on ', date
    do i = 1, 100000000 ! Just a delay
        j = i * i - i
    end do
    call fdate(date)
    print *, 'Program ended on ', date
end program test_fdate
```

6.70 FLOAT — Convert integer to default real

Description:

> FLOAT(I) converts the integer *I* to a default real value.

Standard: F77 and later

Class: Elemental function

Syntax: RESULT = FLOAT(I)

Arguments:

> *I*   The type shall be INTEGER(*).

Return value:

> The return value is of type default REAL.

Example:

```
program test_float
    integer :: i = 1
    if (float(i) /= 1.) call abort
end program test_float
```

See also: Section 6.52 [DBLE], page 68, Section 6.54 [DFLOAT], page 69, Section 6.175 [REAL], page 135

6.71 FGET — Read a single character in stream mode from stdin

Description:

> Read a single character in stream mode from stdin by bypassing normal formatted output. Stream I/O should not be mixed with normal record-oriented (formatted or unformatted) I/O on the same unit; the results are unpredictable.
>
> This intrinsic is provided in both subroutine and function forms; however, only one form can be used in any given program unit.
>
> Note that the FGET intrinsic is provided for backwards compatibility with g77. GNU Fortran provides the Fortran 2003 Stream facility. Programmers should consider the use of new stream IO feature in new code for future portability. See also Chapter 4 [Fortran 2003 status], page 25.

Standard: GNU extension

Class: Subroutine, function

Syntax: `CALL FGET(C [, STATUS])`

Arguments:

          C   The type shall be `CHARACTER`.

          STATUS   (Optional) status flag of type `INTEGER`. Returns 0 on success, -1 on end-of-file, and a system specific positive error code otherwise.

Example:

```
PROGRAM test_fget
  INTEGER, PARAMETER :: strlen = 100
  INTEGER :: status, i = 1
  CHARACTER(len=strlen) :: str = ""

  WRITE (*,*) 'Enter text:'
  DO
    CALL fget(str(i:i), status)
    if (status /= 0 .OR. i > strlen) exit
    i = i + 1
  END DO
  WRITE (*,*) TRIM(str)
END PROGRAM
```

See also: Section 6.72 [FGETC], page 80, Section 6.76 [FPUT], page 82, Section 6.77 [FPUTC], page 83

6.72 FGETC — Read a single character in stream mode

Description:

Read a single character in stream mode by bypassing normal formatted output. Stream I/O should not be mixed with normal record-oriented (formatted or unformatted) I/O on the same unit; the results are unpredictable.

This intrinsic is provided in both subroutine and function forms; however, only one form can be used in any given program unit.

Note that the `FGET` intrinsic is provided for backwards compatibility with **g77**. GNU Fortran provides the Fortran 2003 Stream facility. Programmers should consider the use of new stream IO feature in new code for future portability. See also Chapter 4 [Fortran 2003 status], page 25.

Standard: GNU extension

Class: Subroutine, function

Syntax: `CALL FGETC(UNIT, C [, STATUS])`

Arguments:

          UNIT   The type shall be `INTEGER`.

          C   The type shall be `CHARACTER`.

          STATUS   (Optional) status flag of type `INTEGER`. Returns 0 on success, -1 on end-of-file and a system specific positive error code otherwise.

Example:

```
PROGRAM test_fgetc
  INTEGER :: fd = 42, status
  CHARACTER :: c

  OPEN(UNIT=fd, FILE="/etc/passwd", ACTION="READ", STATUS = "OLD")
  DO
    CALL fgetc(fd, c, status)
    IF (status /= 0) EXIT
    call fput(c)
  END DO
  CLOSE(UNIT=fd)
END PROGRAM
```

See also: Section 6.71 [FGET], page 79, Section 6.76 [FPUT], page 82, Section 6.77
[FPUTC], page 83

6.73 FLOOR — Integer floor function

Description:

FLOOR(X) returns the greatest integer less than or equal to X.

Standard: F95 and later

Class: Elemental function

Syntax: RESULT = FLOOR(X [, KIND])

Arguments:

X	The type shall be REAL(*).
KIND	(Optional) An INTEGER(*) initialization expression indicating the kind parameter of the result.

Return value:

The return value is of type INTEGER(KIND)

Example:

```
program test_floor
    real :: x = 63.29
    real :: y = -63.59
    print *, floor(x) ! returns 63
    print *, floor(y) ! returns -64
end program test_floor
```

See also: Section 6.37 [CEILING], page 58, Section 6.160 [NINT], page 127

6.74 FLUSH — Flush I/O unit(s)

Description:

Flushes Fortran unit(s) currently open for output. Without the optional argument, all units are flushed, otherwise just the unit specified.

Standard: GNU extension

Class: Subroutine

Syntax: CALL FLUSH(UNIT)

Arguments:

UNIT   (Optional) The type shall be `INTEGER`.

Note: Beginning with the Fortran 2003 standard, there is a `FLUSH` statement that
                should be preferred over the `FLUSH` intrinsic.

6.75 `FNUM` — File number function

Description:
                `FNUM(UNIT)` returns the POSIX file descriptor number corresponding to the
                open Fortran I/O unit `UNIT`.

Standard: GNU extension

Class: Function

Syntax: `RESULT = FNUM(UNIT)`

Arguments:

UNIT   The type shall be `INTEGER`.

Return value:
                The return value is of type `INTEGER`

Example:

```
program test_fnum
  integer :: i
  open (unit=10, status = "scratch")
  i = fnum(10)
  print *, i
  close (10)
end program test_fnum
```

6.76 `FPUT` — Write a single character in stream mode to stdout

Description:
                Write a single character in stream mode to stdout by bypassing normal for-
                matted output. Stream I/O should not be mixed with normal record-oriented
                (formatted or unformatted) I/O on the same unit; the results are unpredictable.

                This intrinsic is provided in both subroutine and function forms; however, only
                one form can be used in any given program unit.

                Note that the `FGET` intrinsic is provided for backwards compatibility with g77.
                GNU Fortran provides the Fortran 2003 Stream facility. Programmers should
                consider the use of new stream IO feature in new code for future portability.
                See also Chapter 4 [Fortran 2003 status], page 25.

Standard: GNU extension

Class: Subroutine, function

Syntax: `CALL FPUT(C [, STATUS])`

Arguments:

C	The type shall be `CHARACTER`.
STATUS	(Optional) status flag of type `INTEGER`. Returns 0 on success, -1 on end-of-file and a system specific positive error code otherwise.

Example:

```
PROGRAM test_fput
  CHARACTER(len=10) :: str = "gfortran"
  INTEGER :: i
  DO i = 1, len_trim(str)
    CALL fput(str(i:i))
  END DO
END PROGRAM
```

See also: Section 6.77 [FPUTC], page 83, Section 6.71 [FGET], page 79, Section 6.72 [FGETC], page 80

6.77 FPUTC — Write a single character in stream mode

Description:

Write a single character in stream mode by bypassing normal formatted output. Stream I/O should not be mixed with normal record-oriented (formatted or unformatted) I/O on the same unit; the results are unpredictable.

This intrinsic is provided in both subroutine and function forms; however, only one form can be used in any given program unit.

Note that the `FGET` intrinsic is provided for backwards compatibility with **g77**. GNU Fortran provides the Fortran 2003 Stream facility. Programmers should consider the use of new stream IO feature in new code for future portability. See also Chapter 4 [Fortran 2003 status], page 25.

Standard: GNU extension

Class: Subroutine, function

Syntax: `CALL FPUTC(UNIT, C [, STATUS])`

Arguments:

UNIT	The type shall be `INTEGER`.
C	The type shall be `CHARACTER`.
STATUS	(Optional) status flag of type `INTEGER`. Returns 0 on success, -1 on end-of-file and a system specific positive error code otherwise.

Example:

```
PROGRAM test_fputc
  CHARACTER(len=10) :: str = "gfortran"
  INTEGER :: fd = 42, i

  OPEN(UNIT = fd, FILE = "out", ACTION = "WRITE", STATUS="NEW")
  DO i = 1, len_trim(str)
    CALL fputc(fd, str(i:i))
  END DO
```

```
        CLOSE(fd)
      END PROGRAM
```

See also: Section 6.76 [FPUT], page 82, Section 6.71 [FGET], page 79, Section 6.72
              [FGETC], page 80

6.78 FRACTION — Fractional part of the model representation

Description:

   FRACTION(X) returns the fractional part of the model representation of X.

Standard: F95 and later

Class: Elemental function

Syntax: Y = FRACTION(X)

Arguments:

   X   The type of the argument shall be a REAL.

Return value:

   The return value is of the same type and kind as the argument. The fractional part of the model representation of X is returned; it is X * RADIX(X)**(-
   EXPONENT(X)).

Example:

```
program test_fraction
  real :: x
  x = 178.1387e-4
  print *, fraction(x), x * radix(x)**(-exponent(x))
end program test_fraction
```

6.79 FREE — Frees memory

Description:

   Frees memory previously allocated by MALLOC(). The FREE intrinsic is an extension intended to be used with Cray pointers, and is provided in GNU Fortran
   to allow user to compile legacy code. For new code using Fortran 95 pointers,
   the memory de-allocation intrinsic is DEALLOCATE.

Standard: GNU extension

Class: Subroutine

Syntax: CALL FREE(PTR)

Arguments:

   PTR   The type shall be INTEGER. It represents the location of the
                          memory that should be de-allocated.

Return value:

   None

Example: See MALLOC for an example.

See also: Section 6.141 [MALLOC], page 116

6.80 FSEEK — Low level file positioning subroutine

Description:

Moves *UNIT* to the specified *OFFSET*. If *WHENCE* is set to 0, the *OFFSET* is taken as an absolute value SEEK_SET, if set to 1, *OFFSET* is taken to be relative to the current position SEEK_CUR, and if set to 2 relative to the end of the file SEEK_END. On error, *STATUS* is set to a nonzero value. If *STATUS* the seek fails silently.

This intrinsic routine is not fully backwards compatible with g77. In g77, the FSEEK takes a statement label instead of a *STATUS* variable. If FSEEK is used in old code, change

```
CALL FSEEK(UNIT, OFFSET, WHENCE, *label)
```

to

```
INTEGER :: status
CALL FSEEK(UNIT, OFFSET, WHENCE, status)
IF (status /= 0) GOTO label
```

Please note that GNU Fortran provides the Fortran 2003 Stream facility. Programmers should consider the use of new stream IO feature in new code for future portability. See also Chapter 4 [Fortran 2003 status], page 25.

Standard: GNU extension

Class: Subroutine

Syntax: CALL FSEEK(UNIT, OFFSET, WHENCE[, STATUS])

Arguments:

UNIT	Shall be a scalar of type INTEGER.
OFFSET	Shall be a scalar of type INTEGER.
WHENCE	Shall be a scalar of type INTEGER. Its value shall be either 0, 1 or 2.
STATUS	(Optional) shall be a scalar of type INTEGER(4).

Example:

```
PROGRAM test_fseek
  INTEGER, PARAMETER :: SEEK_SET = 0, SEEK_CUR = 1, SEEK_END = 2
  INTEGER :: fd, offset, ierr

  ierr   = 0
  offset = 5
  fd     = 10

  OPEN(UNIT=fd, FILE="fseek.test")
  CALL FSEEK(fd, offset, SEEK_SET, ierr)  ! move to OFFSET
  print *, FTELL(fd), ierr

  CALL FSEEK(fd, 0, SEEK_END, ierr)        ! move to end
  print *, FTELL(fd), ierr

  CALL FSEEK(fd, 0, SEEK_SET, ierr)        ! move to beginning
  print *, FTELL(fd), ierr

  CLOSE(UNIT=fd)
END PROGRAM
```

See also: Section 6.82 [FTELL], page 86

6.81 FSTAT — Get file status

Description:

FSTAT is identical to Section 6.201 [STAT], page 149, except that information about an already opened file is obtained.

The elements in BUFF are the same as described by Section 6.201 [STAT], page 149.

This intrinsic is provided in both subroutine and function forms; however, only one form can be used in any given program unit.

Standard: GNU extension

Class: Subroutine, function

Syntax: `CALL FSTAT(UNIT, BUFF [, STATUS])`

Arguments:

UNIT	An open I/O unit number of type INTEGER.
BUFF	The type shall be INTEGER(4), DIMENSION(13).
STATUS	(Optional) status flag of type INTEGER(4). Returns 0 on success and a system specific error code otherwise.

Example: See Section 6.201 [STAT], page 149 for an example.

See also: To stat a link: Section 6.139 [LSTAT], page 115, to stat a file: Section 6.201 [STAT], page 149

6.82 FTELL — Current stream position

Description:

Retrieves the current position within an open file.

This intrinsic is provided in both subroutine and function forms; however, only one form can be used in any given program unit.

Standard: GNU extension

Class: Subroutine, function

Syntax:

```
CALL FTELL(UNIT, OFFSET)
OFFSET = FTELL(UNIT)
```

Arguments:

OFFSET	Shall of type INTEGER.
UNIT	Shall of type INTEGER.

Return value:

In either syntax, *OFFSET* is set to the current offset of unit number *UNIT*, or to -1 if the unit is not currently open.

Example:

```
PROGRAM test_ftell
  INTEGER :: i
  OPEN(10, FILE="temp.dat")
  CALL ftell(10,i)
  WRITE(*,*) i
END PROGRAM
```

See also: Section 6.80 [FSEEK], page 85

6.83 GAMMA — Gamma function

Description:

GAMMA(X) computes Gamma (Γ) of X. For positive, integer values of X the Gamma function simplifies to the factorial function $\Gamma(x) = (x - 1)!$.

$$\Gamma(x) = \int_0^\infty t^{x-1}\mathrm{e}^{-t}\,\mathrm{d}t$$

Standard: GNU Extension

Class: Elemental function

Syntax: X = GAMMA(X)

Arguments:

X   Shall be of type REAL and neither zero nor a negative integer.

Return value:

The return value is of type REAL of the same kind as X.

Example:

```
program test_gamma
  real :: x = 1.0
  x = gamma(x) ! returns 1.0
end program test_gamma
```

Specific names:

Name	Argument	Return type	Standard
GAMMA(X)	REAL(4) X	REAL(4)	GNU Extension
DGAMMA(X)	REAL(8) X	REAL(8)	GNU Extension

See also: Logarithm of the Gamma function: Section 6.126 [LGAMMA], page 108

6.84 GERROR — Get last system error message

Description:

Returns the system error message corresponding to the last system error. This resembles the functionality of strerror(3) in C.

Standard: GNU extension

Class: Subroutine

Syntax: CALL GERROR(RESULT)

Arguments:

RESULT   Shall of type CHARACTER(*).

Example:

```
PROGRAM test_gerror
  CHARACTER(len=100) :: msg
  CALL gerror(msg)
  WRITE(*,*) msg
END PROGRAM
```

See also: Section 6.107 [IERRNO], page 99, Section 6.165 [PERROR], page 130

6.85 GETARG — Get command line arguments

Description:

Retrieve the Nth argument that was passed on the command line when the containing program was invoked.

This intrinsic routine is provided for backwards compatibility with GNU Fortran 77. In new code, programmers should consider the use of the Section 6.87 [GET_COMMAND_ARGUMENT], page 89 intrinsic defined by the Fortran 2003 standard.

Standard: GNU extension

Class: Subroutine

Syntax: CALL GETARG(POS, VALUE)

Arguments:

POS   Shall be of type INTEGER and not wider than the default integer kind; $POS \geq 0$

VALUE   Shall be of type CHARACTER(*).

Return value:

After GETARG returns, the *VALUE* argument holds the *POS*th command line argument. If *VALUE* can not hold the argument, it is truncated to fit the length of *VALUE*. If there are less than *POS* arguments specified at the command line, *VALUE* will be filled with blanks. If *POS* = 0, *VALUE* is set to the name of the program (on systems that support this feature).

Example:

```
PROGRAM test_getarg
  INTEGER :: i
  CHARACTER(len=32) :: arg

  DO i = 1, iargc()
    CALL getarg(i, arg)
    WRITE (*,*) arg
  END DO
END PROGRAM
```

See also: GNU Fortran 77 compatibility function: Section 6.100 [IARGC], page 96

F2003 functions and subroutines: Section 6.86 [GET_COMMAND], page 89, Section 6.87 [GET_COMMAND_ARGUMENT], page 89, Section 6.42 [COMMAND_ARGUMENT_COUNT], page 62

6.86 GET_COMMAND — Get the entire command line

Description:

Retrieve the entire command line that was used to invoke the program.

Standard: F2003

Class: Subroutine

Syntax: CALL GET_COMMAND(CMD)

Arguments:

CMD   Shall be of type CHARACTER(*).

Return value:

Stores the entire command line that was used to invoke the program in *ARG*.
If *ARG* is not large enough, the command will be truncated.

Example:

```
PROGRAM test_get_command
  CHARACTER(len=255) :: cmd
  CALL get_command(cmd)
  WRITE (*,*) TRIM(cmd)
END PROGRAM
```

See also: Section 6.87 [GET_COMMAND_ARGUMENT], page 89, Section 6.42 [COM-
MAND_ARGUMENT_COUNT], page 62

6.87 GET_COMMAND_ARGUMENT — Get command line arguments

Description:

Retrieve the Nth argument that was passed on the command line when the
containing program was invoked.

Standard: F2003

Class: Subroutine

Syntax: CALL GET_COMMAND_ARGUMENT(N, ARG)

Arguments:

N   Shall be of type INTEGER(4), $N \geq 0$
ARG   Shall be of type CHARACTER(*).

Return value:

After GET_COMMAND_ARGUMENT returns, the *ARG* argument holds the Nth command line argument. If *ARG* can not hold the argument, it is truncated to fit
the length of *ARG*. If there are less than N arguments specified at the command
line, *ARG* will be filled with blanks. If $N = 0$, *ARG* is set to the name of the
program (on systems that support this feature).

Example:

```
PROGRAM test_get_command_argument
  INTEGER :: i
  CHARACTER(len=32) :: arg
```

```
      i = 0
      DO
        CALL get_command_argument(i, arg)
        IF (LEN_TRIM(arg) == 0) EXIT

        WRITE (*,*) TRIM(arg)
        i = i+1
      END DO
    END PROGRAM
```

See also: Section 6.86 [GET_COMMAND], page 89, Section 6.42 [COM-MAND_ARGUMENT_COUNT], page 62

6.88 GETCWD — Get current working directory

Description:

Get current working directory.

This intrinsic is provided in both subroutine and function forms; however, only one form can be used in any given program unit.

Standard: GNU extension

Class: Subroutine, function

Syntax: CALL GETCWD(CWD [, STATUS])

Arguments:

CWD	The type shall be CHARACTER(*).
STATUS	(Optional) status flag. Returns 0 on success, a system specific and nonzero error code otherwise.

Example:

```
    PROGRAM test_getcwd
      CHARACTER(len=255) :: cwd
      CALL getcwd(cwd)
      WRITE(*,*) TRIM(cwd)
    END PROGRAM
```

See also: Section 6.39 [CHDIR], page 59

6.89 GETENV — Get an environmental variable

Description:

Get the *VALUE* of the environmental variable *ENVVAR*.

This intrinsic routine is provided for backwards compatibility with GNU Fortran 77. In new code, programmers should consider the use of the Section 6.90 [GET_ENVIRONMENT_VARIABLE], page 91 intrinsic defined by the Fortran 2003 standard.

Standard: GNU extension

Class: Subroutine

Syntax: CALL GETENV(ENVVAR, VALUE)

Arguments:

ENVVAR	Shall be of type CHARACTER(*).
VALUE	Shall be of type CHARACTER(*).

Return value:

Stores the value of *ENVVAR* in *VALUE*. If *VALUE* is not large enough to hold the data, it is truncated. If *ENVVAR* is not set, *VALUE* will be filled with blanks.

Example:

```
PROGRAM test_getenv
  CHARACTER(len=255) :: homedir
  CALL getenv("HOME", homedir)
  WRITE (*,*) TRIM(homedir)
END PROGRAM
```

See also: Section 6.90 [GET_ENVIRONMENT_VARIABLE], page 91

6.90 GET_ENVIRONMENT_VARIABLE — Get an environmental variable

Description:

Get the *VALUE* of the environmental variable *ENVVAR*.

Standard: F2003

Class: Subroutine

Syntax: CALL GET_ENVIRONMENT_VARIABLE(ENVVAR, VALUE)

Arguments:

ENVVAR	Shall be of type CHARACTER(*).
VALUE	Shall be of type CHARACTER(*).

Return value:

Stores the value of *ENVVAR* in *VALUE*. If *VALUE* is not large enough to hold the data, it is truncated. If *ENVVAR* is not set, *VALUE* will be filled with blanks.

Example:

```
PROGRAM test_getenv
  CHARACTER(len=255) :: homedir
  CALL get_environment_variable("HOME", homedir)
  WRITE (*,*) TRIM(homedir)
END PROGRAM
```

6.91 GETGID — Group ID function

Description:

Returns the numerical group ID of the current process.

Standard: GNU extension

Class: Function

Syntax: RESULT = GETGID()

Return value:
      The return value of `GETGID` is an `INTEGER` of the default kind.

Example: See `GETPID` for an example.

See also: Section 6.93 [GETPID], page 92, Section 6.94 [GETUID], page 93

6.92 `GETLOG` — Get login name

Description:
      Gets the username under which the program is running.

Standard: GNU extension

Class: Subroutine

Syntax: `CALL GETLOG(LOGIN)`

Arguments:
      LOGIN   Shall be of type `CHARACTER(*)`.

Return value:
      Stores the current user name in *LOGIN*. (On systems where POSIX functions
      `geteuid` and `getpwuid` are not available, and the `getlogin` function is not
      implemented either, this will return a blank string.)

Example:

```
PROGRAM TEST_GETLOG
  CHARACTER(32) :: login
  CALL GETLOG(login)
  WRITE(*,*) login
END PROGRAM
```

See also: Section 6.94 [GETUID], page 93

6.93 `GETPID` — Process ID function

Description:
      Returns the numerical process identifier of the current process.

Standard: GNU extension

Class: Function

Syntax: `RESULT = GETPID()`

Return value:
      The return value of `GETPID` is an `INTEGER` of the default kind.

Example:

```
program info
  print *, "The current process ID is ", getpid()
  print *, "Your numerical user ID is ", getuid()
  print *, "Your numerical group ID is ", getgid()
end program info
```

See also: Section 6.91 [GETGID], page 91, Section 6.94 [GETUID], page 93

6.94 GETUID — User ID function

Description:

Returns the numerical user ID of the current process.

Standard: GNU extension

Class: Function

Syntax: RESULT = GETUID()

Return value:

The return value of GETUID is an INTEGER of the default kind.

Example: See GETPID for an example.

See also: Section 6.93 [GETPID], page 92, Section 6.92 [GETLOG], page 92

6.95 GMTIME — Convert time to GMT info

Description:

Given a system time value *STIME* (as provided by the TIME8() intrinsic), fills *TARRAY* with values extracted from it appropriate to the UTC time zone (Universal Coordinated Time, also known in some countries as GMT, Greenwich Mean Time), using gmtime(3).

Standard: GNU extension

Class: Subroutine

Syntax: CALL GMTIME(STIME, TARRAY)

Arguments:

STIME   An INTEGER(*) scalar expression corresponding to a system time, with INTENT(IN).

TARRAY   A default INTEGER array with 9 elements, with INTENT(OUT).

Return value:

The elements of *TARRAY* are assigned as follows:

1. Seconds after the minute, range 0–59 or 0–61 to allow for leap seconds

2. Minutes after the hour, range 0–59

3. Hours past midnight, range 0–23

4. Day of month, range 0–31

5. Number of months since January, range 0–12

6. Years since 1900

7. Number of days since Sunday, range 0–6

8. Days since January 1

9. Daylight savings indicator: positive if daylight savings is in effect, zero if not, and negative if the information is not available.

See also: Section 6.50 [CTIME], page 66, Section 6.140 [LTIME], page 116, Section 6.208 [TIME], page 154, Section 6.209 [TIME8], page 155

6.96 HOSTNM — Get system host name

Description:

Retrieves the host name of the system on which the program is running.

This intrinsic is provided in both subroutine and function forms; however, only one form can be used in any given program unit.

Standard: GNU extension

Class: Subroutine, function

Syntax:

```
CALL HOSTNM(NAME[, STATUS])
STATUS = HOSTNM(NAME)
```

Arguments:

NAME	Shall of type CHARACTER(*).
STATUS	(Optional) status flag of type INTEGER. Returns 0 on success, or a system specific error code otherwise.

Return value:

In either syntax, *NAME* is set to the current hostname if it can be obtained, or to a blank string otherwise.

6.97 HUGE — Largest number of a kind

Description:

HUGE(X) returns the largest number that is not an infinity in the model of the type of X.

Standard: F95 and later

Class: Inquiry function

Syntax: RESULT = HUGE(X)

Arguments:

X	Shall be of type REAL or INTEGER.

Return value:

The return value is of the same type and kind as *X*

Example:

```
program test_huge_tiny
  print *, huge(0), huge(0.0), huge(0.0d0)
  print *, tiny(0.0), tiny(0.0d0)
end program test_huge_tiny
```

6.98 IACHAR — Code in ASCII collating sequence

Description:

IACHAR(C) returns the code for the ASCII character in the first character position of C.

Standard: F95 and later

Class: Elemental function

Syntax: `RESULT = IACHAR(C [, KIND])`

Arguments:

        C   Shall be a scalar `CHARACTER`, with `INTENT(IN)`

        KIND   (Optional) An `INTEGER` initialization expression indicating the kind parameter of the result.

Return value:

The return value is of type `INTEGER` and of kind *KIND*. If *KIND* is absent, the return value is of default integer kind.

Example:

```
program test_iachar
  integer i
  i = iachar(' ')
end program test_iachar
```

Note: See Section 6.104 [ICHAR], page 97 for a discussion of converting between numerical values and formatted string representations.

See also: Section 6.5 [ACHAR], page 39, Section 6.38 [CHAR], page 59, Section 6.104 [ICHAR], page 97

6.99 `IAND` — Bitwise logical and

Description:

Bitwise logical `AND`.

Standard: F95 and later

Class: Elemental function

Syntax: `RESULT = IAND(I, J)`

Arguments:

        I   The type shall be `INTEGER(*)`.

        J   The type shall be `INTEGER(*)`, of the same kind as *I*. (As a GNU extension, different kinds are also permitted.)

Return value:

The return type is `INTEGER(*)`, of the same kind as the arguments. (If the argument kinds differ, it is of the same kind as the larger argument.)

Example:

```
PROGRAM test_iand
  INTEGER :: a, b
  DATA a / Z'F' /, b / Z'3' /
  WRITE (*,*) IAND(a, b)
END PROGRAM
```

See also: Section 6.112 [IOR], page 102, Section 6.106 [IEOR], page 99, Section 6.102 [IBITS], page 97, Section 6.103 [IBSET], page 97, Section 6.101 [IBCLR], page 96, Section 6.161 [NOT], page 128

6.100 IARGC — Get the number of command line arguments

Description:

IARGC() returns the number of arguments passed on the command line when the containing program was invoked.

This intrinsic routine is provided for backwards compatibility with GNU Fortran 77. In new code, programmers should consider the use of the Section 6.42 [COMMAND_ARGUMENT_COUNT], page 62 intrinsic defined by the Fortran 2003 standard.

Standard: GNU extension

Class: Function

Syntax: RESULT = IARGC()

Arguments:

None.

Return value:

The number of command line arguments, type INTEGER(4).

Example: See Section 6.85 [GETARG], page 88

See also: GNU Fortran 77 compatibility subroutine: Section 6.85 [GETARG], page 88

F2003 functions and subroutines: Section 6.86 [GET_COMMAND], page 89, Section 6.87 [GET_COMMAND_ARGUMENT], page 89, Section 6.42 [COMMAND_ARGUMENT_COUNT], page 62

6.101 IBCLR — Clear bit

Description:

IBCLR returns the value of I with the bit at position POS set to zero.

Standard: F95 and later

Class: Elemental function

Syntax: RESULT = IBCLR(I, POS)

Arguments:

I	The type shall be INTEGER(*).
POS	The type shall be INTEGER(*).

Return value:

The return value is of type INTEGER(*) and of the same kind as I.

See also: Section 6.102 [IBITS], page 97, Section 6.103 [IBSET], page 97, Section 6.99 [IAND], page 95, Section 6.112 [IOR], page 102, Section 6.106 [IEOR], page 99, Section 6.157 [MVBITS], page 126

6.102 IBITS — Bit extraction

Description:

IBITS extracts a field of length *LEN* from *I*, starting from bit position *POS* and extending left for *LEN* bits. The result is right-justified and the remaining bits are zeroed. The value of POS+LEN must be less than or equal to the value BIT_SIZE(I).

Standard: F95 and later

Class: Elemental function

Syntax: RESULT = IBITS(I, POS, LEN)

Arguments:

I	The type shall be INTEGER(*).
POS	The type shall be INTEGER(*).
LEN	The type shall be INTEGER(*).

Return value:

The return value is of type INTEGER(*) and of the same kind as *I*.

See also: Section 6.30 [BIT_SIZE], page 54, Section 6.101 [IBCLR], page 96, Section 6.103 [IBSET], page 97, Section 6.99 [IAND], page 95, Section 6.112 [IOR], page 102, Section 6.106 [IEOR], page 99

6.103 IBSET — Set bit

Description:

IBSET returns the value of *I* with the bit at position *POS* set to one.

Standard: F95 and later

Class: Elemental function

Syntax: RESULT = IBSET(I, POS)

Arguments:

I	The type shall be INTEGER(*).
POS	The type shall be INTEGER(*).

Return value:

The return value is of type INTEGER(*) and of the same kind as *I*.

See also: Section 6.101 [IBCLR], page 96, Section 6.102 [IBITS], page 97, Section 6.99 [IAND], page 95, Section 6.112 [IOR], page 102, Section 6.106 [IEOR], page 99, Section 6.157 [MVBITS], page 126

6.104 ICHAR — Character-to-integer conversion function

Description:

ICHAR(C) returns the code for the character in the first character position of C in the system's native character set. The correspondence between characters and their codes is not necessarily the same across different GNU Fortran implementations.

Standard: F95 and later

Class: Elemental function

Syntax: `RESULT = ICHAR(C [, KIND])`

Arguments:

C	Shall be a scalar `CHARACTER`, with `INTENT(IN)`
KIND	(Optional) An `INTEGER` initialization expression indicating the kind parameter of the result.

Return value:

The return value is of type `INTEGER` and of kind *KIND*. If *KIND* is absent, the return value is of default integer kind.

Example:

```
program test_ichar
  integer i
  i = ichar(' ')
end program test_ichar
```

Note: No intrinsic exists to convert between a numeric value and a formatted character string representation – for instance, given the `CHARACTER` value `'154'`, obtaining an `INTEGER` or `REAL` value with the value 154, or vice versa. Instead, this functionality is provided by internal-file I/O, as in the following example:

```
program read_val
  integer value
  character(len=10) string, string2
  string = '154'

  ! Convert a string to a numeric value
  read (string,'(I10)') value
  print *, value

  ! Convert a value to a formatted string
  write (string2,'(I10)') value
  print *, string2
end program read_val
```

See also: Section 6.5 [ACHAR], page 39, Section 6.38 [CHAR], page 59, Section 6.98 [IACHAR], page 94

6.105 IDATE — Get current local time subroutine (day/month/year)

Description:

IDATE(TARRAY) Fills *TARRAY* with the numerical values at the current local time. The day (in the range 1-31), month (in the range 1-12), and year appear in elements 1, 2, and 3 of *TARRAY*, respectively. The year has four significant digits.

Standard: GNU extension

Class: Subroutine

Syntax: `CALL IDATE(TARRAY)`

Arguments:

      TARRAY   The type shall be `INTEGER, DIMENSION(3)` and the kind shall
                             be the default integer kind.

Return value:

      Does not return.

Example:

```
program test_idate
  integer, dimension(3) :: tarray
  call idate(tarray)
  print *, tarray(1)
  print *, tarray(2)
  print *, tarray(3)
end program test_idate
```

6.106 `IEOR` — Bitwise logical exclusive or

Description:

      `IEOR` returns the bitwise boolean exclusive-OR of *I* and *J*.

Standard: F95 and later

Class: Elemental function

Syntax: `RESULT = IEOR(I, J)`

Arguments:

      I   The type shall be `INTEGER(*)`.
      J   The type shall be `INTEGER(*)`, of the same kind as *I*. (As a
                      GNU extension, different kinds are also permitted.)

Return value:

      The return type is `INTEGER(*)`, of the same kind as the arguments. (If the
      argument kinds differ, it is of the same kind as the larger argument.)

See also: Section 6.112 [IOR], page 102, Section 6.99 [IAND], page 95, Section 6.102
             [IBITS], page 97, Section 6.103 [IBSET], page 97, Section 6.101 [IBCLR],
             page 96, Section 6.161 [NOT], page 128

6.107 `IERRNO` — Get the last system error number

Description:

      Returns the last system error number, as given by the C `errno()` function.

Standard: GNU extension

Class: Function

Syntax: `RESULT = IERRNO()`

Arguments:

      None.

Return value:

      The return value is of type `INTEGER` and of the default integer kind.

See also: Section 6.165 [PERROR], page 130

6.108 INDEX — Position of a substring within a string

Description:

Returns the position of the start of the first occurrence of string *SUBSTRING* as a substring in *STRING*, counting from one. If *SUBSTRING* is not present in *STRING*, zero is returned. If the *BACK* argument is present and true, the return value is the start of the last occurrence rather than the first.

Standard: F77 and later

Class: Elemental function

Syntax: RESULT = INDEX(STRING, SUBSTRING [, BACK [, KIND]])

Arguments:

STRING	Shall be a scalar CHARACTER(*), with INTENT(IN)
SUBSTRING	Shall be a scalar CHARACTER(*), with INTENT(IN)
BACK	(Optional) Shall be a scalar LOGICAL(*), with INTENT(IN)
KIND	(Optional) An INTEGER initialization expression indicating the kind parameter of the result.

Return value:

The return value is of type INTEGER and of kind *KIND*. If *KIND* is absent, the return value is of default integer kind.

See also: Section 6.182 [SCAN], page 139, Section 6.219 [VERIFY], page 159

6.109 INT — Convert to integer type

Description:

Convert to integer type

Standard: F77 and later

Class: Elemental function

Syntax: RESULT = INT(A [, KIND))

Arguments:

A	Shall be of type INTEGER(*), REAL(*), or COMPLEX(*).
KIND	(Optional) An INTEGER(*) initialization expression indicating the kind parameter of the result.

Return value:

These functions return a INTEGER(*) variable or array under the following rules:

(A)   If A is of type INTEGER(*), INT(A) = A

(B)   If A is of type REAL(*) and $|A| < 1$, INT(A) equals 0. If $|A| \geq 1$, then INT(A) equals the largest integer that does not exceed the range of A and whose sign is the same as the sign of A.

(C)   If A is of type COMPLEX(*), rule B is applied to the real part of A.

Example:

```
program test_int
  integer :: i = 42
  complex :: z = (-3.7, 1.0)
  print *, int(i)
  print *, int(z), int(z,8)
end program
```

Specific names:

Name	Argument	Return type	Standard
IFIX(A)	REAL(4) A	INTEGER	F77 and later
IDINT(A)	REAL(8) A	INTEGER	F77 and later

6.110 INT2 — Convert to 16-bit integer type

Description:

Convert to a KIND=2 integer type. This is equivalent to the standard INT intrinsic with an optional argument of KIND=2, and is only included for backwards compatibility.

The SHORT intrinsic is equivalent to INT2.

Standard: GNU extension.

Class: Elemental function

Syntax: RESULT = INT2(A)

Arguments:

A   Shall be of type INTEGER(*), REAL(*), or COMPLEX(*).

Return value:

The return value is a INTEGER(2) variable.

See also: Section 6.109 [INT], page 100, Section 6.111 [INT8], page 101, Section 6.137 [LONG], page 114

6.111 INT8 — Convert to 64-bit integer type

Description:

Convert to a KIND=8 integer type. This is equivalent to the standard INT intrinsic with an optional argument of KIND=8, and is only included for backwards compatibility.

Standard: GNU extension.

Class: Elemental function

Syntax: RESULT = INT8(A)

Arguments:

A   Shall be of type INTEGER(*), REAL(*), or COMPLEX(*).

Return value:

The return value is a INTEGER(8) variable.

See also: Section 6.109 [INT], page 100, Section 6.110 [INT2], page 101, Section 6.137 [LONG], page 114

6.112 `IOR` — Bitwise logical or

Description:

IOR returns the bitwise boolean inclusive-OR of *I* and *J*.

Standard: F95 and later

Class: Elemental function

Syntax: `RESULT = IOR(I, J)`

Arguments:

    I   The type shall be `INTEGER(*)`.

    J   The type shall be `INTEGER(*)`, of the same kind as *I*. (As a GNU extension, different kinds are also permitted.)

Return value:

The return type is `INTEGER(*)`, of the same kind as the arguments. (If the argument kinds differ, it is of the same kind as the larger argument.)

See also: Section 6.106 [IEOR], page 99, Section 6.99 [IAND], page 95, Section 6.102 [IBITS], page 97, Section 6.103 [IBSET], page 97, Section 6.101 [IBCLR], page 96, Section 6.161 [NOT], page 128

6.113 `IRAND` — Integer pseudo-random number

Description:

IRAND(FLAG) returns a pseudo-random number from a uniform distribution between 0 and a system-dependent limit (which is in most cases 2147483647). If *FLAG* is 0, the next number in the current sequence is returned; if *FLAG* is 1, the generator is restarted by `CALL SRAND(0)`; if *FLAG* has any other value, it is used as a new seed with `SRAND`.

This intrinsic routine is provided for backwards compatibility with GNU Fortran 77. It implements a simple modulo generator as provided by g77. For new code, one should consider the use of Section 6.172 [RANDOM_NUMBER], page 133 as it implements a superior algorithm.

Standard: GNU extension

Class: Function

Syntax: `RESULT = IRAND(FLAG)`

Arguments:

    FLAG   Shall be a scalar `INTEGER` of kind 4.

Return value:

The return value is of `INTEGER(kind=4)` type.

Example:

```
program test_irand
  integer,parameter :: seed = 86456

  call srand(seed)
  print *, irand(), irand(), irand(), irand()
  print *, irand(seed), irand(), irand(), irand()
end program test_irand
```

6.114 IS_IOSTAT_END — Test for end-of-file value

Description:

IS_IOSTAT_END tests whether an variable has the value of the I/O status "end of file". The function is equivalent to comparing the variable with the IOSTAT_END parameter of the intrinsic module ISO_FORTRAN_ENV.

Standard: Fortran 2003.

Class: Elemental function

Syntax: RESULT = IS_IOSTAT_END(I)

Arguments:

I   Shall be of the type INTEGER.

Return value:

Returns a LOGICAL of the default kind, which .TRUE. if *I* has the value which indicates an end of file condition for IOSTAT= specifiers, and is .FALSE. otherwise.

Example:

```
PROGRAM iostat
  IMPLICIT NONE
  INTEGER :: stat, i
  OPEN(88, FILE='test.dat')
  READ(88, *, IOSTAT=stat) i
  IF(IS_IOSTAT_END(stat)) STOP 'END OF FILE'
END PROGRAM
```

6.115 IS_IOSTAT_EOR — Test for end-of-record value

Description:

IS_IOSTAT_EOR tests whether an variable has the value of the I/O status "end of record". The function is equivalent to comparing the variable with the IOSTAT_EOR parameter of the intrinsic module ISO_FORTRAN_ENV.

Standard: Fortran 2003.

Class: Elemental function

Syntax: RESULT = IS_IOSTAT_EOR(I)

Arguments:

I   Shall be of the type INTEGER.

Return value:

Returns a LOGICAL of the default kind, which .TRUE. if *I* has the value which indicates an end of file condition for IOSTAT= specifiers, and is .FALSE. otherwise.

Example:

```
PROGRAM iostat
  IMPLICIT NONE
  INTEGER :: stat, i(50)
  OPEN(88, FILE='test.dat', FORM='UNFORMATTED')
```

```
READ(88, IOSTAT=stat) i
IF(IS_IOSTAT_EOR(stat)) STOP 'END OF RECORD'
END PROGRAM
```

6.116 ISATTY — Whether a unit is a terminal device.

Description:

Determine whether a unit is connected to a terminal device.

Standard: GNU extension.

Class: Function

Syntax: RESULT = ISATTY(UNIT)

Arguments:

UNIT   Shall be a scalar INTEGER(*).

Return value:

Returns .TRUE. if the *UNIT* is connected to a terminal device, .FALSE. otherwise.

Example:

```
PROGRAM test_isatty
  INTEGER(kind=1) :: unit
  DO unit = 1, 10
    write(*,*) isatty(unit=unit)
  END DO
END PROGRAM
```

See also: Section 6.214 [TTYNAM], page 157

6.117 ISHFT — Shift bits

Description:

ISHFT returns a value corresponding to *I* with all of the bits shifted *SHIFT* places. A value of *SHIFT* greater than zero corresponds to a left shift, a value of zero corresponds to no shift, and a value less than zero corresponds to a right shift. If the absolute value of *SHIFT* is greater than BIT_SIZE(I), the value is undefined. Bits shifted out from the left end or right end are lost; zeros are shifted in from the opposite end.

Standard: F95 and later

Class: Elemental function

Syntax: RESULT = ISHFT(I, SHIFT)

Arguments:

I   The type shall be INTEGER(*).
SHIFT   The type shall be INTEGER(*).

Return value:

The return value is of type INTEGER(*) and of the same kind as *I*.

See also: Section 6.118 [ISHFTC], page 105

6.118 ISHFTC — Shift bits circularly

Description:

ISHFTC returns a value corresponding to *I* with the rightmost *SIZE* bits shifted circularly *SHIFT* places; that is, bits shifted out one end are shifted into the opposite end. A value of *SHIFT* greater than zero corresponds to a left shift, a value of zero corresponds to no shift, and a value less than zero corresponds to a right shift. The absolute value of *SHIFT* must be less than *SIZE*. If the *SIZE* argument is omitted, it is taken to be equivalent to BIT_SIZE(I).

Standard: F95 and later

Class: Elemental function

Syntax: RESULT = ISHFTC(I, SHIFT [, SIZE])

Arguments:

I	The type shall be INTEGER(*).
SHIFT	The type shall be INTEGER(*).
SIZE	(Optional) The type shall be INTEGER(*); the value must be greater than zero and less than or equal to BIT_SIZE(I).

Return value:

The return value is of type INTEGER(*) and of the same kind as *I*.

See also: Section 6.117 [ISHFT], page 104

6.119 ISNAN — Test for a NaN

Description:

ISNAN tests whether a floating-point value is an IEEE Not-a-Number (NaN).

Standard: GNU extension

Class: Elemental function

Syntax: ISNAN(X)

Arguments:

X	Variable of the type REAL.

Return value:

Returns a default-kind LOGICAL. The returned value is TRUE if *X* is a NaN and FALSE otherwise.

Example:

```
program test_nan
  implicit none
  real :: x
  x = -1.0
  x = sqrt(x)
  if (isnan(x)) stop '"x" is a NaN'
end program test_nan
```

6.120 ITIME — Get current local time subroutine (hour/minutes/seconds)

Description:

IDATE(TARRAY) Fills *TARRAY* with the numerical values at the current local time. The hour (in the range 1-24), minute (in the range 1-60), and seconds (in the range 1-60) appear in elements 1, 2, and 3 of *TARRAY*, respectively.

Standard: GNU extension

Class: Subroutine

Syntax: CALL ITIME(TARRAY)

Arguments:

TARRAY   The type shall be INTEGER, DIMENSION(3) and the kind shall be the default integer kind.

Return value:

Does not return.

Example:

```
program test_itime
  integer, dimension(3) :: tarray
  call itime(tarray)
  print *, tarray(1)
  print *, tarray(2)
  print *, tarray(3)
end program test_itime
```

6.121 KILL — Send a signal to a process

Description:
Standard: Sends the signal specified by *SIGNAL* to the process *PID*. See kill(2).

This intrinsic is provided in both subroutine and function forms; however, only one form can be used in any given program unit.

Class: Subroutine, function

Syntax: CALL KILL(PID, SIGNAL [, STATUS])

Arguments:

PID	Shall be a scalar INTEGER, with INTENT(IN)
SIGNAL	Shall be a scalar INTEGER, with INTENT(IN)
STATUS	(Optional) status flag of type INTEGER(4) or INTEGER(8). Returns 0 on success, or a system-specific error code otherwise.

See also: Section 6.2 [ABORT], page 37, Section 6.66 [EXIT], page 77

6.122 KIND — Kind of an entity

Description:

KIND(X) returns the kind value of the entity *X*.

Standard: F95 and later

Class: Inquiry function

Syntax: K = KIND(X)

Arguments:

    X   Shall be of type LOGICAL, INTEGER, REAL, COMPLEX or CHARACTER.

Return value:

The return value is a scalar of type INTEGER and of the default integer kind.

Example:

```
program test_kind
  integer,parameter :: kc = kind(' ')
  integer,parameter :: kl = kind(.true.)

  print *, "The default character kind is ", kc
  print *, "The default logical kind is ", kl
end program test_kind
```

6.123 LBOUND — Lower dimension bounds of an array

Description:

Returns the lower bounds of an array, or a single lower bound along the *DIM* dimension.

Standard: F95 and later

Class: Inquiry function

Syntax: RESULT = LBOUND(ARRAY [, DIM [, KIND]])

Arguments:

  ARRAY   Shall be an array, of any type.
  DIM   (Optional) Shall be a scalar INTEGER(*).
  KIND   (Optional) An INTEGER initialization expression indicating the kind parameter of the result.

Return value:

The return value is of type INTEGER and of kind *KIND*. If *KIND* is absent, the return value is of default integer kind. If *DIM* is absent, the result is an array of the lower bounds of *ARRAY*. If *DIM* is present, the result is a scalar corresponding to the lower bound of the array along that dimension. If *ARRAY* is an expression rather than a whole array or array structure component, or if it has a zero extent along the relevant dimension, the lower bound is taken to be 1.

See also: Section 6.215 [UBOUND], page 158

6.124 LEN — Length of a character entity

Description:

Returns the length of a character string. If *STRING* is an array, the length of an element of *STRING* is returned. Note that *STRING* need not be defined when this intrinsic is invoked, since only the length, not the content, of *STRING* is needed.

Standard: F77 and later

Class: Inquiry function

Syntax: `L = LEN(STRING [, KIND])`

Arguments:

STRING	Shall be a scalar or array of type `CHARACTER(*)`, with `INTENT(IN)`
KIND	(Optional) An `INTEGER` initialization expression indicating the kind parameter of the result.

Return value:

The return value is of type `INTEGER` and of kind *KIND*. If *KIND* is absent, the return value is of default integer kind.

See also: Section 6.125 [LEN_TRIM], page 108, Section 6.8 [ADJUSTL], page 41, Section 6.9 [ADJUSTR], page 41

6.125 `LEN_TRIM` — Length of a character entity without trailing blank characters

Description:

Returns the length of a character string, ignoring any trailing blanks.

Standard: F95 and later

Class: Elemental function

Syntax: `RESULT = LEN_TRIM(STRING [, KIND])`

Arguments:

STRING	Shall be a scalar of type `CHARACTER(*)`, with `INTENT(IN)`
KIND	(Optional) An `INTEGER` initialization expression indicating the kind parameter of the result.

Return value:

The return value is of type `INTEGER` and of kind *KIND*. If *KIND* is absent, the return value is of default integer kind.

See also: Section 6.124 [LEN], page 107, Section 6.8 [ADJUSTL], page 41, Section 6.9 [ADJUSTR], page 41

6.126 `LGAMMA` — Logarithm of the Gamma function

Description:

`GAMMA(X)` computes the natural logrithm of the absolute value of the Gamma (Γ) function.

Standard: GNU Extension

Class: Elemental function

Syntax: `X = LGAMMA(X)`

Arguments:

X   Shall be of type `REAL` and neither zero nor a negative integer.

Return value:

The return value is of type `REAL` of the same kind as *X*.

Example:

```
program test_log_gamma
  real :: x = 1.0
  x = lgamma(x) ! returns 0.0
end program test_log_gamma
```

Specific names:

Name	Argument	Return type	Standard
LGAMMA(X)	REAL(4) X	REAL(4)	GNU Extension
ALGAMA(X)	REAL(4) X	REAL(4)	GNU Extension
DLGAMA(X)	REAL(8) X	REAL(8)	GNU Extension

See also: Gamma function: Section 6.83 [GAMMA], page 87

6.127 LGE — Lexical greater than or equal

Description:

Determines whether one string is lexically greater than or equal to another string, where the two strings are interpreted as containing ASCII character codes. If the String A and String B are not the same length, the shorter is compared as if spaces were appended to it to form a value that has the same length as the longer.

In general, the lexical comparison intrinsics LGE, LGT, LLE, and LLT differ from the corresponding intrinsic operators .GE., .GT., .LE., and .LT., in that the latter use the processor's character ordering (which is not ASCII on some targets), whereas the former always use the ASCII ordering.

Standard: F77 and later

Class: Elemental function

Syntax: `RESULT = LGE(STRING_A, STRING_B)`

Arguments:

STRING_A   Shall be of default `CHARACTER` type.
STRING_B   Shall be of default `CHARACTER` type.

Return value:

Returns `.TRUE.` if STRING_A >= STRING_B, and `.FALSE.` otherwise, based on the ASCII ordering.

See also: Section 6.128 [LGT], page 110, Section 6.130 [LLE], page 111, Section 6.131 [LLT], page 111

6.128 LGT — Lexical greater than

Description:

Determines whether one string is lexically greater than another string, where the two strings are interpreted as containing ASCII character codes. If the String A and String B are not the same length, the shorter is compared as if spaces were appended to it to form a value that has the same length as the longer.

In general, the lexical comparison intrinsics LGE, LGT, LLE, and LLT differ from the corresponding intrinsic operators .GE., .GT., .LE., and .LT., in that the latter use the processor's character ordering (which is not ASCII on some targets), whereas the former always use the ASCII ordering.

Standard: F77 and later

Class: Elemental function

Syntax: RESULT = LGT(STRING_A, STRING_B)

Arguments:

STRING_A	Shall be of default CHARACTER type.
STRING_B	Shall be of default CHARACTER type.

Return value:

Returns .TRUE. if STRING_A > STRING_B, and .FALSE. otherwise, based on the ASCII ordering.

See also: Section 6.127 [LGE], page 109, Section 6.130 [LLE], page 111, Section 6.131 [LLT], page 111

6.129 LINK — Create a hard link

Description:

Makes a (hard) link from file *PATH1* to *PATH2*. A null character (CHAR(0)) can be used to mark the end of the names in *PATH1* and *PATH2*; otherwise, trailing blanks in the file names are ignored. If the *STATUS* argument is supplied, it contains 0 on success or a nonzero error code upon return; see link(2).

This intrinsic is provided in both subroutine and function forms; however, only one form can be used in any given program unit.

Standard: GNU extension

Class: Subroutine, function

Syntax:

CALL LINK(PATH1, PATH2 [, STATUS])
STATUS = LINK(PATH1, PATH2)

Arguments:

PATH1	Shall be of default CHARACTER type.
PATH2	Shall be of default CHARACTER type.
STATUS	(Optional) Shall be of default INTEGER type.

See also: Section 6.203 [SYMLNK], page 151, Section 6.217 [UNLINK], page 158

6.130 LLE — Lexical less than or equal

Description:

Determines whether one string is lexically less than or equal to another string, where the two strings are interpreted as containing ASCII character codes. If the String A and String B are not the same length, the shorter is compared as if spaces were appended to it to form a value that has the same length as the longer.

In general, the lexical comparison intrinsics LGE, LGT, LLE, and LLT differ from the corresponding intrinsic operators .GE., .GT., .LE., and .LT., in that the latter use the processor's character ordering (which is not ASCII on some targets), whereas the former always use the ASCII ordering.

Standard: F77 and later

Class: Elemental function

Syntax: RESULT = LLE(STRING_A, STRING_B)

Arguments:

STRING_A   Shall be of default CHARACTER type.
STRING_B   Shall be of default CHARACTER type.

Return value:

Returns .TRUE. if STRING_A <= STRING_B, and .FALSE. otherwise, based on the ASCII ordering.

See also: Section 6.127 [LGE], page 109, Section 6.128 [LGT], page 110, Section 6.131 [LLT], page 111

6.131 LLT — Lexical less than

Description:

Determines whether one string is lexically less than another string, where the two strings are interpreted as containing ASCII character codes. If the String A and String B are not the same length, the shorter is compared as if spaces were appended to it to form a value that has the same length as the longer.

In general, the lexical comparison intrinsics LGE, LGT, LLE, and LLT differ from the corresponding intrinsic operators .GE., .GT., .LE., and .LT., in that the latter use the processor's character ordering (which is not ASCII on some targets), whereas the former always use the ASCII ordering.

Standard: F77 and later

Class: Elemental function

Syntax: RESULT = LLT(STRING_A, STRING_B)

Arguments:

STRING_A   Shall be of default CHARACTER type.
STRING_B   Shall be of default CHARACTER type.

Return value:

Returns .TRUE. if STRING_A < STRING_B, and .FALSE. otherwise, based on the ASCII ordering.

See also: Section 6.127 [LGE], page 109, Section 6.128 [LGT], page 110, Section 6.130 [LLE], page 111

6.132 LNBLNK — Index of the last non-blank character in a string

Description:

Returns the length of a character string, ignoring any trailing blanks. This is identical to the standard LEN_TRIM intrinsic, and is only included for backwards compatibility.

Standard: GNU extension

Class: Elemental function

Syntax: RESULT = LNBLNK(STRING)

Arguments:

STRING   Shall be a scalar of type CHARACTER(*), with INTENT(IN)

Return value:

The return value is of INTEGER(kind=4) type.

See also: Section 6.108 [INDEX intrinsic], page 100, Section 6.125 [LEN_TRIM], page 108

6.133 LOC — Returns the address of a variable

Description:

LOC(X) returns the address of X as an integer.

Standard: GNU extension

Class: Inquiry function

Syntax: RESULT = LOC(X)

Arguments:

X   Variable of any type.

Return value:

The return value is of type INTEGER, with a KIND corresponding to the size (in bytes) of a memory address on the target machine.

Example:

```
program test_loc
  integer :: i
  real :: r
  i = loc(r)
  print *, i
end program test_loc
```

6.134 `LOG` — Logarithm function

Description:

LOG(X) computes the logarithm of *X*.

Standard: F77 and later

Class: Elemental function

Syntax: RESULT = LOG(X)

Arguments:

X   The type shall be REAL(*) or COMPLEX(*).

Return value:

The return value is of type REAL(*) or COMPLEX(*). The kind type parameter is the same as *X*.

Example:

```
program test_log
  real(8) :: x = 1.0_8
  complex :: z = (1.0, 2.0)
  x = log(x)
  z = log(z)
end program test_log
```

Specific names:

Name	Argument	Return type	Standard
ALOG(X)	REAL(4) X	REAL(4)	f95, gnu
DLOG(X)	REAL(8) X	REAL(8)	f95, gnu
CLOG(X)	COMPLEX(4) X	COMPLEX(4)	f95, gnu
ZLOG(X)	COMPLEX(8) X	COMPLEX(8)	f95, gnu
CDLOG(X)	COMPLEX(8) X	COMPLEX(8)	f95, gnu

6.135 `LOG10` — Base 10 logarithm function

Description:

LOG10(X) computes the base 10 logarithm of *X*.

Standard: F77 and later

Class: Elemental function

Syntax: RESULT = LOG10(X)

Arguments:

X   The type shall be REAL(*).

Return value:

The return value is of type REAL(*) or COMPLEX(*). The kind type parameter is the same as *X*.

Example:

```
program test_log10
  real(8) :: x = 10.0_8
  x = log10(x)
end program test_log10
```

Specific names:

Name	Argument	Return type	Standard
ALOG10(X)	REAL(4) X	REAL(4)	F95 and later
DLOG10(X)	REAL(8) X	REAL(8)	F95 and later

6.136 LOGICAL — Convert to logical type

Description:

Converts one kind of LOGICAL variable to another.

Standard: F95 and later

Class: Elemental function

Syntax: RESULT = LOGICAL(L [, KIND])

Arguments:

L   The type shall be LOGICAL(*).

KIND   (Optional) An INTEGER(*) initialization expression indicating the kind parameter of the result.

Return value:

The return value is a LOGICAL value equal to *L*, with a kind corresponding to *KIND*, or of the default logical kind if *KIND* is not given.

See also: Section 6.109 [INT], page 100, Section 6.175 [REAL], page 135, Section 6.41 [CMPLX], page 61

6.137 LONG — Convert to integer type

Description:

Convert to a KIND=4 integer type, which is the same size as a C long integer. This is equivalent to the standard INT intrinsic with an optional argument of KIND=4, and is only included for backwards compatibility.

Standard: GNU extension.

Class: Elemental function

Syntax: RESULT = LONG(A)

Arguments:

A   Shall be of type INTEGER(*), REAL(*), or COMPLEX(*).

Return value:

The return value is a INTEGER(4) variable.

See also: Section 6.109 [INT], page 100, Section 6.110 [INT2], page 101, Section 6.111 [INT8], page 101

6.138 LSHIFT — Left shift bits

Description:

LSHIFT returns a value corresponding to *I* with all of the bits shifted left by *SHIFT* places. If the absolute value of *SHIFT* is greater than BIT_SIZE(I), the value is undefined. Bits shifted out from the left end are lost; zeros are shifted in from the opposite end.

This function has been superseded by the ISHFT intrinsic, which is standard in Fortran 95 and later.

Standard: GNU extension

Class: Elemental function

Syntax: RESULT = LSHIFT(I, SHIFT)

Arguments:

I	The type shall be INTEGER(*).
SHIFT	The type shall be INTEGER(*).

Return value:

The return value is of type INTEGER(*) and of the same kind as *I*.

See also: Section 6.117 [ISHFT], page 104, Section 6.118 [ISHFTC], page 105, Section 6.180 [RSHIFT], page 138

6.139 LSTAT — Get file status

Description:

LSTAT is identical to Section 6.201 [STAT], page 149, except that if path is a symbolic link, then the link itself is statted, not the file that it refers to.

The elements in BUFF are the same as described by Section 6.201 [STAT], page 149.

This intrinsic is provided in both subroutine and function forms; however, only one form can be used in any given program unit.

Standard: GNU extension

Class: Subroutine, function

Syntax: CALL LSTAT(FILE, BUFF [, STATUS])

Arguments:

FILE	The type shall be CHARACTER(*), a valid path within the file system.
BUFF	The type shall be INTEGER(4), DIMENSION(13).
STATUS	(Optional) status flag of type INTEGER(4). Returns 0 on success and a system specific error code otherwise.

Example: See Section 6.201 [STAT], page 149 for an example.

See also: To stat an open file: Section 6.81 [FSTAT], page 86, to stat a file: Section 6.201 [STAT], page 149

6.140 LTIME — Convert time to local time info

Description:

Given a system time value *STIME* (as provided by the `TIME8()` intrinsic), fills *TARRAY* with values extracted from it appropriate to the local time zone using `localtime(3)`.

Standard: GNU extension

Class: Subroutine

Syntax: `CALL LTIME(STIME, TARRAY)`

Arguments:

STIME	An `INTEGER(*)` scalar expression corresponding to a system time, with `INTENT(IN)`.
TARRAY	A default `INTEGER` array with 9 elements, with `INTENT(OUT)`.

Return value:

The elements of *TARRAY* are assigned as follows:

1. Seconds after the minute, range 0–59 or 0–61 to allow for leap seconds
2. Minutes after the hour, range 0–59
3. Hours past midnight, range 0–23
4. Day of month, range 0–31
5. Number of months since January, range 0–12
6. Years since 1900
7. Number of days since Sunday, range 0–6
8. Days since January 1
9. Daylight savings indicator: positive if daylight savings is in effect, zero if not, and negative if the information is not available.

See also: Section 6.50 [CTIME], page 66, Section 6.95 [GMTIME], page 93, Section 6.208 [TIME], page 154, Section 6.209 [TIME8], page 155

6.141 MALLOC — Allocate dynamic memory

Description:

`MALLOC(SIZE)` allocates *SIZE* bytes of dynamic memory and returns the address of the allocated memory. The `MALLOC` intrinsic is an extension intended to be used with Cray pointers, and is provided in GNU Fortran to allow the user to compile legacy code. For new code using Fortran 95 pointers, the memory allocation intrinsic is `ALLOCATE`.

Standard: GNU extension

Class: Function

Syntax: `PTR = MALLOC(SIZE)`

Arguments:

SIZE	The type shall be `INTEGER(*)`.

Return value:

> The return value is of type `INTEGER(K)`, with K such that variables of type `INTEGER(K)` have the same size as C pointers (`sizeof(void *)`).

Example: The following example demonstrates the use of `MALLOC` and `FREE` with Cray pointers. This example is intended to run on 32-bit systems, where the default integer kind is suitable to store pointers; on 64-bit systems, ptr_x would need to be declared as `integer(kind=8)`.

```
program test_malloc
  integer i
  integer ptr_x
  real*8 x(*), z
  pointer(ptr_x,x)

  ptr_x = malloc(20*8)
  do i = 1, 20
    x(i) = sqrt(1.0d0 / i)
  end do
  z = 0
  do i = 1, 20
    z = z + x(i)
    print *, z
  end do
  call free(ptr_x)
end program test_malloc
```

See also: Section 6.79 [FREE], page 84

6.142 MATMUL — matrix multiplication

Description:

> Performs a matrix multiplication on numeric or logical arguments.

Standard: F95 and later

Class: Transformational function

Syntax: `RESULT = MATMUL(MATRIX_A, MATRIX_B)`

Arguments:

> *MATRIX_A*   An array of `INTEGER(*)`, `REAL(*)`, `COMPLEX(*)`, or `LOGICAL(*)` type, with a rank of one or two.
>
> *MATRIX_B*   An array of `INTEGER(*)`, `REAL(*)`, or `COMPLEX(*)` type if *MATRIX_A* is of a numeric type; otherwise, an array of `LOGICAL(*)` type. The rank shall be one or two, and the first (or only) dimension of *MATRIX_B* shall be equal to the last (or only) dimension of *MATRIX_A*.

Return value:

> The matrix product of *MATRIX_A* and *MATRIX_B*. The type and kind of the result follow the usual type and kind promotion rules, as for the `*` or `.AND.` operators.

See also:

6.143 `MAX` — Maximum value of an argument list

Description:

Returns the argument with the largest (most positive) value.

Standard: F77 and later

Class: Elemental function

Syntax: `RESULT = MAX(A1, A2 [, A3 [, ...]]])`

Arguments:

A1	The type shall be `INTEGER(*)` or `REAL(*)`.
A2, A3, ...	An expression of the same type and kind as *A1*. (As a GNU extension, arguments of different kinds are permitted.)

Return value:

The return value corresponds to the maximum value among the arguments, and has the same type and kind as the first argument.

Specific names:

Name	Argument	Return type	Standard
`MAX0(I)`	`INTEGER(4) I`	`INTEGER(4)`	F77 and later
`AMAX0(I)`	`INTEGER(4) I`	`REAL(MAX(X))`	F77 and later
`MAX1(X)`	`REAL(*) X`	`INT(MAX(X))`	F77 and later
`AMAX1(X)`	`REAL(4) X`	`REAL(4)`	F77 and later
`DMAX1(X)`	`REAL(8) X`	`REAL(8)`	F77 and later

See also: Section 6.145 [MAXLOC], page 119 Section 6.146 [MAXVAL], page 119, Section 6.150 [MIN], page 121

6.144 `MAXEXPONENT` — Maximum exponent of a real kind

Description:

`MAXEXPONENT(X)` returns the maximum exponent in the model of the type of `X`.

Standard: F95 and later

Class: Inquiry function

Syntax: `RESULT = MAXEXPONENT(X)`

Arguments:

X	Shall be of type `REAL`.

Return value:

The return value is of type `INTEGER` and of the default integer kind.

Example:

```
program exponents
  real(kind=4) :: x
  real(kind=8) :: y

  print *, minexponent(x), maxexponent(x)
  print *, minexponent(y), maxexponent(y)
end program exponents
```

6.145 MAXLOC — Location of the maximum value within an array

Description:

Determines the location of the element in the array with the maximum value, or, if the *DIM* argument is supplied, determines the locations of the maximum element along each row of the array in the *DIM* direction. If *MASK* is present, only the elements for which *MASK* is .TRUE. are considered. If more than one element in the array has the maximum value, the location returned is that of the first such element in array element order. If the array has zero size, or all of the elements of *MASK* are .FALSE., then the result is an array of zeroes. Similarly, if *DIM* is supplied and all of the elements of *MASK* along a given row are zero, the result value for that row is zero.

Standard: F95 and later

Class: Transformational function

Syntax:

```
RESULT = MAXLOC(ARRAY, DIM [, MASK])
RESULT = MAXLOC(ARRAY [, MASK])
```

Arguments:

ARRAY	Shall be an array of type INTEGER(*), REAL(*), or CHARACTER(*).
DIM	(Optional) Shall be a scalar of type INTEGER(*), with a value between one and the rank of *ARRAY*, inclusive. It may not be an optional dummy argument.
MASK	Shall be an array of type LOGICAL(*), and conformable with *ARRAY*.

Return value:

If *DIM* is absent, the result is a rank-one array with a length equal to the rank of *ARRAY*. If *DIM* is present, the result is an array with a rank one less than the rank of *ARRAY*, and a size corresponding to the size of *ARRAY* with the *DIM* dimension removed. If *DIM* is present and *ARRAY* has a rank of one, the result is a scalar. In all cases, the result is of default INTEGER type.

See also: Section 6.143 [MAX], page 118, Section 6.146 [MAXVAL], page 119

6.146 MAXVAL — Maximum value of an array

Description:

Determines the maximum value of the elements in an array value, or, if the *DIM* argument is supplied, determines the maximum value along each row of the array in the *DIM* direction. If *MASK* is present, only the elements for which *MASK* is .TRUE. are considered. If the array has zero size, or all of the elements of *MASK* are .FALSE., then the result is the most negative number of the type and kind of *ARRAY* if *ARRAY* is numeric, or a string of nulls if *ARRAY* is of character type.

Standard: F95 and later

Class: Transformational function

Syntax:

```
RESULT = MAXVAL(ARRAY, DIM [, MASK])
RESULT = MAXVAL(ARRAY [, MASK])
```

Arguments:

ARRAY	Shall be an array of type `INTEGER(*)`, `REAL(*)`, or `CHARACTER(*)`.
DIM	(Optional) Shall be a scalar of type `INTEGER(*)`, with a value between one and the rank of *ARRAY*, inclusive. It may not be an optional dummy argument.
MASK	Shall be an array of type `LOGICAL(*)`, and conformable with *ARRAY*.

Return value:

If *DIM* is absent, or if *ARRAY* has a rank of one, the result is a scalar. If *DIM* is present, the result is an array with a rank one less than the rank of *ARRAY*, and a size corresponding to the size of *ARRAY* with the *DIM* dimension removed. In all cases, the result is of the same type and kind as *ARRAY*.

See also: Section 6.143 [MAX], page 118, Section 6.145 [MAXLOC], page 119

6.147 `MCLOCK` — **Time function**

Description:

Returns the number of clock ticks since the start of the process, based on the UNIX function `clock(3)`.

This intrinsic is not fully portable, such as to systems with 32-bit `INTEGER` types but supporting times wider than 32 bits. Therefore, the values returned by this intrinsic might be, or become, negative, or numerically less than previous values, during a single run of the compiled program.

Standard: GNU extension

Class: Function

Syntax: `RESULT = MCLOCK()`

Return value:

The return value is a scalar of type `INTEGER(4)`, equal to the number of clock ticks since the start of the process, or `-1` if the system does not support `clock(3)`.

See also: Section 6.50 [CTIME], page 66, Section 6.95 [GMTIME], page 93, Section 6.140 [LTIME], page 116, Section 6.147 [MCLOCK], page 120, Section 6.208 [TIME], page 154

6.148 `MCLOCK8` — **Time function (64-bit)**

Description:

Returns the number of clock ticks since the start of the process, based on the UNIX function `clock(3)`.

Warning: this intrinsic does not increase the range of the timing values over that returned by `clock(3)`. On a system with a 32-bit `clock(3)`, `MCLOCK8()` will return a 32-bit value, even though it is converted to a 64-bit `INTEGER(8)` value. That means overflows of the 32-bit value can still occur. Therefore, the values returned by this intrinsic might be or become negative or numerically less than previous values during a single run of the compiled program.

Standard: GNU extension

Class: Function

Syntax: `RESULT = MCLOCK8()`

Return value:

The return value is a scalar of type `INTEGER(8)`, equal to the number of clock ticks since the start of the process, or `-1` if the system does not support `clock(3)`.

See also: Section 6.50 [CTIME], page 66, Section 6.95 [GMTIME], page 93, Section 6.140 [LTIME], page 116, Section 6.147 [MCLOCK], page 120, Section 6.209 [TIME8], page 155

6.149 MERGE — Merge variables

Description:

Select values from two arrays according to a logical mask. The result is equal to *TSOURCE* if *MASK* is `.TRUE.`, or equal to *FSOURCE* if it is `.FALSE.`.

Standard: F95 and later

Class: Elemental function

Syntax: `RESULT = MERGE(TSOURCE, FSOURCE, MASK)`

Arguments:

TSOURCE	May be of any type.
FSOURCE	Shall be of the same type and type parameters as *TSOURCE*.
MASK	Shall be of type `LOGICAL(*)`.

Return value:

The result is of the same type and type parameters as *TSOURCE*.

6.150 MIN — Minimum value of an argument list

Description:

Returns the argument with the smallest (most negative) value.

Standard: F77 and later

Class: Elemental function

Syntax: `RESULT = MIN(A1, A2 [, A3, ...])`

Arguments:

A1	The type shall be `INTEGER(*)` or `REAL(*)`.
A2, A3, ...	An expression of the same type and kind as *A1*. (As a GNU extension, arguments of different kinds are permitted.)

Return value:

> The return value corresponds to the maximum value among the arguments, and has the same type and kind as the first argument.

Specific names:

Name	Argument	Return type	Standard
MIN0(I)	INTEGER(4) I	INTEGER(4)	F77 and later
AMIN0(I)	INTEGER(4) I	REAL(MIN(X))	F77 and later
MIN1(X)	REAL(*) X	INT(MIN(X))	F77 and later
AMIN1(X)	REAL(4) X	REAL(4)	F77 and later
DMIN1(X)	REAL(8) X	REAL(8)	F77 and later

See also: Section 6.143 [MAX], page 118, Section 6.152 [MINLOC], page 122, Section 6.153 [MINVAL], page 123

6.151 MINEXPONENT — Minimum exponent of a real kind

Description:

> MINEXPONENT(X) returns the minimum exponent in the model of the type of X.

Standard: F95 and later

Class: Inquiry function

Syntax: RESULT = MINEXPONENT(X)

Arguments:

> X   Shall be of type REAL.

Return value:

> The return value is of type INTEGER and of the default integer kind.

Example: See MAXEXPONENT for an example.

6.152 MINLOC — Location of the minimum value within an array

Description:

> Determines the location of the element in the array with the minimum value, or, if the *DIM* argument is supplied, determines the locations of the minimum element along each row of the array in the *DIM* direction. If *MASK* is present, only the elements for which *MASK* is .TRUE. are considered. If more than one element in the array has the minimum value, the location returned is that of the first such element in array element order. If the array has zero size, or all of the elements of *MASK* are .FALSE., then the result is an array of zeroes. Similarly, if *DIM* is supplied and all of the elements of *MASK* along a given row are zero, the result value for that row is zero.

Standard: F95 and later

Class: Transformational function

Syntax:

```
RESULT = MINLOC(ARRAY, DIM [, MASK])
RESULT = MINLOC(ARRAY [, MASK])
```

Arguments:

ARRAY	Shall be an array of type `INTEGER(*)`, `REAL(*)`, or `CHARACTER(*)`.
DIM	(Optional) Shall be a scalar of type `INTEGER(*)`, with a value between one and the rank of *ARRAY*, inclusive. It may not be an optional dummy argument.
MASK	Shall be an array of type `LOGICAL(*)`, and conformable with *ARRAY*.

Return value:

If *DIM* is absent, the result is a rank-one array with a length equal to the rank of *ARRAY*. If *DIM* is present, the result is an array with a rank one less than the rank of *ARRAY*, and a size corresponding to the size of *ARRAY* with the *DIM* dimension removed. If *DIM* is present and *ARRAY* has a rank of one, the result is a scalar. In all cases, the result is of default `INTEGER` type.

See also: Section 6.150 [MIN], page 121, Section 6.153 [MINVAL], page 123

6.153 MINVAL — Minimum value of an array

Description:

Determines the minimum value of the elements in an array value, or, if the *DIM* argument is supplied, determines the minimum value along each row of the array in the *DIM* direction. If *MASK* is present, only the elements for which *MASK* is `.TRUE.` are considered. If the array has zero size, or all of the elements of *MASK* are `.FALSE.`, then the result is `HUGE(ARRAY)` if *ARRAY* is numeric, or a string of `CHAR(255)` characters if *ARRAY* is of character type.

Standard: F95 and later

Class: Transformational function

Syntax:

```
RESULT = MINVAL(ARRAY, DIM [, MASK])
RESULT = MINVAL(ARRAY [, MASK])
```

Arguments:

ARRAY	Shall be an array of type `INTEGER(*)`, `REAL(*)`, or `CHARACTER(*)`.
DIM	(Optional) Shall be a scalar of type `INTEGER(*)`, with a value between one and the rank of *ARRAY*, inclusive. It may not be an optional dummy argument.
MASK	Shall be an array of type `LOGICAL(*)`, and conformable with *ARRAY*.

Return value:

If *DIM* is absent, or if *ARRAY* has a rank of one, the result is a scalar. If *DIM* is present, the result is an array with a rank one less than the rank of *ARRAY*, and a size corresponding to the size of *ARRAY* with the *DIM* dimension removed. In all cases, the result is of the same type and kind as *ARRAY*.

See also: Section 6.150 [MIN], page 121, Section 6.152 [MINLOC], page 122

6.154 MOD — Remainder function

Description:
MOD(A,P) computes the remainder of the division of A by P. It is calculated as A - (INT(A/P) * P).

Standard: F77 and later

Class: Elemental function

Syntax: RESULT = MOD(A, P)

Arguments:
A   Shall be a scalar of type INTEGER or REAL
P   Shall be a scalar of the same type as *A* and not equal to zero

Return value:
The kind of the return value is the result of cross-promoting the kinds of the arguments.

Example:
```
program test_mod
  print *, mod(17,3)
  print *, mod(17.5,5.5)
  print *, mod(17.5d0,5.5)
  print *, mod(17.5,5.5d0)

  print *, mod(-17,3)
  print *, mod(-17.5,5.5)
  print *, mod(-17.5d0,5.5)
  print *, mod(-17.5,5.5d0)

  print *, mod(17,-3)
  print *, mod(17.5,-5.5)
  print *, mod(17.5d0,-5.5)
  print *, mod(17.5,-5.5d0)
end program test_mod
```

Specific names:

Name	Arguments	Return type	Standard
AMOD(A,P)	REAL(4)	REAL(4)	F95 and later
DMOD(A,P)	REAL(8)	REAL(8)	F95 and later

6.155 MODULO — Modulo function

Description:
MODULO(A,P) computes the *A* modulo *P*.

Standard: F95 and later

Class: Elemental function

Syntax: `RESULT = MODULO(A, P)`

Arguments:

        A   Shall be a scalar of type `INTEGER` or `REAL`

        P   Shall be a scalar of the same type and kind as *A*

Return value:

The type and kind of the result are those of the arguments.

If *A* and *P* are of type `INTEGER`:

    `MODULO(A,P)` has the value R such that `A=Q*P+R`, where Q is an integer and R is between 0 (inclusive) and P (exclusive).

If *A* and *P* are of type `REAL`:

    `MODULO(A,P)` has the value of `A - FLOOR (A / P) * P`.

In all cases, if P is zero the result is processor-dependent.

Example:

```
program test_modulo
  print *, modulo(17,3)
  print *, modulo(17.5,5.5)

  print *, modulo(-17,3)
  print *, modulo(-17.5,5.5)

  print *, modulo(17,-3)
  print *, modulo(17.5,-5.5)
end program
```

6.156 `MOVE_ALLOC` — Move allocation from one object to another

Description:

`MOVE_ALLOC(SRC, DEST)` moves the allocation from *SRC* to *DEST*. *SRC* will become deallocated in the process.

Standard: F2003 and later

Class: Subroutine

Syntax: `CALL MOVE_ALLOC(SRC, DEST)`

Arguments:

        SRC   `ALLOCATABLE, INTENT(INOUT)`, may be of any type and kind.

        DEST   `ALLOCATABLE, INTENT(OUT)`, shall be of the same type, kind and rank as *SRC*

Return value:

None

Example:

```
program test_move_alloc
    integer, allocatable :: a(:), b(:)

    allocate(a(3))
```

```
        a = [ 1, 2, 3 ]
        call move_alloc(a, b)
        print *, allocated(a), allocated(b)
        print *, b
    end program test_move_alloc
```

6.157 MVBITS — Move bits from one integer to another

Description:

Moves *LEN* bits from positions *FROMPOS* through FROMPOS+LEN-1 of *FROM* to positions *TOPOS* through TOPOS+LEN-1 of *TO*. The portion of argument *TO* not affected by the movement of bits is unchanged. The values of FROMPOS+LEN-1 and TOPOS+LEN-1 must be less than BIT_SIZE(FROM).

Standard: F95 and later

Class: Elemental subroutine

Syntax: CALL MVBITS(FROM, FROMPOS, LEN, TO, TOPOS)

Arguments:

FROM	The type shall be INTEGER(*).
FROMPOS	The type shall be INTEGER(*).
LEN	The type shall be INTEGER(*).
TO	The type shall be INTEGER(*), of the same kind as *FROM*.
TOPOS	The type shall be INTEGER(*).

See also: Section 6.101 [IBCLR], page 96, Section 6.103 [IBSET], page 97, Section 6.102 [IBITS], page 97, Section 6.99 [IAND], page 95, Section 6.112 [IOR], page 102, Section 6.106 [IEOR], page 99

6.158 NEAREST — Nearest representable number

Description:

NEAREST(X, S) returns the processor-representable number nearest to X in the direction indicated by the sign of S.

Standard: F95 and later

Class: Elemental function

Syntax: RESULT = NEAREST(X, S)

Arguments:

X	Shall be of type REAL.
S	(Optional) shall be of type REAL and not equal to zero.

Return value:

The return value is of the same type as X. If S is positive, NEAREST returns the processor-representable number greater than X and nearest to it. If S is negative, NEAREST returns the processor-representable number smaller than X and nearest to it.

Example:

```
program test_nearest
  real :: x, y
  x = nearest(42.0, 1.0)
  y = nearest(42.0, -1.0)
  write (*,"(3(G20.15))") x, y, x - y
end program test_nearest
```

6.159 NEW_LINE — New line character

Description:

NEW_LINE(C) returns the new-line character.

Standard: F2003 and later

Class: Inquiry function

Syntax: RESULT = NEW_LINE(C)

Arguments:

        C   The argument shall be a scalar or array of the type CHARACTER.

Return value:

Returns a *CHARACTER* scalar of length one with the new-line character of the same kind as parameter *C*.

Example:

```
program newline
  implicit none
  write(*,'(A)') 'This is record 1.'//NEW_LINE('A')//'This is record 2.'
end program newline
```

6.160 NINT — Nearest whole number

Description:

NINT(X) rounds its argument to the nearest whole number.

Standard: F77 and later

Class: Elemental function

Syntax: RESULT = NINT(X)

Arguments:

        X   The type of the argument shall be REAL.

Return value:

Returns *A* with the fractional portion of its magnitude eliminated by rounding to the nearest whole number and with its sign preserved, converted to an INTEGER of the default kind.

Example:

```
program test_nint
  real(4) x4
  real(8) x8
  x4 = 1.234E0_4
```

```
x8 = 4.321_8
print *, nint(x4), idnint(x8)
end program test_nint
```

Specific names:

Name	Argument	Standard
IDNINT(X)	REAL(8)	F95 and later

See also: Section 6.37 [CEILING], page 58, Section 6.73 [FLOOR], page 81

6.161 NOT — Logical negation

Description:

NOT returns the bitwise boolean inverse of *I*.

Standard: F95 and later

Class: Elemental function

Syntax: RESULT = NOT(I)

Arguments:

I	The type shall be INTEGER(*).

Return value:

The return type is INTEGER(*), of the same kind as the argument.

See also: Section 6.99 [IAND], page 95, Section 6.106 [IEOR], page 99, Section 6.112 [IOR], page 102, Section 6.102 [IBITS], page 97, Section 6.103 [IBSET], page 97, Section 6.101 [IBCLR], page 96

6.162 NULL — Function that returns an disassociated pointer

Description:

Returns a disassociated pointer.

If *MOLD* is present, a disassociated pointer of the same type is returned, otherwise the type is determined by context.

In Fortran 95, *MOLD* is optional. Please note that F2003 includes cases where it is required.

Standard: F95 and later

Class: Transformational function

Syntax: PTR => NULL([MOLD])

Arguments:

MOLD	(Optional) shall be a pointer of any association status and of any type.

Return value:

A disassociated pointer.

Example:

```
REAL, POINTER, DIMENSION(:) :: VEC => NULL ()
```

See also: Section 6.20 [ASSOCIATED], page 48

6.163 OR — Bitwise logical OR

Description:

Bitwise logical OR.

This intrinsic routine is provided for backwards compatibility with GNU Fortran 77. For integer arguments, programmers should consider the use of the Section 6.112 [IOR], page 102 intrinsic defined by the Fortran standard.

Standard: GNU extension

Class: Function

Syntax: RESULT = OR(X, Y)

Arguments:

    X   The type shall be either INTEGER(*) or LOGICAL.

    Y   The type shall be either INTEGER(*) or LOGICAL.

Return value:

The return type is either INTEGER(*) or LOGICAL after cross-promotion of the arguments.

Example:

```
PROGRAM test_or
  LOGICAL :: T = .TRUE., F = .FALSE.
  INTEGER :: a, b
  DATA a / Z'F' /, b / Z'3' /

  WRITE (*,*) OR(T, T), OR(T, F), OR(F, T), OR(F, F)
  WRITE (*,*) OR(a, b)
END PROGRAM
```

See also: F95 elemental function: Section 6.112 [IOR], page 102

6.164 PACK — Pack an array into an array of rank one

Description:

Stores the elements of *ARRAY* in an array of rank one.

The beginning of the resulting array is made up of elements whose *MASK* equals TRUE. Afterwards, positions are filled with elements taken from *VECTOR*.

Standard: F95 and later

Class: Transformational function

Syntax: RESULT = PACK(ARRAY, MASK[,VECTOR])

Arguments:

    ARRAY   Shall be an array of any type.

    MASK   Shall be an array of type LOGICAL and of the same size as *ARRAY*. Alternatively, it may be a LOGICAL scalar.

VECTOR (Optional) shall be an array of the same type as *ARRAY* and of rank one. If present, the number of elements in *VECTOR* shall be equal to or greater than the number of true elements in *MASK*. If *MASK* is scalar, the number of elements in *VEC-TOR* shall be equal to or greater than the number of elements in *ARRAY*.

Return value:

The result is an array of rank one and the same type as that of *ARRAY*. If *VECTOR* is present, the result size is that of *VECTOR*, the number of `TRUE` values in *MASK* otherwise.

Example: Gathering nonzero elements from an array:

```
PROGRAM test_pack_1
  INTEGER :: m(6)
  m = (/ 1, 0, 0, 0, 5, 0 /)
  WRITE(*, FMT="(6(I0, ' '))") pack(m, m /= 0)  ! "1 5"
END PROGRAM
```

Gathering nonzero elements from an array and appending elements from *VEC-TOR*:

```
PROGRAM test_pack_2
  INTEGER :: m(4)
  m = (/ 1, 0, 0, 2 /)
  WRITE(*, FMT="(4(I0, ' '))") pack(m, m /= 0, (/ 0, 0, 3, 4 /))  ! "1 2 3 4"
END PROGRAM
```

See also: Section 6.218 [UNPACK], page 159

6.165 PERROR — Print system error message

Description:

Prints (on the C `stderr` stream) a newline-terminated error message corresponding to the last system error. This is prefixed by *STRING*, a colon and a space. See `perror(3)`.

Standard: GNU extension

Class: Subroutine

Syntax: `CALL PERROR(STRING)`

Arguments:

STRING A scalar of default `CHARACTER` type.

See also: Section 6.107 [IERRNO], page 99

6.166 PRECISION — Decimal precision of a real kind

Description:

`PRECISION(X)` returns the decimal precision in the model of the type of `X`.

Standard: F95 and later

Class: Inquiry function

Syntax: RESULT = PRECISION(X)

Arguments:

         X   Shall be of type REAL or COMPLEX.

Return value:

      The return value is of type INTEGER and of the default integer kind.

Example:

```
program prec_and_range
  real(kind=4) :: x(2)
  complex(kind=8) :: y

  print *, precision(x), range(x)
  print *, precision(y), range(y)
end program prec_and_range
```

6.167 PRESENT — Determine whether an optional dummy argument is specified

Description:

      Determines whether an optional dummy argument is present.

Standard: F95 and later

Class: Inquiry function

Syntax: RESULT = PRESENT(A)

Arguments:

         A   May be of any type and may be a pointer, scalar or array value, or a dummy procedure. It shall be the name of an optional dummy argument accessible within the current subroutine or function.

Return value:

      Returns either TRUE if the optional argument A is present, or FALSE otherwise.

Example:

```
PROGRAM test_present
  WRITE(*,*) f(), f(42)        ! "F T"
CONTAINS
  LOGICAL FUNCTION f(x)
    INTEGER, INTENT(IN), OPTIONAL :: x
    f = PRESENT(x)
  END FUNCTION
END PROGRAM
```

6.168 PRODUCT — Product of array elements

Description:

      Multiplies the elements of *ARRAY* along dimension *DIM* if the corresponding element in *MASK* is TRUE.

Standard: F95 and later

Class: Transformational function

Syntax: RESULT = PRODUCT(ARRAY[, MASK]) RESULT = PRODUCT(ARRAY, DIM[, MASK])

Arguments:

ARRAY	Shall be an array of type INTEGER(*), REAL(*) or COMPLEX(*).
DIM	(Optional) shall be a scalar of type INTEGER with a value in the range from 1 to n, where n equals the rank of *ARRAY*.
MASK	(Optional) shall be of type LOGICAL and either be a scalar or an array of the same shape as *ARRAY*.

Return value:

The result is of the same type as *ARRAY*.

If *DIM* is absent, a scalar with the product of all elements in *ARRAY* is returned. Otherwise, an array of rank n-1, where n equals the rank of *ARRAY*, and a shape similar to that of *ARRAY* with dimension *DIM* dropped is returned.

Example:

```
PROGRAM test_product
  INTEGER :: x(5) = (/ 1, 2, 3, 4 ,5 /)
  print *, PRODUCT(x)                  ! all elements, product = 120
  print *, PRODUCT(x, MASK=MOD(x, 2)==1) ! odd elements, product = 15
END PROGRAM
```

See also: Section 6.202 [SUM], page 151

6.169 RADIX — Base of a model number

Description:

RADIX(X) returns the base of the model representing the entity *X*.

Standard: F95 and later

Class: Inquiry function

Syntax: RESULT = RADIX(X)

Arguments:

X	Shall be of type INTEGER or REAL

Return value:

The return value is a scalar of type INTEGER and of the default integer kind.

Example:

```
program test_radix
  print *, "The radix for the default integer kind is", radix(0)
  print *, "The radix for the default real kind is", radix(0.0)
end program test_radix
```

6.170 RAN — Real pseudo-random number

Description:

For compatibility with HP FORTRAN 77/iX, the RAN intrinsic is provided as an alias for RAND. See Section 6.171 [RAND], page 133 for complete documentation.

Standard: GNU extension

Class: Function

See also: Section 6.171 [RAND], page 133, Section 6.172 [RANDOM_NUMBER], page 133

6.171 RAND — Real pseudo-random number

Description:

RAND(FLAG) returns a pseudo-random number from a uniform distribution between 0 and 1. If *FLAG* is 0, the next number in the current sequence is returned; if *FLAG* is 1, the generator is restarted by CALL SRAND(0); if *FLAG* has any other value, it is used as a new seed with SRAND.

This intrinsic routine is provided for backwards compatibility with GNU Fortran 77. It implements a simple modulo generator as provided by g77. For new code, one should consider the use of Section 6.172 [RANDOM_NUMBER], page 133 as it implements a superior algorithm.

Standard: GNU extension

Class: Function

Syntax: RESULT = RAND(FLAG)

Arguments:

FLAG   Shall be a scalar INTEGER of kind 4.

Return value:

The return value is of REAL type and the default kind.

Example:

```
program test_rand
  integer,parameter :: seed = 86456

  call srand(seed)
  print *, rand(), rand(), rand(), rand()
  print *, rand(seed), rand(), rand(), rand()
end program test_rand
```

See also: Section 6.200 [SRAND], page 149, Section 6.172 [RANDOM_NUMBER], page 133

6.172 RANDOM_NUMBER — Pseudo-random number

Description:

Returns a single pseudorandom number or an array of pseudorandom numbers from the uniform distribution over the range $0 \leq x < 1$.

The runtime-library implements George Marsaglia's KISS (Keep It Simple Stupid) random number generator (RNG). This RNG combines:

1. The congruential generator $x(n) = 69069 \cdot x(n-1) + 1327217885$ with a period of 2^{32},

2. A 3-shift shift-register generator with a period of $2^{32} - 1$,

3. Two 16-bit multiply-with-carry generators with a period of $597273182964842497 > 2^{59}$.

The overall period exceeds 2^{123}.

Please note, this RNG is thread safe if used within OpenMP directives, i. e. its state will be consistent while called from multiple threads. However, the KISS generator does not create random numbers in parallel from multiple sources, but in sequence from a single source. If an OpenMP-enabled application heavily relies on random numbers, one should consider employing a dedicated parallel random number generator instead.

Standard: F95 and later

Class: Subroutine

Syntax: `RANDOM_NUMBER(HARVEST)`

Arguments:

    HARVEST   Shall be a scalar or an array of type `REAL(*)`.

Example:

```
program test_random_number
  REAL :: r(5,5)
  CALL init_random_seed()           ! see example of RANDOM_SEED
  CALL RANDOM_NUMBER(r)
end program
```

See also: Section 6.173 [RANDOM_SEED], page 134

6.173 RANDOM_SEED — Initialize a pseudo-random number sequence

Description:

    Restarts or queries the state of the pseudorandom number generator used by `RANDOM_NUMBER`.

    If `RANDOM_SEED` is called without arguments, it is initialized to a default state. The example below shows how to initialize the random seed based on the system's time.

Standard: F95 and later

Class: Subroutine

Syntax: `CALL RANDOM_SEED(SIZE, PUT, GET)`

Arguments:

    SIZE   (Optional) Shall be a scalar and of type default `INTEGER`, with `INTENT(OUT)`. It specifies the minimum size of the arrays used with the *PUT* and *GET* arguments.

PUT	(Optional) Shall be an array of type default `INTEGER` and rank one. It is `INTENT(IN)` and the size of the array must be larger than or equal to the number returned by the *SIZE* argument.
GET	(Optional) Shall be an array of type default `INTEGER` and rank one. It is `INTENT(OUT)` and the size of the array must be larger than or equal to the number returned by the *SIZE* argument.

Example:

```
SUBROUTINE init_random_seed()
  INTEGER :: i, n, clock
  INTEGER, DIMENSION(:), ALLOCATABLE :: seed

  CALL RANDOM_SEED(size = n)
  ALLOCATE(seed(n))

  CALL SYSTEM_CLOCK(COUNT=clock)

  seed = clock + 37 * (/ (i - 1, i = 1, n) /)
  CALL RANDOM_SEED(PUT = seed)

  DEALLOCATE(seed)
END SUBROUTINE
```

See also: Section 6.172 [RANDOM_NUMBER], page 133

6.174 RANGE — Decimal exponent range of a real kind

Description:

RANGE(X) returns the decimal exponent range in the model of the type of X.

Standard: F95 and later

Class: Inquiry function

Syntax: `RESULT = RANGE(X)`

Arguments:

X	Shall be of type `REAL` or `COMPLEX`.

Return value:

The return value is of type `INTEGER` and of the default integer kind.

Example: See `PRECISION` for an example.

6.175 REAL — Convert to real type

Description:

REAL(X [, KIND]) converts its argument X to a real type. The REALPART(X) function is provided for compatibility with g77, and its use is strongly discouraged.

Standard: F77 and later

Class: Elemental function

Syntax:

```
RESULT = REAL(X [, KIND])
RESULT = REALPART(Z)
```

Arguments:

X	Shall be `INTEGER(*)`, `REAL(*)`, or `COMPLEX(*)`.
KIND	(Optional) An `INTEGER(*)` initialization expression indicating the kind parameter of the result.

Return value:

These functions return a `REAL(*)` variable or array under the following rules:

(A)   `REAL(X)` is converted to a default real type if *X* is an integer or real variable.

(B)   `REAL(X)` is converted to a real type with the kind type parameter of *X* if *X* is a complex variable.

(C)   `REAL(X, KIND)` is converted to a real type with kind type parameter *KIND* if *X* is a complex, integer, or real variable.

Example:

```
program test_real
  complex :: x = (1.0, 2.0)
  print *, real(x), real(x,8), realpart(x)
end program test_real
```

See also: Section 6.52 [DBLE], page 68, Section 6.54 [DFLOAT], page 69, Section 6.70 [FLOAT], page 79

6.176 `RENAME` — Rename a file

Description:

Renames a file from file *PATH1* to *PATH2*. A null character (`CHAR(0)`) can be used to mark the end of the names in *PATH1* and *PATH2*; otherwise, trailing blanks in the file names are ignored. If the *STATUS* argument is supplied, it contains 0 on success or a nonzero error code upon return; see `rename(2)`.

This intrinsic is provided in both subroutine and function forms; however, only one form can be used in any given program unit.

Standard: GNU extension

Class: Subroutine, function

Syntax:

```
CALL RENAME(PATH1, PATH2 [, STATUS])
STATUS = RENAME(PATH1, PATH2)
```

Arguments:

PATH1	Shall be of default `CHARACTER` type.
PATH2	Shall be of default `CHARACTER` type.
STATUS	(Optional) Shall be of default `INTEGER` type.

See also: Section 6.129 [LINK], page 110

6.177 REPEAT — Repeated string concatenation

Description:

Concatenates *NCOPIES* copies of a string.

Standard: F95 and later

Class: Transformational function

Syntax: `RESULT = REPEAT(STRING, NCOPIES)`

Arguments:

STRING	Shall be scalar and of type `CHARACTER(*)`.
NCOPIES	Shall be scalar and of type `INTEGER(*)`.

Return value:

A new scalar of type `CHARACTER` built up from *NCOPIES* copies of *STRING*.

Example:

```
program test_repeat
  write(*,*) repeat("x", 5)   ! "xxxxx"
end program
```

6.178 RESHAPE — Function to reshape an array

Description:

Reshapes *SOURCE* to correspond to *SHAPE*. If necessary, the new array may be padded with elements from *PAD* or permuted as defined by *ORDER*.

Standard: F95 and later

Class: Transformational function

Syntax: `RESULT = RESHAPE(SOURCE, SHAPE[, PAD, ORDER])`

Arguments:

SOURCE	Shall be an array of any type.
SHAPE	Shall be of type `INTEGER` and an array of rank one. Its values must be positive or zero.
PAD	(Optional) shall be an array of the same type as *SOURCE*.
ORDER	(Optional) shall be of type `INTEGER` and an array of the same shape as *SHAPE*. Its values shall be a permutation of the numbers from 1 to n, where n is the size of *SHAPE*. If *ORDER* is absent, the natural ordering shall be assumed.

Return value:

The result is an array of shape *SHAPE* with the same type as *SOURCE*.

Example:

```
PROGRAM test_reshape
  INTEGER, DIMENSION(4) :: x
  WRITE(*,*) SHAPE(x)                    ! prints "4"
  WRITE(*,*) SHAPE(RESHAPE(x, (/2, 2/)))  ! prints "2 2"
END PROGRAM
```

See also: Section 6.188 [SHAPE], page 142

6.179 RRSPACING — Reciprocal of the relative spacing

Description:

RRSPACING(X) returns the reciprocal of the relative spacing of model numbers near *X*.

Standard: F95 and later

Class: Elemental function

Syntax: RESULT = RRSPACING(X)

Arguments:

    X   Shall be of type REAL.

Return value:

The return value is of the same type and kind as *X*. The value returned is equal to ABS(FRACTION(X)) * FLOAT(RADIX(X))**DIGITS(X).

See also: Section 6.197 [SPACING], page 147

6.180 RSHIFT — Right shift bits

Description:

RSHIFT returns a value corresponding to *I* with all of the bits shifted right by *SHIFT* places. If the absolute value of *SHIFT* is greater than BIT_SIZE(I), the value is undefined. Bits shifted out from the left end are lost; zeros are shifted in from the opposite end.

This function has been superseded by the ISHFT intrinsic, which is standard in Fortran 95 and later.

Standard: GNU extension

Class: Elemental function

Syntax: RESULT = RSHIFT(I, SHIFT)

Arguments:

    I   The type shall be INTEGER(*).
    SHIFT   The type shall be INTEGER(*).

Return value:

The return value is of type INTEGER(*) and of the same kind as *I*.

See also: Section 6.117 [ISHFT], page 104, Section 6.118 [ISHFTC], page 105, Section 6.138 [LSHIFT], page 115

6.181 SCALE — Scale a real value

Description:

SCALE(X,I) returns X * RADIX(X)**I.

Standard: F95 and later

Class: Elemental function

Syntax: `RESULT = SCALE(X, I)`

Arguments:

X	The type of the argument shall be a `REAL`.
I	The type of the argument shall be a `INTEGER`.

Return value:

The return value is of the same type and kind as X. Its value is `X * RADIX(X)**I`.

Example:

```
program test_scale
  real :: x = 178.1387e-4
  integer :: i = 5
  print *, scale(x,i), x*radix(x)**i
end program test_scale
```

6.182 SCAN — Scan a string for the presence of a set of characters

Description:

Scans a *STRING* for any of the characters in a *SET* of characters.

If *BACK* is either absent or equals **FALSE**, this function returns the position of the leftmost character of *STRING* that is in *SET*. If *BACK* equals **TRUE**, the rightmost position is returned. If no character of *SET* is found in *STRING*, the result is zero.

Standard: F95 and later

Class: Elemental function

Syntax: `RESULT = SCAN(STRING, SET[, BACK [, KIND]])`

Arguments:

STRING	Shall be of type `CHARACTER(*)`.
SET	Shall be of type `CHARACTER(*)`.
BACK	(Optional) shall be of type `LOGICAL`.
KIND	(Optional) An `INTEGER` initialization expression indicating the kind parameter of the result.

Return value:

The return value is of type `INTEGER` and of kind *KIND*. If *KIND* is absent, the return value is of default integer kind.

Example:

```
PROGRAM test_scan
  WRITE(*,*) SCAN("FORTRAN", "AO")          ! 2, found 'O'
  WRITE(*,*) SCAN("FORTRAN", "AO", .TRUE.)  ! 6, found 'A'
  WRITE(*,*) SCAN("FORTRAN", "C++")         ! 0, found none
END PROGRAM
```

See also: Section 6.108 [INDEX intrinsic], page 100, Section 6.219 [VERIFY], page 159

6.183 SECNDS — Time function

Description:

SECNDS(X) gets the time in seconds from the real-time system clock. X is a reference time, also in seconds. If this is zero, the time in seconds from midnight is returned. This function is non-standard and its use is discouraged.

Standard: GNU extension

Class: Function

Syntax: RESULT = SECNDS (X)

Arguments:

T	Shall be of type REAL(4).
X	Shall be of type REAL(4).

Return value:

None

Example:

```
program test_secnds
    integer :: i
    real(4) :: t1, t2
    print *, secnds (0.0)     ! seconds since midnight
    t1 = secnds (0.0)         ! reference time
    do i = 1, 10000000        ! do something
    end do
    t2 = secnds (t1)          ! elapsed time
    print *, "Something took ", t2, " seconds."
end program test_secnds
```

6.184 SECOND — CPU time function

Description:

Returns a REAL(4) value representing the elapsed CPU time in seconds. This provides the same functionality as the standard CPU_TIME intrinsic, and is only included for backwards compatibility.

This intrinsic is provided in both subroutine and function forms; however, only one form can be used in any given program unit.

Standard: GNU extension

Class: Subroutine, function

Syntax:

CALL SECOND(TIME)
TIME = SECOND()

Arguments:

TIME	Shall be of type REAL(4).

Return value:

In either syntax, *TIME* is set to the process's current runtime in seconds.

See also: Section 6.48 [CPU_TIME], page 65

6.185 SELECTED_INT_KIND — Choose integer kind

Description:

SELECTED_INT_KIND(I) return the kind value of the smallest integer type that can represent all values ranging from -10^I (exclusive) to 10^I (exclusive). If there is no integer kind that accommodates this range, SELECTED_INT_KIND returns -1.

Standard: F95 and later

Class: Transformational function

Syntax: RESULT = SELECTED_INT_KIND(I)

Arguments:

    I   Shall be a scalar and of type INTEGER.

Example:

```
program large_integers
  integer,parameter :: k5 = selected_int_kind(5)
  integer,parameter :: k15 = selected_int_kind(15)
  integer(kind=k5) :: i5
  integer(kind=k15) :: i15

  print *, huge(i5), huge(i15)

  ! The following inequalities are always true
  print *, huge(i5) >= 10_k5**5-1
  print *, huge(i15) >= 10_k15**15-1
end program large_integers
```

6.186 SELECTED_REAL_KIND — Choose real kind

Description:

SELECTED_REAL_KIND(P,R) return the kind value of a real data type with decimal precision greater of at least P digits and exponent range greater at least R.

Standard: F95 and later

Class: Transformational function

Syntax: RESULT = SELECTED_REAL_KIND(P, R)

Arguments:

    P   (Optional) shall be a scalar and of type INTEGER.
    R   (Optional) shall be a scalar and of type INTEGER.

At least one argument shall be present.

Return value:

SELECTED_REAL_KIND returns the value of the kind type parameter of a real data type with decimal precision of at least P digits and a decimal exponent range of at least R. If more than one real data type meet the criteria, the kind of the data type with the smallest decimal precision is returned. If no real data type matches the criteria, the result is

-1 if the processor does not support a real data type with a
precision greater than or equal to P

-2 if the processor does not support a real type with an exponent
range greater than or equal to R

-3 if neither is supported.

Example:

```
program real_kinds
  integer,parameter :: p6 = selected_real_kind(6)
  integer,parameter :: p10r100 = selected_real_kind(10,100)
  integer,parameter :: r400 = selected_real_kind(r=400)
  real(kind=p6) :: x
  real(kind=p10r100) :: y
  real(kind=r400) :: z

  print *, precision(x), range(x)
  print *, precision(y), range(y)
  print *, precision(z), range(z)
end program real_kinds
```

6.187 SET_EXPONENT — Set the exponent of the model

Description:

SET_EXPONENT(X, I) returns the real number whose fractional part is that that
of X and whose exponent part is I.

Standard: F95 and later

Class: Elemental function

Syntax: RESULT = SET_EXPONENT(X, I)

Arguments:

X	Shall be of type REAL.
I	Shall be of type INTEGER.

Return value:

The return value is of the same type and kind as X. The real number whose
fractional part is that that of X and whose exponent part if I is returned; it is
FRACTION(X) * RADIX(X)**I.

Example:

```
PROGRAM test_setexp
  REAL :: x = 178.1387e-4
  INTEGER :: i = 17
  PRINT *, SET_EXPONENT(x, i), FRACTION(x) * RADIX(x)**i
END PROGRAM
```

6.188 SHAPE — Determine the shape of an array

Description:

Determines the shape of an array.

Standard: F95 and later

Class: Inquiry function

Syntax: `RESULT = SHAPE(SOURCE)`

Arguments:

SOURCE   Shall be an array or scalar of any type. If *SOURCE* is a pointer it must be associated and allocatable arrays must be allocated.

Return value:

An `INTEGER` array of rank one with as many elements as *SOURCE* has dimensions. The elements of the resulting array correspond to the extend of *SOURCE* along the respective dimensions. If *SOURCE* is a scalar, the result is the rank one array of size zero.

Example:

```
PROGRAM test_shape
  INTEGER, DIMENSION(-1:1, -1:2) :: A
  WRITE(*,*) SHAPE(A)          ! (/ 3, 4 /)
  WRITE(*,*) SIZE(SHAPE(42))   ! (/ /)
END PROGRAM
```

See also: Section 6.178 [RESHAPE], page 137, Section 6.193 [SIZE], page 145

6.189 `SIGN` — Sign copying function

Description:

`SIGN(A,B)` returns the value of *A* with the sign of *B*.

Standard: F77 and later

Class: Elemental function

Syntax: `RESULT = SIGN(A, B)`

Arguments:

A   Shall be of type `INTEGER` or `REAL`
B   Shall be of the same type and kind as *A*

Return value:

The kind of the return value is that of *A* and *B*. If $B \geq 0$ then the result is `ABS(A)`, else it is `-ABS(A)`.

Example:

```
program test_sign
  print *, sign(-12,1)
  print *, sign(-12,0)
  print *, sign(-12,-1)

  print *, sign(-12.,1.)
  print *, sign(-12.,0.)
  print *, sign(-12.,-1.)
end program test_sign
```

Specific names:

Name	Arguments	Return type	Standard
ISIGN(A,P)	INTEGER(4)	INTEGER(4)	f95, gnu
DSIGN(A,P)	REAL(8)	REAL(8)	f95, gnu

6.190 SIGNAL — Signal handling subroutine (or function)

Description:

SIGNAL(NUMBER, HANDLER [, STATUS]) causes external subroutine *HANDLER* to be executed with a single integer argument when signal *NUMBER* occurs. If *HANDLER* is an integer, it can be used to turn off handling of signal *NUMBER* or revert to its default action. See signal(2).

If SIGNAL is called as a subroutine and the *STATUS* argument is supplied, it is set to the value returned by signal(2).

Standard: GNU extension

Class: Subroutine, function

Syntax:

```
CALL SIGNAL(NUMBER, HANDLER [, STATUS])
STATUS = SIGNAL(NUMBER, HANDLER)
```

Arguments:

NUMBER	Shall be a scalar integer, with INTENT(IN)
HANDLER	Signal handler (INTEGER FUNCTION or SUBROUTINE) or dummy/global INTEGER scalar. INTEGER. It is INTENT(IN).
STATUS	(Optional) *STATUS* shall be a scalar integer. It has INTENT(OUT).

Return value:

The SIGNAL function returns the value returned by signal(2).

Example:

```
program test_signal
  intrinsic signal
  external handler_print

  call signal (12, handler_print)
  call signal (10, 1)

  call sleep (30)
end program test_signal
```

6.191 SIN — Sine function

Description:

SIN(X) computes the sine of *X*.

Standard: F77 and later

Class: Elemental function

Syntax: RESULT = SIN(X)

Arguments:

X	The type shall be REAL(*) or COMPLEX(*).

Return value:

The return value has same type and kind as *X*.

Example:

```
program test_sin
  real :: x = 0.0
  x = sin(x)
end program test_sin
```

Specific names:

Name	Argument	Return type	Standard
DSIN(X)	REAL(8) X	REAL(8)	f95, gnu
CSIN(X)	COMPLEX(4) X	COMPLEX(4)	f95, gnu
ZSIN(X)	COMPLEX(8) X	COMPLEX(8)	f95, gnu
CDSIN(X)	COMPLEX(8) X	COMPLEX(8)	f95, gnu

See also: Section 6.18 [ASIN], page 47

6.192 SINH — Hyperbolic sine function

Description:

SINH(X) computes the hyperbolic sine of *X*.

Standard: F95 and later

Class: Elemental function

Syntax: RESULT = SINH(X)

Arguments:

X   The type shall be REAL(*).

Return value:

The return value is of type REAL(*).

Example:

```
program test_sinh
  real(8) :: x = - 1.0_8
  x = sinh(x)
end program test_sinh
```

Specific names:

Name	Argument	Return type	Standard
DSINH(X)	REAL(8) X	REAL(8)	F95 and later

See also: Section 6.19 [ASINH], page 48

6.193 SIZE — Determine the size of an array

Description:

Determine the extent of *ARRAY* along a specified dimension *DIM*, or the total number of elements in *ARRAY* if *DIM* is absent.

Standard: F95 and later

Class: Inquiry function

Syntax: RESULT = SIZE(ARRAY[, DIM [, KIND]])

Arguments:

ARRAY	Shall be an array of any type. If *ARRAY* is a pointer it must be associated and allocatable arrays must be allocated.
DIM	(Optional) shall be a scalar of type INTEGER and its value shall be in the range from 1 to n, where n equals the rank of *ARRAY*.
KIND	(Optional) An INTEGER initialization expression indicating the kind parameter of the result.

Return value:

The return value is of type INTEGER and of kind *KIND*. If *KIND* is absent, the return value is of default integer kind.

Example:

```
PROGRAM test_size
  WRITE(*,*) SIZE((/ 1, 2 /))    ! 2
END PROGRAM
```

See also: Section 6.188 [SHAPE], page 142, Section 6.178 [RESHAPE], page 137

6.194 SIZEOF — Size in bytes of an expression

Description:

SIZEOF(X) calculates the number of bytes of storage the expression X occupies.

Standard: GNU extension

Class: Intrinsic function

Syntax: N = SIZEOF(X)

Arguments:

X	The argument shall be of any type, rank or shape.

Return value:

The return value is of type integer and of the system-dependent kind *C_SIZE_T* (from the *ISO_C_BINDING* module). Its value is the number of bytes occupied by the argument. If the argument has the POINTER attribute, the number of bytes of the storage area pointed to is returned. If the argument is of a derived type with POINTER or ALLOCATABLE components, the return value doesn't account for the sizes of the data pointed to by these components.

Example:

```
integer :: i
real :: r, s(5)
print *, (sizeof(s)/sizeof(r) == 5)
end
```

The example will print .TRUE. unless you are using a platform where default REAL variables are unusually padded.

6.195 SLEEP — Sleep for the specified number of seconds

Description:

Calling this subroutine causes the process to pause for *SECONDS* seconds.

Standard: GNU extension

Class: Subroutine

Syntax: `CALL SLEEP(SECONDS)`

Arguments:

SECONDS   The type shall be of default `INTEGER`.

Example:

```
program test_sleep
  call sleep(5)
end
```

6.196 SNGL — Convert double precision real to default real

Description:

`SNGL(A)` converts the double precision real *A* to a default real value. This is an archaic form of `REAL` that is specific to one type for *A*.

Standard: F77 and later

Class: Elemental function

Syntax: `RESULT = SNGL(A)`

Arguments:

A   The type shall be a double precision `REAL`.

Return value:

The return value is of type default `REAL`.

See also: Section 6.52 [DBLE], page 68

6.197 SPACING — Smallest distance between two numbers of a given type

Description:

Determines the distance between the argument *X* and the nearest adjacent number of the same type.

Standard: F95 and later

Class: Elemental function

Syntax: `RESULT = SPACING(X)`

Arguments:

X   Shall be of type `REAL(*)`.

Return value:

The result is of the same type as the input argument *X*.

Example:

```
PROGRAM test_spacing
   INTEGER, PARAMETER :: SGL = SELECTED_REAL_KIND(p=6, r=37)
   INTEGER, PARAMETER :: DBL = SELECTED_REAL_KIND(p=13, r=200)

   WRITE(*,*) spacing(1.0_SGL)    ! "1.1920929E-07"        on i686
   WRITE(*,*) spacing(1.0_DBL)    ! "2.220446049250313E-016" on i686
END PROGRAM
```

See also: Section 6.179 [RRSPACING], page 138

6.198 SPREAD — Add a dimension to an array

Description:

Replicates a *SOURCE* array *NCOPIES* times along a specified dimension *DIM*.

Standard: F95 and later

Class: Transformational function

Syntax: RESULT = SPREAD(SOURCE, DIM, NCOPIES)

Arguments:

SOURCE	Shall be a scalar or an array of any type and a rank less than seven.
DIM	Shall be a scalar of type INTEGER with a value in the range from 1 to n+1, where n equals the rank of *SOURCE*.
NCOPIES	Shall be a scalar of type INTEGER.

Return value:

The result is an array of the same type as *SOURCE* and has rank n+1 where n equals the rank of *SOURCE*.

Example:

```
PROGRAM test_spread
   INTEGER :: a = 1, b(2) = (/ 1, 2 /)
   WRITE(*,*) SPREAD(A, 1, 2)          ! "1 1"
   WRITE(*,*) SPREAD(B, 1, 2)          ! "1 1 2 2"
END PROGRAM
```

See also: Section 6.218 [UNPACK], page 159

6.199 SQRT — Square-root function

Description:

SQRT(X) computes the square root of *X*.

Standard: F77 and later

Class: Elemental function

Syntax: RESULT = SQRT(X)

Arguments:

X	The type shall be REAL(*) or COMPLEX(*).

Return value:

The return value is of type REAL(*) or COMPLEX(*). The kind type parameter is the same as *X*.

Example:

```
program test_sqrt
  real(8) :: x = 2.0_8
  complex :: z = (1.0, 2.0)
  x = sqrt(x)
  z = sqrt(z)
end program test_sqrt
```

Specific names:

Name	Argument	Return type	Standard
DSQRT(X)	REAL(8) X	REAL(8)	F95 and later
CSQRT(X)	COMPLEX(4) X	COMPLEX(4)	F95 and later
ZSQRT(X)	COMPLEX(8) X	COMPLEX(8)	GNU extension
CDSQRT(X)	COMPLEX(8) X	COMPLEX(8)	GNU extension

6.200 SRAND — Reinitialize the random number generator

Description:

SRAND reinitializes the pseudo-random number generator called by RAND and IRAND. The new seed used by the generator is specified by the required argument *SEED*.

Standard: GNU extension

Class: Subroutine

Syntax: CALL SRAND(SEED)

Arguments:

SEED   Shall be a scalar INTEGER(kind=4).

Return value:

Does not return.

Example: See RAND and IRAND for examples.

Notes: The Fortran 2003 standard specifies the intrinsic RANDOM_SEED to initialize the pseudo-random numbers generator and RANDOM_NUMBER to generate pseudo-random numbers. Please note that in GNU Fortran, these two sets of intrinsics (RAND, IRAND and SRAND on the one hand, RANDOM_NUMBER and RANDOM_SEED on the other hand) access two independent pseudo-random number generators.

See also: Section 6.171 [RAND], page 133, Section 6.173 [RANDOM_SEED], page 134, Section 6.172 [RANDOM_NUMBER], page 133

6.201 STAT — Get file status

Description:

This function returns information about a file. No permissions are required on the file itself, but execute (search) permission is required on all of the directories in path that lead to the file.

The elements that are obtained and stored in the array BUFF:

buff(1)	Device ID
buff(2)	Inode number
buff(3)	File mode
buff(4)	Number of links
buff(5)	Owner's uid
buff(6)	Owner's gid
buff(7)	ID of device containing directory entry for file (0 if not available)
buff(8)	File size (bytes)
buff(9)	Last access time
buff(10)	Last modification time
buff(11)	Last file status change time
buff(12)	Preferred I/O block size (-1 if not available)
buff(13)	Number of blocks allocated (-1 if not available)

Not all these elements are relevant on all systems. If an element is not relevant, it is returned as 0.

This intrinsic is provided in both subroutine and function forms; however, only one form can be used in any given program unit.

Standard: GNU extension

Class: Subroutine, function

Syntax: `CALL STAT(FILE,BUFF[,STATUS])`

Arguments:

FILE	The type shall be `CHARACTER(*)`, a valid path within the file system.
BUFF	The type shall be `INTEGER(4)`, `DIMENSION(13)`.
STATUS	(Optional) status flag of type `INTEGER(4)`. Returns 0 on success and a system specific error code otherwise.

Example:

```
PROGRAM test_stat
  INTEGER, DIMENSION(13) :: buff
  INTEGER :: status

  CALL STAT("/etc/passwd", buff, status)

  IF (status == 0) THEN
    WRITE (*, FMT="('Device ID:',              T30, I19)") buff(1)
    WRITE (*, FMT="('Inode number:',           T30, I19)") buff(2)
    WRITE (*, FMT="('File mode (octal):',       T30, O19)") buff(3)
    WRITE (*, FMT="('Number of links:',        T30, I19)") buff(4)
    WRITE (*, FMT="('Owner''s uid:',            T30, I19)") buff(5)
    WRITE (*, FMT="('Owner''s gid:',            T30, I19)") buff(6)
    WRITE (*, FMT="('Device where located:',    T30, I19)") buff(7)
    WRITE (*, FMT="('File size:',              T30, I19)") buff(8)
    WRITE (*, FMT="('Last access time:',       T30, A19)") CTIME(buff(9))
    WRITE (*, FMT="('Last modification time',  T30, A19)") CTIME(buff(10))
    WRITE (*, FMT="('Last status change time:', T30, A19)") CTIME(buff(11))
```

```
            WRITE (*, FMT="('Preferred block size:',    T30, I19)") buff(12)
            WRITE (*, FMT="('No. of blocks allocated:', T30, I19)") buff(13)
          END IF
        END PROGRAM
```

See also: To stat an open file: Section 6.81 [FSTAT], page 86, to stat a link: Section 6.139 [LSTAT], page 115

6.202 SUM — Sum of array elements

Description:

Adds the elements of *ARRAY* along dimension *DIM* if the corresponding element in *MASK* is TRUE.

Standard: F95 and later

Class: Transformational function

Syntax: RESULT = SUM(ARRAY[, MASK]) RESULT = SUM(ARRAY, DIM[, MASK])

Arguments:

ARRAY	Shall be an array of type INTEGER(*), REAL(*) or COMPLEX(*).
DIM	(Optional) shall be a scalar of type INTEGER with a value in the range from 1 to n, where n equals the rank of *ARRAY*.
MASK	(Optional) shall be of type LOGICAL and either be a scalar or an array of the same shape as *ARRAY*.

Return value:

The result is of the same type as *ARRAY*.

If *DIM* is absent, a scalar with the sum of all elements in *ARRAY* is returned. Otherwise, an array of rank n-1, where n equals the rank of *ARRAY*,and a shape similar to that of *ARRAY* with dimension *DIM* dropped is returned.

Example:

```
        PROGRAM test_sum
          INTEGER :: x(5) = (/ 1, 2, 3, 4 ,5 /)
          print *, SUM(x)                    ! all elements, sum = 15
          print *, SUM(x, MASK=MOD(x, 2)==1) ! odd elements, sum = 9
        END PROGRAM
```

See also: Section 6.168 [PRODUCT], page 131

6.203 SYMLNK — Create a symbolic link

Description:

Makes a symbolic link from file *PATH1* to *PATH2*. A null character (CHAR(0)) can be used to mark the end of the names in *PATH1* and *PATH2*; otherwise, trailing blanks in the file names are ignored. If the *STATUS* argument is supplied, it contains 0 on success or a nonzero error code upon return; see symlink(2). If the system does not supply symlink(2), ENOSYS is returned.

This intrinsic is provided in both subroutine and function forms; however, only one form can be used in any given program unit.

Standard: GNU extension

Class: Subroutine, function

Syntax:

```
CALL SYMLNK(PATH1, PATH2 [, STATUS])
STATUS = SYMLNK(PATH1, PATH2)
```

Arguments:
PATH1	Shall be of default **CHARACTER** type.
PATH2	Shall be of default **CHARACTER** type.
STATUS	(Optional) Shall be of default **INTEGER** type.

See also: Section 6.129 [LINK], page 110, Section 6.217 [UNLINK], page 158

6.204 SYSTEM — Execute a shell command

Description:

Passes the command *COMMAND* to a shell (see system(3)). If argument *STATUS* is present, it contains the value returned by system(3), which is presumably 0 if the shell command succeeded. Note that which shell is used to invoke the command is system-dependent and environment-dependent.

This intrinsic is provided in both subroutine and function forms; however, only one form can be used in any given program unit.

Standard: GNU extension

Class: Subroutine, function

Syntax:

```
CALL SYSTEM(COMMAND [, STATUS])
STATUS = SYSTEM(COMMAND)
```

Arguments:
COMMAND	Shall be of default **CHARACTER** type.
STATUS	(Optional) Shall be of default **INTEGER** type.

See also:

6.205 SYSTEM_CLOCK — Time function

Description:

Determines the *COUNT* of milliseconds of wall clock time since the Epoch (00:00:00 UTC, January 1, 1970) modulo *COUNT_MAX*, *COUNT_RATE* determines the number of clock ticks per second. *COUNT_RATE* and *COUNT_MAX* are constant and specific to gfortran.

If there is no clock, *COUNT* is set to -HUGE(COUNT), and *COUNT_RATE* and *COUNT_MAX* are set to zero

Standard: F95 and later

Class: Subroutine

Syntax: `CALL SYSTEM_CLOCK([COUNT, COUNT_RATE, COUNT_MAX])`

Arguments:
Arguments:

           COUNT   (Optional) shall be a scalar of type default `INTEGER` with `INTENT(OUT)`.

           COUNT_RATE(Optional) shall be a scalar of type default `INTEGER` with `INTENT(OUT)`.

           COUNT_MAX (Optional) shall be a scalar of type default `INTEGER` with `INTENT(OUT)`.

Example:

```
PROGRAM test_system_clock
  INTEGER :: count, count_rate, count_max
  CALL SYSTEM_CLOCK(count, count_rate, count_max)
  WRITE(*,*) count, count_rate, count_max
END PROGRAM
```

See also: Section 6.51 [DATE_AND_TIME], page 67, Section 6.48 [CPU_TIME], page 65

6.206 TAN — Tangent function

Description:

      `TAN(X)` computes the tangent of *X*.

Standard: F77 and later

Class: Elemental function

Syntax: `RESULT = TAN(X)`

Arguments:

      X   The type shall be `REAL(*)`.

Return value:

      The return value is of type `REAL(*)`. The kind type parameter is the same as *X*.

Example:

```
program test_tan
  real(8) :: x = 0.165_8
  x = tan(x)
end program test_tan
```

Specific names:

Name	Argument	Return type	Standard
DTAN(X)	REAL(8) X	REAL(8)	F95 and later

See also: Section 6.21 [ATAN], page 49

6.207 TANH — Hyperbolic tangent function

Description:

      `TANH(X)` computes the hyperbolic tangent of *X*.

Standard: F77 and later

Class: Elemental function

Syntax: X = TANH(X)

Arguments:

        X   The type shall be `REAL(*)`.

Return value:

    The return value is of type `REAL(*)` and lies in the range $-1 \leq tanh(x) \leq 1$.

Example:

```
program test_tanh
  real(8) :: x = 2.1_8
  x = tanh(x)
end program test_tanh
```

Specific names:

Name	Argument	Return type	Standard
DTANH(X)	REAL(8) X	REAL(8)	F95 and later

See also: Section 6.23 [ATANH], page 50

6.208 TIME — Time function

Description:

    Returns the current time encoded as an integer (in the manner of the UNIX function `time(3)`). This value is suitable for passing to `CTIME()`, `GMTIME()`, and `LTIME()`.

    This intrinsic is not fully portable, such as to systems with 32-bit `INTEGER` types but supporting times wider than 32 bits. Therefore, the values returned by this intrinsic might be, or become, negative, or numerically less than previous values, during a single run of the compiled program.

    See Section 6.209 [TIME8], page 155, for information on a similar intrinsic that might be portable to more GNU Fortran implementations, though to fewer Fortran compilers.

Standard: GNU extension

Class: Function

Syntax: RESULT = TIME()

Return value:

    The return value is a scalar of type `INTEGER(4)`.

See also: Section 6.50 [CTIME], page 66, Section 6.95 [GMTIME], page 93, Section 6.140 [LTIME], page 116, Section 6.147 [MCLOCK], page 120, Section 6.209 [TIME8], page 155

6.209 `TIME8` — Time function (64-bit)

Description:

Returns the current time encoded as an integer (in the manner of the UNIX function `time(3)`). This value is suitable for passing to `CTIME()`, `GMTIME()`, and `LTIME()`.

Warning: this intrinsic does not increase the range of the timing values over that returned by `time(3)`. On a system with a 32-bit `time(3)`, `TIME8()` will return a 32-bit value, even though it is converted to a 64-bit `INTEGER(8)` value. That means overflows of the 32-bit value can still occur. Therefore, the values returned by this intrinsic might be or become negative or numerically less than previous values during a single run of the compiled program.

Standard: GNU extension

Class: Function

Syntax: `RESULT = TIME8()`

Return value:

The return value is a scalar of type `INTEGER(8)`.

See also: Section 6.50 [CTIME], page 66, Section 6.95 [GMTIME], page 93, Section 6.140 [LTIME], page 116, Section 6.148 [MCLOCK8], page 120, Section 6.208 [TIME], page 154

6.210 `TINY` — Smallest positive number of a real kind

Description:

`TINY(X)` returns the smallest positive (non zero) number in the model of the type of `X`.

Standard: F95 and later

Class: Inquiry function

Syntax: `RESULT = TINY(X)`

Arguments:

X Shall be of type `REAL`.

Return value:

The return value is of the same type and kind as X

Example: See `HUGE` for an example.

6.211 `TRANSFER` — Transfer bit patterns

Description:

Interprets the bitwise representation of *SOURCE* in memory as if it is the representation of a variable or array of the same type and type parameters as *MOLD*.

This is approximately equivalent to the C concept of *casting* one type to another.

Standard: F95 and later

Class: Transformational function

Syntax: `RESULT = TRANSFER(SOURCE, MOLD[, SIZE])`

Arguments:

SOURCE	Shall be a scalar or an array of any type.
MOLD	Shall be a scalar or an array of any type.
SIZE	(Optional) shall be a scalar of type `INTEGER`.

Return value:

The result has the same type as *MOLD*, with the bit level representation of *SOURCE*. If *SIZE* is present, the result is a one-dimensional array of length *SIZE*. If *SIZE* is absent but *MOLD* is an array (of any size or shape), the result is a one- dimensional array of the minimum length needed to contain the entirety of the bitwise representation of *SOURCE*. If *SIZE* is absent and *MOLD* is a scalar, the result is a scalar.

If the bitwise representation of the result is longer than that of *SOURCE*, then the leading bits of the result correspond to those of *SOURCE* and any trailing bits are filled arbitrarily.

When the resulting bit representation does not correspond to a valid representation of a variable of the same type as *MOLD*, the results are undefined, and subsequent operations on the result cannot be guaranteed to produce sensible behavior. For example, it is possible to create `LOGICAL` variables for which `VAR` and `.NOT.VAR` both appear to be true.

Example:

```
PROGRAM test_transfer
  integer :: x = 2143289344
  print *, transfer(x, 1.0)    ! prints "NaN" on i686
END PROGRAM
```

6.212 TRANSPOSE — Transpose an array of rank two

Description:

Transpose an array of rank two. Element (i, j) of the result has the value `MATRIX(j, i)`, for all i, j.

Standard: F95 and later

Class: Transformational function

Syntax: `RESULT = TRANSPOSE(MATRIX)`

Arguments:

MATRIX	Shall be an array of any type and have a rank of two.

Return value:

The result has the the same type as *MATRIX*, and has shape (/ m, n /) if *MATRIX* has shape (/ n, m /).

6.213 TRIM — Remove trailing blank characters of a string

Description:

Removes trailing blank characters of a string.

Standard: F95 and later

Class: Transformational function

Syntax: RESULT = TRIM(STRING)

Arguments:

STRING   Shall be a scalar of type CHARACTER(*).

Return value:

A scalar of type CHARACTER(*) which length is that of *STRING* less the number of trailing blanks.

Example:

```
PROGRAM test_trim
  CHARACTER(len=10), PARAMETER :: s = "GFORTRAN  "
  WRITE(*,*) LEN(s), LEN(TRIM(s))  ! "10 8", with/without trailing blanks
END PROGRAM
```

See also: Section 6.8 [ADJUSTL], page 41, Section 6.9 [ADJUSTR], page 41

6.214 TTYNAM — Get the name of a terminal device.

Description:

Get the name of a terminal device. For more information, see ttyname(3).

This intrinsic is provided in both subroutine and function forms; however, only one form can be used in any given program unit.

Standard: GNU extension

Class: Subroutine, function

Syntax:

CALL TTYNAM(UNIT, NAME)
NAME = TTYNAM(UNIT)

Arguments:

UNIT   Shall be a scalar INTEGER(*).
NAME   Shall be of type CHARACTER(*).

Example:

```
PROGRAM test_ttynam
  INTEGER :: unit
  DO unit = 1, 10
    IF (isatty(unit=unit)) write(*,*) ttynam(unit)
  END DO
END PROGRAM
```

See also: Section 6.116 [ISATTY], page 104

6.215 UBOUND — Upper dimension bounds of an array

Description:

Returns the upper bounds of an array, or a single upper bound along the *DIM* dimension.

Standard: F95 and later

Class: Inquiry function

Syntax: `RESULT = UBOUND(ARRAY [, DIM [, KIND]])`

Arguments:

ARRAY	Shall be an array, of any type.
DIM	(Optional) Shall be a scalar `INTEGER(*)`.
KIND	(Optional) An `INTEGER` initialization expression indicating the kind parameter of the result.

Return value:

The return value is of type `INTEGER` and of kind *KIND*. If *KIND* is absent, the return value is of default integer kind. If *DIM* is absent, the result is an array of the upper bounds of *ARRAY*. If *DIM* is present, the result is a scalar corresponding to the upper bound of the array along that dimension. If *ARRAY* is an expression rather than a whole array or array structure component, or if it has a zero extent along the relevant dimension, the upper bound is taken to be the number of elements along the relevant dimension.

See also: Section 6.123 [LBOUND], page 107

6.216 UMASK — Set the file creation mask

Description:

Sets the file creation mask to *MASK* and returns the old value in argument *OLD* if it is supplied. See `umask(2)`.

Standard: GNU extension

Class: Subroutine

Syntax: `CALL UMASK(MASK [, OLD])`

Arguments:

MASK	Shall be a scalar of type `INTEGER(*)`.
MASK	(Optional) Shall be a scalar of type `INTEGER(*)`.

6.217 UNLINK — Remove a file from the file system

Description:

Unlinks the file *PATH*. A null character (`CHAR(0)`) can be used to mark the end of the name in *PATH*; otherwise, trailing blanks in the file name are ignored. If the *STATUS* argument is supplied, it contains 0 on success or a nonzero error code upon return; see `unlink(2)`.

This intrinsic is provided in both subroutine and function forms; however, only one form can be used in any given program unit.

Standard: GNU extension

Class: Subroutine, function

Syntax:

```
CALL UNLINK(PATH [, STATUS])
STATUS = UNLINK(PATH)
```

Arguments:

PATH	Shall be of default CHARACTER type.
STATUS	(Optional) Shall be of default INTEGER type.

See also: Section 6.129 [LINK], page 110, Section 6.203 [SYMLNK], page 151

6.218 UNPACK — Unpack an array of rank one into an array

Description:

Store the elements of *VECTOR* in an array of higher rank.

Standard: F95 and later

Class: Transformational function

Syntax: RESULT = UNPACK(VECTOR, MASK, FIELD)

Arguments:

VECTOR	Shall be an array of any type and rank one. It shall have at least as many elements as *MASK* has TRUE values.
MASK	Shall be an array of type LOGICAL.
FIELD	Shall be of the sam type as *VECTOR* and have the same shape as *MASK*.

Return value:

The resulting array corresponds to *FIELD* with TRUE elements of *MASK* replaced by values from *VECTOR* in array element order.

Example:

```
PROGRAM test_unpack
  integer :: vector(2)  = (/1,1/)
  logical :: mask(4)  = (/ .TRUE., .FALSE., .FALSE., .TRUE. /)
  integer :: field(2,2) = 0, unity(2,2)

  ! result: unity matrix
  unity = unpack(vector, reshape(mask, (/2,2/)), field)
END PROGRAM
```

See also: Section 6.164 [PACK], page 129, Section 6.198 [SPREAD], page 148

6.219 VERIFY — Scan a string for the absence of a set of characters

Description:

Verifies that all the characters in a *SET* are present in a *STRING*.

If *BACK* is either absent or equals FALSE, this function returns the position of the leftmost character of *STRING* that is not in *SET*. If *BACK* equals TRUE, the rightmost position is returned. If all characters of *SET* are found in *STRING*, the result is zero.

Standard: F95 and later

Class: Elemental function

Syntax: `RESULT = VERIFY(STRING, SET[, BACK [, KIND]])`

Arguments:

STRING	Shall be of type `CHARACTER(*)`.
SET	Shall be of type `CHARACTER(*)`.
BACK	(Optional) shall be of type `LOGICAL`.
KIND	(Optional) An `INTEGER` initialization expression indicating the kind parameter of the result.

Return value:

The return value is of type `INTEGER` and of kind *KIND*. If *KIND* is absent, the return value is of default integer kind.

Example:

```
 PROGRAM test_verify
    WRITE(*,*) VERIFY("FORTRAN", "AO")          ! 1, found 'F'
    WRITE(*,*) VERIFY("FORTRAN", "FOO")         ! 3, found 'R'
    WRITE(*,*) VERIFY("FORTRAN", "C++")         ! 1, found 'F'
    WRITE(*,*) VERIFY("FORTRAN", "C++", .TRUE.) ! 7, found 'N'
    WRITE(*,*) VERIFY("FORTRAN", "FORTRAN")     ! 0' found none
 END PROGRAM
```

See also: Section 6.182 [SCAN], page 139, Section 6.108 [INDEX intrinsic], page 100

6.220 `XOR` — Bitwise logical exclusive OR

Description:

Bitwise logical exclusive or.

This intrinsic routine is provided for backwards compatibility with GNU Fortran 77. For integer arguments, programmers should consider the use of the Section 6.106 [IEOR], page 99 intrinsic defined by the Fortran standard.

Standard: GNU extension

Class: Function

Syntax: `RESULT = XOR(X, Y)`

Arguments:

X	The type shall be either `INTEGER(*)` or `LOGICAL`.
Y	The type shall be either `INTEGER(*)` or `LOGICAL`.

Return value:

The return type is either `INTEGER(*)` or `LOGICAL` after cross-promotion of the arguments.

Example:

```
PROGRAM test_xor
  LOGICAL :: T = .TRUE., F = .FALSE.
  INTEGER :: a, b
  DATA a / Z'F' /, b / Z'3' /

  WRITE (*,*) XOR(T, T), XOR(T, F), XOR(F, T), XOR(F, F)
  WRITE (*,*) XOR(a, b)
END PROGRAM
```

See also: F95 elemental function: Section 6.106 [IEOR], page 99

7 Intrinsic Modules

7.1 ISO_FORTRAN_ENV

Standard: Fortran 2003

The `ISO_FORTRAN_ENV` module provides the following scalar default-integer named constants:

CHARACTER_STORAGE_SIZE:
> Size in bits of the character storage unit.

ERROR_UNIT:
> Indentifies the preconnected unit used for error reporting.

FILE_STORAGE_SIZE:
> Size in bits of the file-storage unit.

INPUT_UNIT:
> Indentifies the preconnected unit indentified by the asterisk (∗) in `READ` statement.

IOSTAT_END:
> The value assigned to the variable passed to the IOSTAT= specifier of an input/output statement if an end-of-file condition occurred.

IOSTAT_EOR:
> The value assigned to the variable passed to the IOSTAT= specifier of an input/output statement if an end-of-record condition occurred.

NUMERIC_STORAGE_SIZE:
> The size in bits of the numeric storage unit.

OUTPUT_UNIT:
> Indentifies the preconnected unit indentified by the asterisk (∗) in `WRITE` statement.

7.2 ISO_C_BINDING

Standard: Fortran 2003

The following intrinsic procedures are provided by the module; their definition can be found in the section Intrinsic Procedures of this manual.

C_ASSOCIATED
C_F_POINTER
C_F_PROCPOINTER
C_FUNLOC

C_LOC

The `ISO_C_BINDING` module provides the following named constants of the type integer, which can be used as KIND type parameter. Note that GNU Fortran currently does not support the `C_INT_FAST`... KIND type parameters (marked by an asterix (∗) in the list below). The `C_INT_FAST...` parameters have therefore the value −2 and cannot be used as KIND type parameter of the `INTEGER` type.

Fortran Type	Named constant	C type
INTEGER	C_INT	int
INTEGER	C_SHORT	short int
INTEGER	C_LONG	long int
INTEGER	C_LONG_LONG	long long int
INTEGER	C_SIGNED_CHAR	signed char/unsigned char
INTEGER	C_SIZE_T	size_t
INTEGER	C_INT8_T	int8_t
INTEGER	C_INT16_T	int16_t
INTEGER	C_INT32_T	int32_t
INTEGER	C_INT64_T	int64_t
INTEGER	C_INT_LEAST8_T	int_least8_t
INTEGER	C_INT_LEAST16_T	int_least16_t
INTEGER	C_INT_LEAST32_T	int_least32_t
INTEGER	C_INT_LEAST64_T	int_least64_t
INTEGER	C_INT_FAST8_T*	int_fast8_t
INTEGER	C_INT_FAST16_T*	int_fast16_t
INTEGER	C_INT_FAST32_T*	int_fast32_t
INTEGER	C_INT_FAST64_T*	int_fast64_t
INTEGER	C_INTMAX_T	intmax_t
INTEGER	C_INTPTR_T	intptr_t
REAL	C_FLOAT	float
REAL	C_DOUBLE	double
REAL	C_LONG_DOUBLE	long double
COMPLEX	C_FLOAT_COMPLEX	float _Complex
COMPLEX	C_DOUBLE_COMPLEX	double _Complex
COMPLEX	C_LONG_DOUBLE_COMPLEX	long double _Complex
LOGICAL	C_BOOL	_Bool
CHARACTER	C_CHAR	char

Additionally, the following (`CHARACTER(KIND=C_CHAR)`) are defined.

Name	C definition	Value
C_NULL_CHAR	null character	'\0'
C_ALERT	alert	'\a'
C_BACKSPACE	backspace	'\b'
C_FORM_FEED	form feed	'\f'
C_NEW_LINE	new line	'\n'
C_CARRIAGE_RETURN	carriage return	'\r'
C_HORIZONTAL_TAB	horizontal tab	'\t'
C_VERTICAL_TAB	vertical tab	'\v'

7.3 OpenMP Modules `OMP_LIB` and `OMP_LIB_KINDS`

Standard: OpenMP Application Program Interface v2.5

The OpenMP Fortran runtime library routines are provided both in a form of two Fortran 90 modules, named `OMP_LIB` and `OMP_LIB_KINDS`, and in a form of a Fortran **include** file named 'omp_lib.h'. The procedures provided by `OMP_LIB` can be found in the Section "Introduction" in *GNU OpenMP runtime library* manual, the named constants defined in the `OMP_LIB_KINDS` module are listed below.

For details refer to the actual OpenMP Application Program Interface v2.5.

`OMP_LIB_KINDS` provides the following scalar default-integer named constants:

```
omp_integer_kind
omp_logical_kind
omp_lock_kind
omp_nest_lock_kind
```

Contributing

Free software is only possible if people contribute to efforts to create it. We're always in need of more people helping out with ideas and comments, writing documentation and contributing code.

If you want to contribute to GNU Fortran, have a look at the long lists of projects you can take on. Some of these projects are small, some of them are large; some are completely orthogonal to the rest of what is happening on GNU Fortran, but others are "mainstream" projects in need of enthusiastic hackers. All of these projects are important! We'll eventually get around to the things here, but they are also things doable by someone who is willing and able.

Contributors to GNU Fortran

Most of the parser was hand-crafted by *Andy Vaught*, who is also the initiator of the whole project. Thanks Andy! Most of the interface with GCC was written by *Paul Brook*.

The following individuals have contributed code and/or ideas and significant help to the GNU Fortran project (in alphabetical order):

- Janne Blomqvist
- Steven Bosscher
- Paul Brook
- Tobias Burnus
- François-Xavier Coudert
- Bud Davis
- Jerry DeLisle
- Erik Edelmann
- Bernhard Fischer
- Daniel Franke
- Richard Guenther
- Richard Henderson
- Katherine Holcomb
- Jakub Jelinek
- Niels Kristian Bech Jensen
- Steven Johnson
- Steven G. Kargl
- Thomas Koenig
- Asher Langton
- H. J. Lu
- Toon Moene
- Brooks Moses
- Andrew Pinski
- Tim Prince

- Christopher D. Rickett
- Richard Sandiford
- Tobias Schlüter
- Roger Sayle
- Paul Thomas
- Andy Vaught
- Feng Wang
- Janus Weil

The following people have contributed bug reports, smaller or larger patches, and much needed feedback and encouragement for the GNU Fortran project:

- Bill Clodius
- Dominique d'Humières
- Kate Hedstrom
- Erik Schnetter

Many other individuals have helped debug, test and improve the GNU Fortran compiler over the past few years, and we welcome you to do the same! If you already have done so, and you would like to see your name listed in the list above, please contact us.

Projects

Help build the test suite

> Solicit more code for donation to the test suite: the more extensive the testsuite, the smaller the risk of breaking things in the future! We can keep code private on request.

Bug hunting/squishing

> Find bugs and write more test cases! Test cases are especially very welcome, because it allows us to concentrate on fixing bugs instead of isolating them. Going through the bugzilla database at `http://gcc.gnu.org/bugzilla/` to reduce testcases posted there and add more information (for example, for which version does the testcase work, for which versions does it fail?) is also very helpful.

Proposed Extensions

Here's a list of proposed extensions for the GNU Fortran compiler, in no particular order. Most of these are necessary to be fully compatible with existing Fortran compilers, but they are not part of the official J3 Fortran 95 standard.

Compiler extensions:

- User-specified alignment rules for structures.
- Flag to generate `Makefile` info.
- Automatically extend single precision constants to double.

- Compile code that conserves memory by dynamically allocating common and module storage either on stack or heap.
- Compile flag to generate code for array conformance checking (suggest -CC).
- User control of symbol names (underscores, etc).
- Compile setting for maximum size of stack frame size before spilling parts to static or heap.
- Flag to force local variables into static space.
- Flag to force local variables onto stack.

Environment Options

- Pluggable library modules for random numbers, linear algebra. LA should use BLAS calling conventions.
- Environment variables controlling actions on arithmetic exceptions like overflow, underflow, precision loss—Generate NaN, abort, default. action.
- Set precision for fp units that support it (i387).
- Variable for setting fp rounding mode.
- Variable to fill uninitialized variables with a user-defined bit pattern.
- Environment variable controlling filename that is opened for that unit number.
- Environment variable to clear/trash memory being freed.
- Environment variable to control tracing of allocations and frees.
- Environment variable to display allocated memory at normal program end.
- Environment variable for filename for * IO-unit.
- Environment variable for temporary file directory.
- Environment variable forcing standard output to be line buffered (unix).

GNU General Public License

Version 3, 29 June 2007

Copyright © 2007 Free Software Foundation, Inc. http://fsf.org/

Everyone is permitted to copy and distribute verbatim copies of this license document, but changing it is not allowed.

Preamble

The GNU General Public License is a free, copyleft license for software and other kinds of works.

The licenses for most software and other practical works are designed to take away your freedom to share and change the works. By contrast, the GNU General Public License is intended to guarantee your freedom to share and change all versions of a program–to make sure it remains free software for all its users. We, the Free Software Foundation, use the GNU General Public License for most of our software; it applies also to any other work released this way by its authors. You can apply it to your programs, too.

When we speak of free software, we are referring to freedom, not price. Our General Public Licenses are designed to make sure that you have the freedom to distribute copies of free software (and charge for them if you wish), that you receive source code or can get it if you want it, that you can change the software or use pieces of it in new free programs, and that you know you can do these things.

To protect your rights, we need to prevent others from denying you these rights or asking you to surrender the rights. Therefore, you have certain responsibilities if you distribute copies of the software, or if you modify it: responsibilities to respect the freedom of others.

For example, if you distribute copies of such a program, whether gratis or for a fee, you must pass on to the recipients the same freedoms that you received. You must make sure that they, too, receive or can get the source code. And you must show them these terms so they know their rights.

Developers that use the GNU GPL protect your rights with two steps: (1) assert copyright on the software, and (2) offer you this License giving you legal permission to copy, distribute and/or modify it.

For the developers' and authors' protection, the GPL clearly explains that there is no warranty for this free software. For both users' and authors' sake, the GPL requires that modified versions be marked as changed, so that their problems will not be attributed erroneously to authors of previous versions.

Some devices are designed to deny users access to install or run modified versions of the software inside them, although the manufacturer can do so. This is fundamentally incompatible with the aim of protecting users' freedom to change the software. The systematic pattern of such abuse occurs in the area of products for individuals to use, which is precisely where it is most unacceptable. Therefore, we have designed this version of the GPL to prohibit the practice for those products. If such problems arise substantially in other domains, we stand ready to extend this provision to those domains in future versions of the GPL, as needed to protect the freedom of users.

Finally, every program is threatened constantly by software patents. States should not allow patents to restrict development and use of software on general-purpose computers, but in those that do, we wish to avoid the special danger that patents applied to a free program could make it effectively proprietary. To prevent this, the GPL assures that patents cannot be used to render the program non-free.

The precise terms and conditions for copying, distribution and modification follow.

TERMS AND CONDITIONS

0. Definitions.

    "This License" refers to version 3 of the GNU General Public License.

    "Copyright" also means copyright-like laws that apply to other kinds of works, such as semiconductor masks.

    "The Program" refers to any copyrightable work licensed under this License. Each licensee is addressed as "you". "Licensees" and "recipients" may be individuals or organizations.

    To "modify" a work means to copy from or adapt all or part of the work in a fashion requiring copyright permission, other than the making of an exact copy. The resulting work is called a "modified version" of the earlier work or a work "based on" the earlier work.

    A "covered work" means either the unmodified Program or a work based on the Program.

    To "propagate" a work means to do anything with it that, without permission, would make you directly or secondarily liable for infringement under applicable copyright law, except executing it on a computer or modifying a private copy. Propagation includes copying, distribution (with or without modification), making available to the public, and in some countries other activities as well.

    To "convey" a work means any kind of propagation that enables other parties to make or receive copies. Mere interaction with a user through a computer network, with no transfer of a copy, is not conveying.

    An interactive user interface displays "Appropriate Legal Notices" to the extent that it includes a convenient and prominently visible feature that (1) displays an appropriate copyright notice, and (2) tells the user that there is no warranty for the work (except to the extent that warranties are provided), that licensees may convey the work under this License, and how to view a copy of this License. If the interface presents a list of user commands or options, such as a menu, a prominent item in the list meets this criterion.

1. Source Code.

    The "source code" for a work means the preferred form of the work for making modifications to it. "Object code" means any non-source form of a work.

    A "Standard Interface" means an interface that either is an official standard defined by a recognized standards body, or, in the case of interfaces specified for a particular programming language, one that is widely used among developers working in that language.

The "System Libraries" of an executable work include anything, other than the work as a whole, that (a) is included in the normal form of packaging a Major Component, but which is not part of that Major Component, and (b) serves only to enable use of the work with that Major Component, or to implement a Standard Interface for which an implementation is available to the public in source code form. A "Major Component", in this context, means a major essential component (kernel, window system, and so on) of the specific operating system (if any) on which the executable work runs, or a compiler used to produce the work, or an object code interpreter used to run it.

The "Corresponding Source" for a work in object code form means all the source code needed to generate, install, and (for an executable work) run the object code and to modify the work, including scripts to control those activities. However, it does not include the work's System Libraries, or general-purpose tools or generally available free programs which are used unmodified in performing those activities but which are not part of the work. For example, Corresponding Source includes interface definition files associated with source files for the work, and the source code for shared libraries and dynamically linked subprograms that the work is specifically designed to require, such as by intimate data communication or control flow between those subprograms and other parts of the work.

The Corresponding Source need not include anything that users can regenerate automatically from other parts of the Corresponding Source.

The Corresponding Source for a work in source code form is that same work.

2. Basic Permissions.

All rights granted under this License are granted for the term of copyright on the Program, and are irrevocable provided the stated conditions are met. This License explicitly affirms your unlimited permission to run the unmodified Program. The output from running a covered work is covered by this License only if the output, given its content, constitutes a covered work. This License acknowledges your rights of fair use or other equivalent, as provided by copyright law.

You may make, run and propagate covered works that you do not convey, without conditions so long as your license otherwise remains in force. You may convey covered works to others for the sole purpose of having them make modifications exclusively for you, or provide you with facilities for running those works, provided that you comply with the terms of this License in conveying all material for which you do not control copyright. Those thus making or running the covered works for you must do so exclusively on your behalf, under your direction and control, on terms that prohibit them from making any copies of your copyrighted material outside their relationship with you.

Conveying under any other circumstances is permitted solely under the conditions stated below. Sublicensing is not allowed; section 10 makes it unnecessary.

3. Protecting Users' Legal Rights From Anti-Circumvention Law.

No covered work shall be deemed part of an effective technological measure under any applicable law fulfilling obligations under article 11 of the WIPO copyright treaty adopted on 20 December 1996, or similar laws prohibiting or restricting circumvention of such measures.

When you convey a covered work, you waive any legal power to forbid circumvention of technological measures to the extent such circumvention is effected by exercising rights under this License with respect to the covered work, and you disclaim any intention to limit operation or modification of the work as a means of enforcing, against the work's users, your or third parties' legal rights to forbid circumvention of technological measures.

4. Conveying Verbatim Copies.

You may convey verbatim copies of the Program's source code as you receive it, in any medium, provided that you conspicuously and appropriately publish on each copy an appropriate copyright notice; keep intact all notices stating that this License and any non-permissive terms added in accord with section 7 apply to the code; keep intact all notices of the absence of any warranty; and give all recipients a copy of this License along with the Program.

You may charge any price or no price for each copy that you convey, and you may offer support or warranty protection for a fee.

5. Conveying Modified Source Versions.

You may convey a work based on the Program, or the modifications to produce it from the Program, in the form of source code under the terms of section 4, provided that you also meet all of these conditions:

   a. The work must carry prominent notices stating that you modified it, and giving a relevant date.

   b. The work must carry prominent notices stating that it is released under this License and any conditions added under section 7. This requirement modifies the requirement in section 4 to "keep intact all notices".

   c. You must license the entire work, as a whole, under this License to anyone who comes into possession of a copy. This License will therefore apply, along with any applicable section 7 additional terms, to the whole of the work, and all its parts, regardless of how they are packaged. This License gives no permission to license the work in any other way, but it does not invalidate such permission if you have separately received it.

   d. If the work has interactive user interfaces, each must display Appropriate Legal Notices; however, if the Program has interactive interfaces that do not display Appropriate Legal Notices, your work need not make them do so.

A compilation of a covered work with other separate and independent works, which are not by their nature extensions of the covered work, and which are not combined with it such as to form a larger program, in or on a volume of a storage or distribution medium, is called an "aggregate" if the compilation and its resulting copyright are not used to limit the access or legal rights of the compilation's users beyond what the individual works permit. Inclusion of a covered work in an aggregate does not cause this License to apply to the other parts of the aggregate.

6. Conveying Non-Source Forms.

You may convey a covered work in object code form under the terms of sections 4 and 5, provided that you also convey the machine-readable Corresponding Source under the terms of this License, in one of these ways:

a. Convey the object code in, or embodied in, a physical product (including a phys-
    ical distribution medium), accompanied by the Corresponding Source fixed on a
    durable physical medium customarily used for software interchange.

b. Convey the object code in, or embodied in, a physical product (including a physi-
    cal distribution medium), accompanied by a written offer, valid for at least three
    years and valid for as long as you offer spare parts or customer support for that
    product model, to give anyone who possesses the object code either (1) a copy of
    the Corresponding Source for all the software in the product that is covered by this
    License, on a durable physical medium customarily used for software interchange,
    for a price no more than your reasonable cost of physically performing this con-
    veying of source, or (2) access to copy the Corresponding Source from a network
    server at no charge.

c. Convey individual copies of the object code with a copy of the written offer to
    provide the Corresponding Source. This alternative is allowed only occasionally
    and noncommercially, and only if you received the object code with such an offer,
    in accord with subsection 6b.

d. Convey the object code by offering access from a designated place (gratis or for
    a charge), and offer equivalent access to the Corresponding Source in the same
    way through the same place at no further charge. You need not require recipients
    to copy the Corresponding Source along with the object code. If the place to
    copy the object code is a network server, the Corresponding Source may be on
    a different server (operated by you or a third party) that supports equivalent
    copying facilities, provided you maintain clear directions next to the object code
    saying where to find the Corresponding Source. Regardless of what server hosts
    the Corresponding Source, you remain obligated to ensure that it is available for
    as long as needed to satisfy these requirements.

e. Convey the object code using peer-to-peer transmission, provided you inform other
    peers where the object code and Corresponding Source of the work are being offered
    to the general public at no charge under subsection 6d.

A separable portion of the object code, whose source code is excluded from the Corresponding Source as a System Library, need not be included in conveying the object
code work.

A "User Product" is either (1) a "consumer product", which means any tangible personal property which is normally used for personal, family, or household purposes, or
(2) anything designed or sold for incorporation into a dwelling. In determining whether
a product is a consumer product, doubtful cases shall be resolved in favor of coverage.
For a particular product received by a particular user, "normally used" refers to a
typical or common use of that class of product, regardless of the status of the particular user or of the way in which the particular user actually uses, or expects or is
expected to use, the product. A product is a consumer product regardless of whether
the product has substantial commercial, industrial or non-consumer uses, unless such
uses represent the only significant mode of use of the product.

"Installation Information" for a User Product means any methods, procedures, autho-
rization keys, or other information required to install and execute modified versions of a
covered work in that User Product from a modified version of its Corresponding Source.

The information must suffice to ensure that the continued functioning of the modified object code is in no case prevented or interfered with solely because modification has been made.

If you convey an object code work under this section in, or with, or specifically for use in, a User Product, and the conveying occurs as part of a transaction in which the right of possession and use of the User Product is transferred to the recipient in perpetuity or for a fixed term (regardless of how the transaction is characterized), the Corresponding Source conveyed under this section must be accompanied by the Installation Information. But this requirement does not apply if neither you nor any third party retains the ability to install modified object code on the User Product (for example, the work has been installed in ROM).

The requirement to provide Installation Information does not include a requirement to continue to provide support service, warranty, or updates for a work that has been modified or installed by the recipient, or for the User Product in which it has been modified or installed. Access to a network may be denied when the modification itself materially and adversely affects the operation of the network or violates the rules and protocols for communication across the network.

Corresponding Source conveyed, and Installation Information provided, in accord with this section must be in a format that is publicly documented (and with an implementation available to the public in source code form), and must require no special password or key for unpacking, reading or copying.

7. Additional Terms.

"Additional permissions" are terms that supplement the terms of this License by making exceptions from one or more of its conditions. Additional permissions that are applicable to the entire Program shall be treated as though they were included in this License, to the extent that they are valid under applicable law. If additional permissions apply only to part of the Program, that part may be used separately under those permissions, but the entire Program remains governed by this License without regard to the additional permissions.

When you convey a copy of a covered work, you may at your option remove any additional permissions from that copy, or from any part of it. (Additional permissions may be written to require their own removal in certain cases when you modify the work.) You may place additional permissions on material, added by you to a covered work, for which you have or can give appropriate copyright permission.

Notwithstanding any other provision of this License, for material you add to a covered work, you may (if authorized by the copyright holders of that material) supplement the terms of this License with terms:

a. Disclaiming warranty or limiting liability differently from the terms of sections 15 and 16 of this License; or

b. Requiring preservation of specified reasonable legal notices or author attributions in that material or in the Appropriate Legal Notices displayed by works containing it; or

c. Prohibiting misrepresentation of the origin of that material, or requiring that modified versions of such material be marked in reasonable ways as different from the original version; or

d. Limiting the use for publicity purposes of names of licensors or authors of the material; or

e. Declining to grant rights under trademark law for use of some trade names, trademarks, or service marks; or

f. Requiring indemnification of licensors and authors of that material by anyone who conveys the material (or modified versions of it) with contractual assumptions of liability to the recipient, for any liability that these contractual assumptions directly impose on those licensors and authors.

All other non-permissive additional terms are considered "further restrictions" within the meaning of section 10. If the Program as you received it, or any part of it, contains a notice stating that it is governed by this License along with a term that is a further restriction, you may remove that term. If a license document contains a further restriction but permits relicensing or conveying under this License, you may add to a covered work material governed by the terms of that license document, provided that the further restriction does not survive such relicensing or conveying.

If you add terms to a covered work in accord with this section, you must place, in the relevant source files, a statement of the additional terms that apply to those files, or a notice indicating where to find the applicable terms.

Additional terms, permissive or non-permissive, may be stated in the form of a separately written license, or stated as exceptions; the above requirements apply either way.

8. Termination.

You may not propagate or modify a covered work except as expressly provided under this License. Any attempt otherwise to propagate or modify it is void, and will automatically terminate your rights under this License (including any patent licenses granted under the third paragraph of section 11).

However, if you cease all violation of this License, then your license from a particular copyright holder is reinstated (a) provisionally, unless and until the copyright holder explicitly and finally terminates your license, and (b) permanently, if the copyright holder fails to notify you of the violation by some reasonable means prior to 60 days after the cessation.

Moreover, your license from a particular copyright holder is reinstated permanently if the copyright holder notifies you of the violation by some reasonable means, this is the first time you have received notice of violation of this License (for any work) from that copyright holder, and you cure the violation prior to 30 days after your receipt of the notice.

Termination of your rights under this section does not terminate the licenses of parties who have received copies or rights from you under this License. If your rights have been terminated and not permanently reinstated, you do not qualify to receive new licenses for the same material under section 10.

9. Acceptance Not Required for Having Copies.

You are not required to accept this License in order to receive or run a copy of the Program. Ancillary propagation of a covered work occurring solely as a consequence of using peer-to-peer transmission to receive a copy likewise does not require acceptance.

However, nothing other than this License grants you permission to propagate or modify any covered work. These actions infringe copyright if you do not accept this License. Therefore, by modifying or propagating a covered work, you indicate your acceptance of this License to do so.

10. Automatic Licensing of Downstream Recipients.

Each time you convey a covered work, the recipient automatically receives a license from the original licensors, to run, modify and propagate that work, subject to this License. You are not responsible for enforcing compliance by third parties with this License.

An "entity transaction" is a transaction transferring control of an organization, or substantially all assets of one, or subdividing an organization, or merging organizations. If propagation of a covered work results from an entity transaction, each party to that transaction who receives a copy of the work also receives whatever licenses to the work the party's predecessor in interest had or could give under the previous paragraph, plus a right to possession of the Corresponding Source of the work from the predecessor in interest, if the predecessor has it or can get it with reasonable efforts.

You may not impose any further restrictions on the exercise of the rights granted or affirmed under this License. For example, you may not impose a license fee, royalty, or other charge for exercise of rights granted under this License, and you may not initiate litigation (including a cross-claim or counterclaim in a lawsuit) alleging that any patent claim is infringed by making, using, selling, offering for sale, or importing the Program or any portion of it.

11. Patents.

A "contributor" is a copyright holder who authorizes use under this License of the Program or a work on which the Program is based. The work thus licensed is called the contributor's "contributor version".

A contributor's "essential patent claims" are all patent claims owned or controlled by the contributor, whether already acquired or hereafter acquired, that would be infringed by some manner, permitted by this License, of making, using, or selling its contributor version, but do not include claims that would be infringed only as a consequence of further modification of the contributor version. For purposes of this definition, "control" includes the right to grant patent sublicenses in a manner consistent with the requirements of this License.

Each contributor grants you a non-exclusive, worldwide, royalty-free patent license under the contributor's essential patent claims, to make, use, sell, offer for sale, import and otherwise run, modify and propagate the contents of its contributor version.

In the following three paragraphs, a "patent license" is any express agreement or commitment, however denominated, not to enforce a patent (such as an express permission to practice a patent or covenant not to sue for patent infringement). To "grant" such a patent license to a party means to make such an agreement or commitment not to enforce a patent against the party.

If you convey a covered work, knowingly relying on a patent license, and the Corresponding Source of the work is not available for anyone to copy, free of charge and under the terms of this License, through a publicly available network server or other readily accessible means, then you must either (1) cause the Corresponding Source to be so available, or (2) arrange to deprive yourself of the benefit of the patent license for this particular work, or (3) arrange, in a manner consistent with the requirements of this License, to extend the patent license to downstream recipients. "Knowingly relying" means you have actual knowledge that, but for the patent license, your conveying the covered work in a country, or your recipient's use of the covered work in a country, would infringe one or more identifiable patents in that country that you have reason to believe are valid.

If, pursuant to or in connection with a single transaction or arrangement, you convey, or propagate by procuring conveyance of, a covered work, and grant a patent license to some of the parties receiving the covered work authorizing them to use, propagate, modify or convey a specific copy of the covered work, then the patent license you grant is automatically extended to all recipients of the covered work and works based on it.

A patent license is "discriminatory" if it does not include within the scope of its coverage, prohibits the exercise of, or is conditioned on the non-exercise of one or more of the rights that are specifically granted under this License. You may not convey a covered work if you are a party to an arrangement with a third party that is in the business of distributing software, under which you make payment to the third party based on the extent of your activity of conveying the work, and under which the third party grants, to any of the parties who would receive the covered work from you, a discriminatory patent license (a) in connection with copies of the covered work conveyed by you (or copies made from those copies), or (b) primarily for and in connection with specific products or compilations that contain the covered work, unless you entered into that arrangement, or that patent license was granted, prior to 28 March 2007.

Nothing in this License shall be construed as excluding or limiting any implied license or other defenses to infringement that may otherwise be available to you under applicable patent law.

12. No Surrender of Others' Freedom.

If conditions are imposed on you (whether by court order, agreement or otherwise) that contradict the conditions of this License, they do not excuse you from the conditions of this License. If you cannot convey a covered work so as to satisfy simultaneously your obligations under this License and any other pertinent obligations, then as a consequence you may not convey it at all. For example, if you agree to terms that obligate you to collect a royalty for further conveying from those to whom you convey the Program, the only way you could satisfy both those terms and this License would be to refrain entirely from conveying the Program.

13. Use with the GNU Affero General Public License.

Notwithstanding any other provision of this License, you have permission to link or combine any covered work with a work licensed under version 3 of the GNU Affero General Public License into a single combined work, and to convey the resulting work. The terms of this License will continue to apply to the part which is the covered work, but the special requirements of the GNU Affero General Public License, section 13, concerning interaction through a network will apply to the combination as such.

14. Revised Versions of this License.

The Free Software Foundation may publish revised and/or new versions of the GNU General Public License from time to time. Such new versions will be similar in spirit to the present version, but may differ in detail to address new problems or concerns.

Each version is given a distinguishing version number. If the Program specifies that a certain numbered version of the GNU General Public License "or any later version" applies to it, you have the option of following the terms and conditions either of that numbered version or of any later version published by the Free Software Foundation. If the Program does not specify a version number of the GNU General Public License, you may choose any version ever published by the Free Software Foundation.

If the Program specifies that a proxy can decide which future versions of the GNU General Public License can be used, that proxy's public statement of acceptance of a version permanently authorizes you to choose that version for the Program.

Later license versions may give you additional or different permissions. However, no additional obligations are imposed on any author or copyright holder as a result of your choosing to follow a later version.

15. Disclaimer of Warranty.

THERE IS NO WARRANTY FOR THE PROGRAM, TO THE EXTENT PERMITTED BY APPLICABLE LAW. EXCEPT WHEN OTHERWISE STATED IN WRITING THE COPYRIGHT HOLDERS AND/OR OTHER PARTIES PROVIDE THE PROGRAM "AS IS" WITHOUT WARRANTY OF ANY KIND, EITHER EXPRESSED OR IMPLIED, INCLUDING, BUT NOT LIMITED TO, THE IMPLIED WARRANTIES OF MERCHANTABILITY AND FITNESS FOR A PARTICULAR PURPOSE. THE ENTIRE RISK AS TO THE QUALITY AND PERFORMANCE OF THE PROGRAM IS WITH YOU. SHOULD THE PROGRAM PROVE DEFECTIVE, YOU ASSUME THE COST OF ALL NECESSARY SERVICING, REPAIR OR CORRECTION.

16. Limitation of Liability.

IN NO EVENT UNLESS REQUIRED BY APPLICABLE LAW OR AGREED TO IN WRITING WILL ANY COPYRIGHT HOLDER, OR ANY OTHER PARTY WHO MODIFIES AND/OR CONVEYS THE PROGRAM AS PERMITTED ABOVE, BE LIABLE TO YOU FOR DAMAGES, INCLUDING ANY GENERAL, SPECIAL, INCIDENTAL OR CONSEQUENTIAL DAMAGES ARISING OUT OF THE USE OR INABILITY TO USE THE PROGRAM (INCLUDING BUT NOT LIMITED TO LOSS OF DATA OR DATA BEING RENDERED INACCURATE OR LOSSES SUSTAINED BY YOU OR THIRD PARTIES OR A FAILURE OF THE PROGRAM TO OPERATE WITH ANY OTHER PROGRAMS), EVEN IF SUCH HOLDER OR OTHER PARTY HAS BEEN ADVISED OF THE POSSIBILITY OF SUCH DAMAGES.

17. Interpretation of Sections 15 and 16.

If the disclaimer of warranty and limitation of liability provided above cannot be given local legal effect according to their terms, reviewing courts shall apply local law that most closely approximates an absolute waiver of all civil liability in connection with the Program, unless a warranty or assumption of liability accompanies a copy of the Program in return for a fee.

END OF TERMS AND CONDITIONS

How to Apply These Terms to Your New Programs

If you develop a new program, and you want it to be of the greatest possible use to the public, the best way to achieve this is to make it free software which everyone can redistribute and change under these terms.

To do so, attach the following notices to the program. It is safest to attach them to the start of each source file to most effectively state the exclusion of warranty; and each file should have at least the "copyright" line and a pointer to where the full notice is found.

```
one line to give the program's name and a brief idea of what it does.
Copyright (C) year name of author

This program is free software: you can redistribute it and/or modify
it under the terms of the GNU General Public License as published by
the Free Software Foundation, either version 3 of the License, or (at
your option) any later version.

This program is distributed in the hope that it will be useful, but
WITHOUT ANY WARRANTY; without even the implied warranty of
MERCHANTABILITY or FITNESS FOR A PARTICULAR PURPOSE.  See the GNU
General Public License for more details.

You should have received a copy of the GNU General Public License
along with this program.  If not, see http://www.gnu.org/licenses/.
```

Also add information on how to contact you by electronic and paper mail.

If the program does terminal interaction, make it output a short notice like this when it starts in an interactive mode:

```
program Copyright (C) year name of author
This program comes with ABSOLUTELY NO WARRANTY; for details type 'show w'.
This is free software, and you are welcome to redistribute it
under certain conditions; type 'show c' for details.
```

The hypothetical commands 'show w' and 'show c' should show the appropriate parts of the General Public License. Of course, your program's commands might be different; for a GUI interface, you would use an "about box".

You should also get your employer (if you work as a programmer) or school, if any, to sign a "copyright disclaimer" for the program, if necessary. For more information on this, and how to apply and follow the GNU GPL, see http://www.gnu.org/licenses/.

The GNU General Public License does not permit incorporating your program into proprietary programs. If your program is a subroutine library, you may consider it more useful to permit linking proprietary applications with the library. If this is what you want to do, use the GNU Lesser General Public License instead of this License. But first, please read http://www.gnu.org/philosophy/why-not-lgpl.html.

GNU Free Documentation License

Version 1.2, November 2002

Copyright © 2000,2001,2002 Free Software Foundation, Inc.
51 Franklin Street, Fifth Floor, Boston, MA 02110-1301, USA

0. PREAMBLE

The purpose of this License is to make a manual, textbook, or other functional and useful document *free* in the sense of freedom: to assure everyone the effective freedom to copy and redistribute it, with or without modifying it, either commercially or non-commercially. Secondarily, this License preserves for the author and publisher a way to get credit for their work, while not being considered responsible for modifications made by others.

This License is a kind of "copyleft", which means that derivative works of the document must themselves be free in the same sense. It complements the GNU General Public License, which is a copyleft license designed for free software.

We have designed this License in order to use it for manuals for free software, because free software needs free documentation: a free program should come with manuals providing the same freedoms that the software does. But this License is not limited to software manuals; it can be used for any textual work, regardless of subject matter or whether it is published as a printed book. We recommend this License principally for works whose purpose is instruction or reference.

1. APPLICABILITY AND DEFINITIONS

This License applies to any manual or other work, in any medium, that contains a notice placed by the copyright holder saying it can be distributed under the terms of this License. Such a notice grants a world-wide, royalty-free license, unlimited in duration, to use that work under the conditions stated herein. The "Document", below, refers to any such manual or work. Any member of the public is a licensee, and is addressed as "you". You accept the license if you copy, modify or distribute the work in a way requiring permission under copyright law.

A "Modified Version" of the Document means any work containing the Document or a portion of it, either copied verbatim, or with modifications and/or translated into another language.

A "Secondary Section" is a named appendix or a front-matter section of the Document that deals exclusively with the relationship of the publishers or authors of the Document to the Document's overall subject (or to related matters) and contains nothing that could fall directly within that overall subject. (Thus, if the Document is in part a textbook of mathematics, a Secondary Section may not explain any mathematics.) The relationship could be a matter of historical connection with the subject or with related matters, or of legal, commercial, philosophical, ethical or political position regarding them.

The "Invariant Sections" are certain Secondary Sections whose titles are designated, as being those of Invariant Sections, in the notice that says that the Document is released under this License. If a section does not fit the above definition of Secondary then it is not allowed to be designated as Invariant. The Document may contain zero Invariant Sections. If the Document does not identify any Invariant Sections then there are none.

The "Cover Texts" are certain short passages of text that are listed, as Front-Cover Texts or Back-Cover Texts, in the notice that says that the Document is released under this License. A Front-Cover Text may be at most 5 words, and a Back-Cover Text may be at most 25 words.

A "Transparent" copy of the Document means a machine-readable copy, represented in a format whose specification is available to the general public, that is suitable for revising the document straightforwardly with generic text editors or (for images composed of pixels) generic paint programs or (for drawings) some widely available drawing editor, and that is suitable for input to text formatters or for automatic translation to a variety of formats suitable for input to text formatters. A copy made in an otherwise Transparent file format whose markup, or absence of markup, has been arranged to thwart or discourage subsequent modification by readers is not Transparent. An image format is not Transparent if used for any substantial amount of text. A copy that is not "Transparent" is called "Opaque".

Examples of suitable formats for Transparent copies include plain ASCII without markup, Texinfo input format, LaTeX input format, SGML or XML using a publicly available DTD, and standard-conforming simple HTML, PostScript or PDF designed for human modification. Examples of transparent image formats include PNG, XCF and JPG. Opaque formats include proprietary formats that can be read and edited only by proprietary word processors, SGML or XML for which the DTD and/or processing tools are not generally available, and the machine-generated HTML, PostScript or PDF produced by some word processors for output purposes only.

The "Title Page" means, for a printed book, the title page itself, plus such following pages as are needed to hold, legibly, the material this License requires to appear in the title page. For works in formats which do not have any title page as such, "Title Page" means the text near the most prominent appearance of the work's title, preceding the beginning of the body of the text.

A section "Entitled XYZ" means a named subunit of the Document whose title either is precisely XYZ or contains XYZ in parentheses following text that translates XYZ in another language. (Here XYZ stands for a specific section name mentioned below, such as "Acknowledgements", "Dedications", "Endorsements", or "History".) To "Preserve the Title" of such a section when you modify the Document means that it remains a section "Entitled XYZ" according to this definition.

The Document may include Warranty Disclaimers next to the notice which states that this License applies to the Document. These Warranty Disclaimers are considered to be included by reference in this License, but only as regards disclaiming warranties: any other implication that these Warranty Disclaimers may have is void and has no effect on the meaning of this License.

2. VERBATIM COPYING

You may copy and distribute the Document in any medium, either commercially or noncommercially, provided that this License, the copyright notices, and the license notice saying this License applies to the Document are reproduced in all copies, and that you add no other conditions whatsoever to those of this License. You may not use technical measures to obstruct or control the reading or further copying of the copies you make or distribute. However, you may accept compensation in exchange for copies. If you distribute a large enough number of copies you must also follow the conditions in section 3.

You may also lend copies, under the same conditions stated above, and you may publicly display copies.

3. COPYING IN QUANTITY

If you publish printed copies (or copies in media that commonly have printed covers) of the Document, numbering more than 100, and the Document's license notice requires Cover Texts, you must enclose the copies in covers that carry, clearly and legibly, all these Cover Texts: Front-Cover Texts on the front cover, and Back-Cover Texts on the back cover. Both covers must also clearly and legibly identify you as the publisher of these copies. The front cover must present the full title with all words of the title equally prominent and visible. You may add other material on the covers in addition. Copying with changes limited to the covers, as long as they preserve the title of the Document and satisfy these conditions, can be treated as verbatim copying in other respects.

If the required texts for either cover are too voluminous to fit legibly, you should put the first ones listed (as many as fit reasonably) on the actual cover, and continue the rest onto adjacent pages.

If you publish or distribute Opaque copies of the Document numbering more than 100, you must either include a machine-readable Transparent copy along with each Opaque copy, or state in or with each Opaque copy a computer-network location from which the general network-using public has access to download using public-standard network protocols a complete Transparent copy of the Document, free of added material. If you use the latter option, you must take reasonably prudent steps, when you begin distribution of Opaque copies in quantity, to ensure that this Transparent copy will remain thus accessible at the stated location until at least one year after the last time you distribute an Opaque copy (directly or through your agents or retailers) of that edition to the public.

It is requested, but not required, that you contact the authors of the Document well before redistributing any large number of copies, to give them a chance to provide you with an updated version of the Document.

4. MODIFICATIONS

You may copy and distribute a Modified Version of the Document under the conditions of sections 2 and 3 above, provided that you release the Modified Version under precisely this License, with the Modified Version filling the role of the Document, thus licensing distribution and modification of the Modified Version to whoever possesses a copy of it. In addition, you must do these things in the Modified Version:

A. Use in the Title Page (and on the covers, if any) a title distinct from that of the Document, and from those of previous versions (which should, if there were any, be listed in the History section of the Document). You may use the same title as a previous version if the original publisher of that version gives permission.

B. List on the Title Page, as authors, one or more persons or entities responsible for authorship of the modifications in the Modified Version, together with at least five of the principal authors of the Document (all of its principal authors, if it has fewer than five), unless they release you from this requirement.

C. State on the Title page the name of the publisher of the Modified Version, as the publisher.

D. Preserve all the copyright notices of the Document.

E. Add an appropriate copyright notice for your modifications adjacent to the other copyright notices.

F. Include, immediately after the copyright notices, a license notice giving the public permission to use the Modified Version under the terms of this License, in the form shown in the Addendum below.

G. Preserve in that license notice the full lists of Invariant Sections and required Cover Texts given in the Document's license notice.

H. Include an unaltered copy of this License.

I. Preserve the section Entitled "History", Preserve its Title, and add to it an item stating at least the title, year, new authors, and publisher of the Modified Version as given on the Title Page. If there is no section Entitled "History" in the Document, create one stating the title, year, authors, and publisher of the Document as given on its Title Page, then add an item describing the Modified Version as stated in the previous sentence.

J. Preserve the network location, if any, given in the Document for public access to a Transparent copy of the Document, and likewise the network locations given in the Document for previous versions it was based on. These may be placed in the "History" section. You may omit a network location for a work that was published at least four years before the Document itself, or if the original publisher of the version it refers to gives permission.

K. For any section Entitled "Acknowledgements" or "Dedications", Preserve the Title of the section, and preserve in the section all the substance and tone of each of the contributor acknowledgements and/or dedications given therein.

L. Preserve all the Invariant Sections of the Document, unaltered in their text and in their titles. Section numbers or the equivalent are not considered part of the section titles.

M. Delete any section Entitled "Endorsements". Such a section may not be included in the Modified Version.

N. Do not retitle any existing section to be Entitled "Endorsements" or to conflict in title with any Invariant Section.

O. Preserve any Warranty Disclaimers.

If the Modified Version includes new front-matter sections or appendices that qualify as Secondary Sections and contain no material copied from the Document, you may at your option designate some or all of these sections as invariant. To do this, add their titles to the list of Invariant Sections in the Modified Version's license notice. These titles must be distinct from any other section titles.

You may add a section Entitled "Endorsements", provided it contains nothing but endorsements of your Modified Version by various parties—for example, statements of peer review or that the text has been approved by an organization as the authoritative definition of a standard.

You may add a passage of up to five words as a Front-Cover Text, and a passage of up to 25 words as a Back-Cover Text, to the end of the list of Cover Texts in the Modified Version. Only one passage of Front-Cover Text and one of Back-Cover Text may be added by (or through arrangements made by) any one entity. If the Document already includes a cover text for the same cover, previously added by you or by arrangement made by the same entity you are acting on behalf of, you may not add another; but you may replace the old one, on explicit permission from the previous publisher that added the old one.

The author(s) and publisher(s) of the Document do not by this License give permission to use their names for publicity for or to assert or imply endorsement of any Modified Version.

5. COMBINING DOCUMENTS

You may combine the Document with other documents released under this License, under the terms defined in section 4 above for modified versions, provided that you include in the combination all of the Invariant Sections of all of the original documents, unmodified, and list them all as Invariant Sections of your combined work in its license notice, and that you preserve all their Warranty Disclaimers.

The combined work need only contain one copy of this License, and multiple identical Invariant Sections may be replaced with a single copy. If there are multiple Invariant Sections with the same name but different contents, make the title of each such section unique by adding at the end of it, in parentheses, the name of the original author or publisher of that section if known, or else a unique number. Make the same adjustment to the section titles in the list of Invariant Sections in the license notice of the combined work.

In the combination, you must combine any sections Entitled "History" in the various original documents, forming one section Entitled "History"; likewise combine any sections Entitled "Acknowledgements", and any sections Entitled "Dedications". You must delete all sections Entitled "Endorsements."

6. COLLECTIONS OF DOCUMENTS

You may make a collection consisting of the Document and other documents released under this License, and replace the individual copies of this License in the various documents with a single copy that is included in the collection, provided that you follow the rules of this License for verbatim copying of each of the documents in all other respects.

You may extract a single document from such a collection, and distribute it individually under this License, provided you insert a copy of this License into the extracted document, and follow this License in all other respects regarding verbatim copying of that document.

7. AGGREGATION WITH INDEPENDENT WORKS

A compilation of the Document or its derivatives with other separate and independent documents or works, in or on a volume of a storage or distribution medium, is called an "aggregate" if the copyright resulting from the compilation is not used to limit the legal rights of the compilation's users beyond what the individual works permit. When the Document is included in an aggregate, this License does not apply to the other works in the aggregate which are not themselves derivative works of the Document.

If the Cover Text requirement of section 3 is applicable to these copies of the Document, then if the Document is less than one half of the entire aggregate, the Document's Cover Texts may be placed on covers that bracket the Document within the aggregate, or the electronic equivalent of covers if the Document is in electronic form. Otherwise they must appear on printed covers that bracket the whole aggregate.

8. TRANSLATION

Translation is considered a kind of modification, so you may distribute translations of the Document under the terms of section 4. Replacing Invariant Sections with translations requires special permission from their copyright holders, but you may include translations of some or all Invariant Sections in addition to the original versions of these Invariant Sections. You may include a translation of this License, and all the license notices in the Document, and any Warranty Disclaimers, provided that you also include the original English version of this License and the original versions of those notices and disclaimers. In case of a disagreement between the translation and the original version of this License or a notice or disclaimer, the original version will prevail.

If a section in the Document is Entitled "Acknowledgements", "Dedications", or "History", the requirement (section 4) to Preserve its Title (section 1) will typically require changing the actual title.

9. TERMINATION

You may not copy, modify, sublicense, or distribute the Document except as expressly provided for under this License. Any other attempt to copy, modify, sublicense or distribute the Document is void, and will automatically terminate your rights under this License. However, parties who have received copies, or rights, from you under this License will not have their licenses terminated so long as such parties remain in full compliance.

10. FUTURE REVISIONS OF THIS LICENSE

The Free Software Foundation may publish new, revised versions of the GNU Free Documentation License from time to time. Such new versions will be similar in spirit to the present version, but may differ in detail to address new problems or concerns. See http://www.gnu.org/copyleft/.

Each version of the License is given a distinguishing version number. If the Document specifies that a particular numbered version of this License "or any later version" applies to it, you have the option of following the terms and conditions either of that specified version or of any later version that has been published (not as a draft) by the Free Software Foundation. If the Document does not specify a version number of this License, you may choose any version ever published (not as a draft) by the Free Software Foundation.

ADDENDUM: How to use this License for your documents

To use this License in a document you have written, include a copy of the License in the document and put the following copyright and license notices just after the title page:

```
Copyright (C)  year  your name.
Permission is granted to copy, distribute and/or modify this document
under the terms of the GNU Free Documentation License, Version 1.2
or any later version published by the Free Software Foundation;
with no Invariant Sections, no Front-Cover Texts, and no Back-Cover
Texts.  A copy of the license is included in the section entitled ''GNU
Free Documentation License''.
```

If you have Invariant Sections, Front-Cover Texts and Back-Cover Texts, replace the "with...Texts." line with this:

```
with the Invariant Sections being list their titles, with
the Front-Cover Texts being list, and with the Back-Cover Texts
being list.
```

If you have Invariant Sections without Cover Texts, or some other combination of the three, merge those two alternatives to suit the situation.

If your document contains nontrivial examples of program code, we recommend releasing these examples in parallel under your choice of free software license, such as the GNU General Public License, to permit their use in free software.

Funding Free Software

If you want to have more free software a few years from now, it makes sense for you to help encourage people to contribute funds for its development. The most effective approach known is to encourage commercial redistributors to donate.

Users of free software systems can boost the pace of development by encouraging for-a-fee distributors to donate part of their selling price to free software developers—the Free Software Foundation, and others.

The way to convince distributors to do this is to demand it and expect it from them. So when you compare distributors, judge them partly by how much they give to free software development. Show distributors they must compete to be the one who gives the most.

To make this approach work, you must insist on numbers that you can compare, such as, "We will donate ten dollars to the Frobnitz project for each disk sold." Don't be satisfied with a vague promise, such as "A portion of the profits are donated," since it doesn't give a basis for comparison.

Even a precise fraction "of the profits from this disk" is not very meaningful, since creative accounting and unrelated business decisions can greatly alter what fraction of the sales price counts as profit. If the price you pay is $50, ten percent of the profit is probably less than a dollar; it might be a few cents, or nothing at all.

Some redistributors do development work themselves. This is useful too; but to keep everyone honest, you need to inquire how much they do, and what kind. Some kinds of development make much more long-term difference than others. For example, maintaining a separate version of a program contributes very little; maintaining the standard version of a program for the whole community contributes much. Easy new ports contribute little, since someone else would surely do them; difficult ports such as adding a new CPU to the GNU Compiler Collection contribute more; major new features or packages contribute the most.

By establishing the idea that supporting further development is "the proper thing to do" when distributing free software for a fee, we can assure a steady flow of resources into making more free software.

Option Index

gfortran's command line options are indexed here without any initial '-' or '--'. Where an option has both positive and negative forms (such as -foption and -fno-option), relevant entries in the manual are indexed under the most appropriate form; it may sometimes be useful to look up both forms.

Keyword Index

LaVergne, TN USA
24 August 2010
194489LV00005B/44/P